The Landauer Principle and Its Implementations in Physics, Chemistry and Biology: Current Status, Critics and Controversies

The Landauer Principle and Its Implementations in Physics, Chemistry and Biology: Current Status, Critics and Controversies

Guest Editor
Edward Bormashenko

Basel • Beijing • Wuhan • Barcelona • Belgrade • Novi Sad • Cluj • Manchester

Guest Editor
Edward Bormashenko
Chemical Engineering Department
Engineering Sciences Faculty
Ariel University
Ariel
Israel

Editorial Office
MDPI AG
Grosspeteranlage 5
4052 Basel, Switzerland

This is a reprint of the Special Issue, published open access by the journal *Entropy* (ISSN 1099-4300), freely accessible at: https://www.mdpi.com/journal/entropy/special_issues/Lan_Prin_II.

For citation purposes, cite each article independently as indicated on the article page online and as indicated below:

Lastname, A.A.; Lastname, B.B. Article Title. *Journal Name* **Year**, *Volume Number*, Page Range.

ISBN 978-3-7258-4141-7 (Hbk)
ISBN 978-3-7258-4142-4 (PDF)
https://doi.org/10.3390/books978-3-7258-4142-4

© 2025 by the authors. Articles in this book are Open Access and distributed under the Creative Commons Attribution (CC BY) license. The book as a whole is distributed by MDPI under the terms and conditions of the Creative Commons Attribution-NonCommercial-NoDerivs (CC BY-NC-ND) license (https://creativecommons.org/licenses/by-nc-nd/4.0/).

Contents

About the Editor vii

Preface ix

Edward Bormashenko
Landauer's Principle: Past, Present and Future
Reprinted from: *Entropy* 2025, 27, 437, https://doi.org/10.3390/e27040437 1

Maria Cristina Diamantini
Landauer Bound and Continuous Phase Transitions
Reprinted from: *Entropy* 2023, 25, 984, https://doi.org/10.3390/e25070984 5

Uğur Çetiner, Oren Raz, Madolyn Britt and Sergei Sukharev
Dissipation during the Gating Cycle of the Bacterial Mechanosensitive Ion Channel Approaches the Landauer Limit
Reprinted from: *Entropy* 2023, 25, 779, https://doi.org/10.3390/e25050779 17

Didier Lairez
Thermodynamical versus Logical Irreversibility: A Concrete Objection to Landauer's Principle
Reprinted from: *Entropy* 2023, 25, 1155, https://doi.org/10.3390/e25081155 29

Cameron Witkowski, Stephen Brown and Kevin Truong
On the Precise Link between Energy and Information
Reprinted from: *Entropy* 2024, 26, 203, https://doi.org/10.3390/e26030203 40

J. Gerhard Müller
Events as Elements of Physical Observation: Experimental Evidence
Reprinted from: *Entropy* 2024, 26, 255, https://doi.org/10.3390/e26030255 54

Edward Bormashenko
Landauer Bound in the Context of Minimal Physical Principles: Meaning, Experimental Verification, Controversies and Perspectives
Reprinted from: *Entropy* 2024, 26, 423, https://doi.org/10.3390/e26050423 66

Yuri J. Alvim and Lucas C. Céleri
Landauer Principle and the Second Law in a Relativistic Communication Scenario
Reprinted from: *Entropy* 2024, 26, 613, https://doi.org/10.3390/e26070613 84

J. Gerhard Müller
Elementary Observations: Building Blocks of Physical Information Gain
Reprinted from: *Entropy* 2024, 26, 619, https://doi.org/10.3390/e26080619 94

Luis Herrera
Modified Landauer Principle According to Tsallis Entropy
Reprinted from: *Entropy* 2024, 26, 931, https://doi.org/10.3390/e26110931 110

Michael Paul Gough
Evidence for Dark Energy Driven by Star Formation: Information Dark Energy?
Reprinted from: *Entropy* 2025, 27, 110, https://doi.org/10.3390/e27020110 118

About the Editor

Edward Bormashenko

Edward Bormashenko is a Professor of Materials Science at Ariel University, Israel. His scientific interests include the foundations of thermodynamics, surface science, materials science, polymer science, the physics of plasma, the physics of computation, and Ramsey theory. He is the author of 350 papers and 5 books.

Preface

This Special Issue addresses the Landauer principle, which is one of the limiting physical principles that constrain the behavior of computing systems; a digital computer is seen as a physical device, which processes bits by switching logical units "on" and "off"—those physical changes are the computation. The Landauer principle restricts the minimal energy necessary for the erasure of one bit of information. This Special Issue addresses a diversity of problems, related to the meaning and applications of the Landauer principle. The interrelation between the Landauer principle and the Second Law of Thermodynamics is addressed.

Edward Bormashenko
Guest Editor

Editorial
Landauer's Principle: Past, Present and Future

Edward Bormashenko

Department of Chemical Engineering, Biotechnology and Materials, Engineering Sciences Faculty, Ariel University, Ariel 407000, Israel; edward@ariel.ac.il; Tel.: +972-074-729-68-63

"Thermodynamics is only physical theory of universal content, which I am convinced will never be overthrown, within the framework of applicability of its basic concepts."

Albert Einstein

The rapid development of computers has led to growing interest in the physical foundations of computation. This interest arises from both applicative and fundamental aspects of computation [1]. It has been hypothesized that the entire universe can be regarded as a giant quantum computer [2]. *Cum grano salis*, even natural evolution can be looked at as a computation that exploits the physical properties of materials [3]. In its most general meaning, computation involves transforming inputs into outputs using a specific set of instructions; we restrict our treatment with a physical framework: a digital computer is seen as physical device, which processes bits by switching logical units "on" and "off"—those physical changes are the computation [4]. A reasonable question that follows from this is what are physical limitations of computation? In other words, what is the minimal energy cost of computation and what is the maximal possible velocity of computation? There are fundamental laws and principles that set the limits of physical systems. Thus, we well expect fundamental limitations on computation to be imposed by nature [5]. From this another question arises: is it possible to break these fundamental limitations under specific circumstances?

Landauer's principle, addressed in this Special Issue, is one of the limiting physical principles which constrains the behavior of computing systems. There exist fundamental laws and principles that set the limits of physical systems [5–7]. These principles include the Abbe diffraction limit [8] and the Heisenberg uncertainty principle [9]. Combining the limiting value of light propagating in a vacuum c with the Heisenberg uncertainty principle yields Bremermann's limit, which enforces a limit on the maximum rate of computation that can be achieved in a self-contained system [10]. Quantum mechanics also gives rise to the Mandelstam–Tamm and Margolus–Levitin limiting principles, which restrict the maximum speed of the dynamical evolution of quantum systems [11–13].

Landauer's principle, in turn, sets a limit the minimum energy necessary for the erasure of one bit of information. Rolf Landauer believed that computation is a physical process; thus, it must obey the laws of physics and, first and foremost, the laws of thermodynamics [14–17]. This thinking led to a new limiting physical principle by establishing a minimal energy cost for the erasure of a single bit of memory from a system operating at the equilibrium temperature T. The minimum amount of heat/energy dissipated when erasing one bit of information is given by

$$W = k_B T ln2 \qquad (1)$$

Landauer's principle also led to the fundamentally important distinction between logic and thermodynamic irreversibility [18]. It should be emphasized that the Landauer bound, given in Equation (1), relates only to a single information-bearing degree of freedom within an entire computing system. Landauer's principle was rigorously and microscopically derived without direct reference to the second law of thermodynamics [19]. The quantum mechanics extension of Landauer's principle has also been demonstrated [20,21]. Elsewhere, the relativistic generalization of Landauer's principle has been introduced [22,23]. The extension of Landauer's principle to many-valued logic was addressed in [24].

Combining the Landauer bound with the Margolus–Levitin limiting principle yields the minimal time that it will take for a device to make a single computing operation (as reported in this Special Issue [7]). The minimal "Margolus–Levitin–Landauer" time necessary for a single computation, denoted by τ_{MLL}, is given by Equation (2):

$$\tau_{MLL} \geq \frac{h}{4\ln 2 k_B T} = \frac{\tau_{PB}}{4 ln 2} \qquad (2)$$

where $\tau_{PB} = \frac{h}{k_B T}$ is the Planck–Boltzmann thermalization time, which is thought to be the fastest relaxation timescale for the thermalization of a given system [25].

Landauer's principle could be interpreted within the global concept aphoristically called "It from bit", which was suggested by John Archibald Wheeler. "It from bit symbolizes the idea that every item of the physical world has at bottom ... an immaterial source and explanation; that what we call reality arises in the last analysis from the posing of yes-no questions and the registering of equipment-evoked responses; in short, that all things physical are information-theoretic in origin and this is a participatory universe" [26]. Landauer's principle provides the "It from Bit" idea with measurable physical content by supplying a bridge between "information" and physically measurable values. This bridge was built in a series of recent papers [22,23,27–29]. According to Herrera [22], changing one bit of information leads to a decrease in the mass of the system by an amount whose minimal value given by Equation (3):

$$\Delta M = \frac{k_B T}{c^2} ln 2 \qquad (3)$$

Generalizations of Landauer's principle have been reported for logically indeterministic operations and non-equilibrium systems [30,31]. The Landauer bound has been successfully tested in a number of experimental investigations [32–34]. Despite this, the meaning and formulation of Landauer's principle have been intensively criticized. It was argued that since it is not independent of the second law of thermodynamics, it is either necessary nor sufficient an exorcism of Maxwell's Demon [35]. Lairez suggested a counterexample with a physical implementation (which uses a two-to-one relation between logic and thermodynamic states) that allows one bit to be erased in a thermodynamic quasi-static manner [36]. Buffoni et al. demonstrated that Landauer's principle, in contrast to widespread opinion, is not the second law of thermodynamics nor equivalent to it, but in fact a stricter bound [37]. The discussion is far from exhausted. It should be emphasized that real, artificial, and natural computers operate far from thermodynamic equilibrium; thus, the Landauer bound arising from classical equilibrium thermodynamics may be broken [38]. Now, let us briefly list the problems that remain:

(i) The exact place of Landauer's principle in the structure of thermodynamics should be clarified.
(ii) A relativistic extension of Landauer's principle remains one of the unsolved problems. The problem of the accurate derivation and grounding of the relativistic transformation of temperature also remains unsolved.

(iii) It is important to implement the Landauer principle in the development of optimal computational protocols, providing minimal energy dissipation, including non-Turing computational devices [39].

Funding: This research received no external funding.

Conflicts of Interest: The author declares no conflicts of interest.

References

1. Adamatzky, A. *Computing in Nonlinear Media and Automata Collectives*; Institute of Physics Publishing: Bristol, UK, 2001.
2. Lloyd, S. *The Universe as Quantum Computer, A Computable Universe: Understanding and Exploring Nature as Computation*; World Scientific: Singapore, 2013.
3. Miller, J.F.; Harding, S.L.; Tufte, G. Evolution-in-materio: Evolving computation in materials. *Evol. Intel.* **2014**, *7*, 49–67. [CrossRef]
4. Piccinini, G.; Maley, C. Computation in physical systems. In *The Stanford Encyclopedia of Philosophy*; Zalta, E.N., Ed.; Metaphysics Research Lab, Stanford University: Stanford, CA, USA, 2010; Available online: https://plato.stanford.edu/archives/sum2021/entries/computation-physicalsystems (accessed on 16 April 2025).
5. Markov, I. Limits on fundamental limits to computation. *Nature* **2014**, *512*, 147–154. [CrossRef]
6. Liu, Y.C.; Huang, K.; Xiao, Y.-F.; Yang, L.; Qiu, C.W. What limits limits? *Nat. Sci. Rev.* **2021**, *8*, nwaa210. [CrossRef]
7. Bormashenko, E. Landauer Bound in the Context of Minimal Physical Principles: Meaning, Experimental Verification, Controversies and Perspectives. *Entropy* **2024**, *26*, 423. [CrossRef] [PubMed]
8. Hecht, E. Modern Optics. In *Optics*, 4th ed.; Addison-Wesley: Reading, MA, USA, 2002; Chapter 13; pp. 609–611.
9. Landau, L.D.; Lifshitz, E.M. *Quantum Mechanics: Non-Relativistic Theory*, 3rd ed.; Pergamon Press: Oxford, UK, 1977; Volume 3, Chapter 2; pp. 46–49.
10. Bremermann, H.J. Optimization through evolution and recombination. In *Self-Organizing Systems 1962*; Yovits, M.C., Jacobi, G.T., Goldstein, G.D., Eds.; Spartan Books: Washington, DC, USA, 1962; pp. 93–106.
11. Mandelstam, L.; Tamm, I. The Uncertainty Relation Between Energy and Time in Non-Relativistic Quantum Mechanics, in Selected Papers; Bolotovskii, B.M., Frenkel, V.Y., Peierls, R., Eds.; Springer: Berlin/Heidelberg, Germany, 1991.
12. Hörnedal, N.; Sönnerborn, O. Margolus-Levitin quantum speed limit for an arbitrary fidelity. *Phys. Rev. Res.* **2023**, *5*, 043234. [CrossRef]
13. Margolus, M.; Levitin, L.B. The maximum speed of dynamical evolution. *Phys. D Nonlinear Phenomena* **1998**, *120*, 188–195. [CrossRef]
14. Landauer, R. Dissipation and heat generation in the computing process. *IBM J. Res. Dev.* **1961**, *5*, 183. [CrossRef]
15. Landauer, R. Information is physical. *Phys. Today* **1991**, *44*, 5, 23–29. [CrossRef]
16. Landauer, R. Minimal energy requirements in communication. *Science* **1996**, *272*, 1914–1918. [CrossRef]
17. Bennett, C.H.; Landauer, R. The fundamental physical limits of computation. *Sci. Am.* **1985**, *253*, 48–57. [CrossRef]
18. Maroney, O.J.E. The (absence of a) relationship between thermodynamic and logical reversibility. *Stud. Hist. Philos. Sci. B* **2005**, *36*, 355–374. [CrossRef]
19. Piechocinska, B. Information erasure. *Phys. Rev. A* **2000**, *61*, 062314. [CrossRef]
20. Parrondo, J.M.R.; Horowitz, J.M.; Sagawa, T. Thermodynamics of information. *Nat. Phys.* **2015**, *11*, 131–139. [CrossRef]
21. Sagawa, T. Thermodynamic and logical reversibilities revisited. *J. Stat. Mech.* **2014**, *2014*, P03025. [CrossRef]
22. Herrera, L. The mass of a bit of information and the Brillouin's principle. *Fluct. Noise Lett.* **2014**, *13*, 1450002. [CrossRef]
23. Herrera, L. Landauer Principle and General Relativity. *Entropy* **2020**, *22*, 340. [CrossRef] [PubMed]
24. Bormashenko, E. Generalization of the Landauer Principle for Computing Devices Based on Many-Valued Logic. *Entropy* **2019**, *21*, 1150. [CrossRef]
25. Hartnoll, S.A.; Mackenzie, A.P. Colloquium: Planckian dissipation in metals. *Rev. Mod. Phys.* **2022**, *94*, 041002. [CrossRef]
26. Wheeler, J.A. Information, physics, quantum: The search for links. In Proceedings of the 3rd International Symposium on Foundations of Quantum Mechanics in the Light of New Technology, Tokyo, Japan, 28–31 August 1989; pp. 354–368.
27. Vopson, M. The mass-energy-information equivalence principle. *AIP Adv.* **2019**, *9*, 095206. [CrossRef]
28. Müller, J.G. Events as Elements of Physical Observation: Experimental Evidence. *Entropy* **2024**, *26*, 255. [CrossRef]
29. Bormashenko, E. The Landauer Principle: Re-Formulation of the Second Thermodynamics Law or a Step to Great Unification? *Entropy* **2019**, *21*, 918. [CrossRef]
30. Maroney, O.J.E. Generalizing Landauer's principle. *Phys. Rev. E* **2009**, *79*, 031105. [CrossRef] [PubMed]
31. Esposito, M.; Van den Broeck, C. Second law and Landauer principle far from equilibrium. *Europhys. Lett.* **2011**, *95*, 40004. [CrossRef]

32. Orlov, A.O.; Lent, C.S.; Thorpe, C.C.; Boechler, G.P.; Snider, G.L. Experimental Test of Landauer's Principle at the Sub-$k_B Y$ Level. *Jpn. J. Appl. Phys.* **2012**, *51*, 06FE10. [CrossRef]
33. Bérut, A.; Arakelyan, A.; Petrosyan, A.; Ciliberto, S.; Dillenschneider, R.; Lutz, E. Experimental verification of Landauer's principle linking information and thermodynamics. *Nature* **2012**, *483*, 187–189. [CrossRef]
34. Jun, Y.; Gavrilov, M.; Bechhoefer, J. High-precision test of Landauer's principle in a feedback trap. *Phys. Rev. Lett.* **2014**, *113*, 190601. [CrossRef]
35. Norton, J.D. Eaters of the lotus: Landauer's principle and the return of Maxwell's demon. *Stud. Hist. Philos. Sci. B* **2005**, *36*, 375–411. [CrossRef]
36. Lairez, D. Thermodynamical versus Logical Irreversibility: A Concrete Objection to Landauer's Principle. *Entropy* **2023**, *25*, 1155. [CrossRef]
37. Buffoni, L.; Campisi, M. Spontaneous Fluctuation-Symmetry Breaking and the Landauer Principle. *J. Stat. Phys.* **2022**, *186*, 31. [CrossRef]
38. Wolpert, D.H. Is stochastic thermodynamics the key to understanding the energy costs of computation? *Proc. Natl. Acad. Sci.* **2024**, *121*, e2321112121. [CrossRef]
39. Jaeger, H.; Noheda, B.; van der Wiel, W.G. Toward a formal theory for computing machines made out of whatever physics offers. *Nat. Commun.* **2023**, *14*, 4911. [CrossRef] [PubMed]

Disclaimer/Publisher's Note: The statements, opinions and data contained in all publications are solely those of the individual author(s) and contributor(s) and not of MDPI and/or the editor(s). MDPI and/or the editor(s) disclaim responsibility for any injury to people or property resulting from any ideas, methods, instructions or products referred to in the content.

Review

Landauer Bound and Continuous Phase Transitions

Maria Cristina Diamantini

NiPS Laboratory, INFN and Dipartimento di Fisica e Geologia, University of Perugia, Via A. Pascoli, I-06100 Perugia, Italy; cristina.diamantini@pg.infn.it

Abstract: In this review, we establish a relation between information erasure and continuous phase transitions. The order parameter, which characterizes these transitions, measures the order of the systems. It varies between 0, when the system is completely disordered, and 1, when the system is completely ordered. This ordering process can be seen as information erasure by resetting a certain number of bits to a standard value. The thermodynamic entropy in the partially ordered phase is given by the information-theoretic expression for the generalized Landauer bound in terms of error probability. We will demonstrate this for the Hopfield neural network model of associative memory, where the Landauer bound sets a lower limit for the work associated with 'remembering' rather than 'forgetting'. Using the relation between the Landauer bound and continuous phase transition, we will be able to extend the bound to analog computing systems. In the case of the erasure of an analog variable, the entropy production per degree of freedom is given by the logarithm of the configurational volume measured in units of its minimal quantum.

Keywords: Landauer bound; continuous phase transitions; analog computing

1. Introduction

Landauer's principle [1–3] tells us that forgetting is costly: the erasing of one bit of information, namely resetting it to a particular memory state, independently of its previous memory state, has an entropic cost of, at least, $kT \ln(2)$ energy (where T is the temperature and k the Boltzmann constant). This is the content of the famous statement that "information is physical" as realized first by Szilard [4] and after by Landauer: information can only be processed by physical systems, computers, and thus it is subject to the laws of thermodynamics of physical systems. The minimum energy expenditure of $kT \ln(2)$ solves the problem of the violation of the second law of Maxwell's demon [5]: the second law is not violated since one has to take into account the cost of erasing the demon's memory. The paradox of Maxwell's demon has also been addressed in a related but slightly different way by Brillouin [6,7], using the idea of negentropy, namely the reverse of entropy, describing a system becoming "more ordered", and its relation with information. A bit of information is obtained by the demon at the price of some negative entropy lost in the environment, which allows the demon to make choices which decrease the entropy in the environment. The relation between the negentropy and the Landauer limit was analyzed in [8,9] considering a system of magnetic skyrmions. There, it was shown that the Landauer bound can be seen as a variation of the negentropy of the skyrmion. Landauer's principle was recently experimentally verified in [10–13].

Since its formulation, many discussions have been devoted to the validity and usefulness of Landauer's principle [14–16], and many attempts have been devoted to possibly beat Landauer's limit since it sets a minimum energy expenditure in computation. More sophisticated formulations have been proposed [17,18], which take into account the role of the conditional entropy to relate Shannon and Gibbs entropy and that lower Landauer's limit. For a review on recent developments on the thermodynamics of information, see [19]. Another possibility to beat this limit is to admit errors during the erasure procedure. In this case, the original Landauer limit and the associated minimum cost of erasure can be lowered. In [20], it was shown that, admitting errors, the Landauer bound can be lowered and the minimum work necessary to stochastically erase one bit becomes

$$\frac{-\Delta S}{k} = \ln 2 + p \ln(p) + (1-p) \ln(1-p), \quad (1)$$

where p is the error probability. This error probability, which can be interpreted as mutual or conditional entropy [21,22], becomes relevant [20] for future nanoscale implementations of switches which must necessarily take into account also their thermal fluctuations.

Information is physical; this statement, as shown in [23], implies that physical systems, which contain order, can encode information bits. Continuous phase transitions represent a paradigmatic example of these physical systems. Continuous phase transitions are characterized by symmetry breaking. The order parameter describes the symmetry broken phase and it is zero in the unbroken phase. These transitions, which are generally driven by temperature in the classical case, are described by the phenomenological Landau theory expressed in terms of the temperature and of the order parameter [24]. As we lower the temperature below the critical temperature T_C, at which the phase transition takes place, the Landau function [24], representing the effective potential, goes from one single minimum to a manifold of minima, e.g., it bifurcates into two minima in the case of Z_2 symmetry breaking, creating a new order and a new configuration space for the system. The work performed on the system to lower the temperature is completely used to lower the entropy and to change the state of the system, making it "more ordered". We call this procedure efficient. To better understand the relation between Landauer erasure and continuous phase transition, let us consider one classical bit of information stored in a bistable potential, exemplified by a particle in a double potential well. The first step of the erasure of the memory corresponds to the lowering of the barrier; note that in this step, the phase space available doubles. This corresponds to the disordered phase with $m = 0$. Then, in general, by applying a tilting force and raising again the barrier will force the particle to be in one of the wells, depending on the tilting force, thus resetting either to zero or to one. This is a non-equilibrium state valid for a time smaller than the relaxation time in the well. In this last step, we have a phase space reduction; we 'compress' two states in one, and this is what causes the heat dissipation. In spontaneous symmetry breaking, something similar happens. Above the critical temperature, all possible degenerate ground states are available, while below the critical temperature, the system 'chooses' one state. In the case of symmetry breaking, an external perturbation, which is generally then set to zero, is what makes the system choose a particular state. In Landauer erasure, this is the role of the tilting in the double-well potential model for a single switch [10].

A particularly interesting example is given by neural networks [25], which are composed of a large number of interacting stochastic bits. Neural networks are the basic elements of associative memories. Contrary to address-oriented memories, recovery of the information is based on the similarity between the stored memory pattern and the presented pattern. The Hopfield model [26] is the most used example of neural networks [25]. The Hopfield model undergoes a phase transition, characterized by order parameter m that goes from zero in the disordered phase to one in the ordered phase. The transition is driven by a fictitious temperature: below T_C, the system becomes ordered. As shown in [23] (and derived in Section 2) this phase transition is akin to an erasure with errors for the N stochastic neurons. The entropy difference between the disordered phase and the partially ordered phase can be exactly written as Equation (1) of [10,20,21], where, in this case, the error probability is related to the order parameter. Note that, while in the Landauer case, the erasure corresponds to forgetting, in the case of the neural networks, it corresponds to remembering.

A phase transition is clearly a collective phenomenon; a single spin cannot have a phase transition, while one can erase a single bit or flip a single spin. However, in the example we chose of the Hopfield model, which, as we will show in the next section, can be mapped in a long range Ising model [25], the bits which compose the associative memory represent the information bearing degrees of freedom. The order parameter m, which characterizes the continuous phase transition, plays the role of the error in an erasure with errors. When the parameter m is equal to one, we have the completely ordered phase corresponding to the erasure without errors. In [23], we showed that the entropy difference between the disordered phase and the completely ordered phase goes approximately $kT \ln 2$ times the number of spins of the network, which coincides with the number of the information bearing degrees of freedom.

The Landauer principle [1] was originally formulated to compute the minimal energy required to erase a bit of information and it applies, thus, to the system in which information is represented by discrete units. What happens for analog computing systems? In [27], the relation between erasure and continuous phase transition allowed us to extend Landauer's principle to systems where information is a continuous variable.

When we erase discrete information, assuming that the conditional entropy is zero [18], the difference in the Shannon entropy between the final state, to which we reset the memory, e.g., to one, and the one in which the system can be in any one of the possible states s_i with probability p_i, is given by

$$\Delta S_S = \sum_i^M p_i \ln p_i , \qquad (2)$$

where M is the finite number of possible logic states. The continuous generalization of the Shannon entropy is defined as [28,29]

$$S_S^{cont} = - \int_{x \in M} p(x) \ln p(x) . \qquad (3)$$

where $p(x)$ is the probability distribution of the relevant degree(s) of freedom. The information-theoretic continuous Shannon entropy, however, requires an appropriate regularization, which adapts the dimensional character of the relevant degrees of freedom to the dimensionless quantity considered in the probability density $p(x)$. This is because the continuous extension of the Shannon entropy, contrary to the discrete entropy, which is an absolute quantity, is not invariant under the change of coordinates [28]. To cure this problem, Jaynes [30–32] proposed to modify Equation (3) by introducing an invariant factor $p_0(M)$, which represents the density of the discrete distribution, which gives $p(x)$ in the continuum limit:

$$S_S^{cont} = - \int_{x \in M} p(x) \ln \frac{p(x)}{p_0(M)} . \qquad (4)$$

The factor $p_0(M)$, introduced as a regularization, arises naturally when we consider the continuous Landauer reset. This factor needs to be introduced to cure the problem of classical continuous entropy, which can be negative and divergent [33,34], and is given by the minimum quantum of configuration volume of the physical system.

In Section 2 of this review, we analyze the relation between continuous phase transitions, characterized by an order parameter, and the Landauer bound [23]. Using the example of the Hopfield model [26], we show that the information-theoretic expression for the entropy production during the erasure process, expressed in terms of the error probability, has the same expressions as the thermodynamic entropy in the partially ordered phase. For the Hopfield model, however, the completely ordered state corresponds to perfect remembering rather than forgetting, so the Landauer bound sets a lower limit for the cost of 'remembering' [35].

In Section 3, using the relation between the Landauer's limit and continuos phase transitions, we extend the results of Section 2 to analog computing systems [27]. In this case, the entropy production per degree of freedom during the erasure of an analog variable is given by the logarithm of the configurational volume measured in units of its minimal quantum. Additionally, in this case, we have a "discretization" of the information bearing degrees of freedom, and an infinite amount of energies will be required to perform a computation with infinite precision.

2. Thermodynamic Entropy in Continuous Phase Transitions and Landauer Bound

Neural networks, using the definition given in [25], "are algorithms for cognitive tasks, such learning and optimization, which are in a loose sense based on concepts derived from research into the nature of the brain". One important task that neural networks perform is pattern recognition: the retrieval of information, contrary to address-oriented memories, is performed by looking at the "similarity" between a pattern, which is presented, and the stored patterns. Associative memories have the advantage of being able to retrieve information even in the case of incomplete or noisy inputs, which is not permitted in traditional computers. The Hopfield model [26,36] is the paradigmatic example of a neural network designed to perform the task of associative pattern retrieval and is largely used in associative memory.

In associative memories, when a new pattern is presented, the network evolves from a totally unknown state to a state which corresponds to the stored pattern. As shown in [25], this is gauged equivalent to a state with all neurons, e.g., equal to +1. The transition between the unknown state and the final state corresponding to the stored pattern is, by definition, the process of remembering rather than forgetting, and the Landauer limit corresponds to the minimum energy necessary for remembering. The noise affects the remembering process: when it is not too large, the network provides the minimum energy required to remember, and when errors become too important, there is a phase transition to a state in which remembering becomes impossible.

The Hopfield model [26] is a directed graph of N binary neurons s_i, $i = 1 \ldots N$, with $s_i = \pm 1$ fully connected by symmetric synapses with coupling strengths $w_{ij} = w_{ji}$ ($w_{ii} = 0$), which can be excitatory (>0) or inhibitory (<0). The state $s_i = +1$ indicates the firing state of the neuron, while $s_i = -1$ indicates the resting state. The network is characterized by an energy function

$$E = -\frac{J}{2} \sum_{i \neq j} w_{ij} s_i s_j, \quad s_i = \pm 1, \quad i,j = 1 \ldots N, \tag{5}$$

where J represents the (positive) coupling constant. The dynamical evolution of the network state is defined by the random sequential updating (in time t) of the neurons according to the rule

$$s_i(t+1) = \text{sign}(h_i(t)), \tag{6}$$
$$h_i(t) = J \sum_{i \neq j} w_{ij} s_j(t), \tag{7}$$

where h_i is the local magnetization. As is standard for neural networks and, thus, for the Hopfield model [25], the temporal evolution proceeds in finite steps, which correspond to the updating of neurons according to the rule Equation (7) in this model. At time $(t+1)$, the neurons are firing or resting depending on the activation function. This process is intrinsically discrete in time. The synaptic coupling strengths are chosen according to the Hebb rule [25]

$$w_{ij} = \frac{1}{N} \sum_{\mu=1 \ldots p} \sigma_i^\mu \sigma_j^\mu, \tag{8}$$

where σ_i^μ, $\mu = 1 \ldots p$ are p binary patterns to be memorized. The synaptic strengths contain all the information of the memory, which is encoded in the interaction between the spins σ_i^μ.

The dynamical evolution of the networks will allow the system, prepared in an initial state s_i^0 (presented pattern), to retrieve the stored pattern σ_i^λ, which most closely "resembles" the presented pattern, namely the one that minimizes the Hamming distance, i.e., the total number of different bits in the two patterns.

Updating the Hopfield network according to the Hebb rule guarantees that the dynamical evolution minimizes the energy of Equation (5): the stored patterns are "attractors" for this dynamic, namely, they are local minima of the energy functional, which is bounded below. This implies that, when an initial pattern is presented, it will evolve until it overlaps with the closest stored pattern and then not evolve anymore. The possibility of remembering depends, however, crucially upon the loading factor $\alpha = p/N$, given by the ratio between the number of stored memories and the number of available bits [25]: above a critical value, the network has a phase transition into a spin glass [36], and remembering becomes impossible.

In what follows, we consider the case of a single stored pattern σ_i. As shown in [25], using the gauge transformation,

$$s_i \to \sigma_i s_i \,, \tag{9}$$

the energy functional Equation (5) becomes

$$E = -\frac{J}{2N} \sum_{i \neq j} s_i s_j \,, \tag{10}$$

the Hopfield model thus reduces to the long-range Ising model, and the stored pattern becomes $\sigma_i = +1$ for all i. Remembering for the network, in this case, is equivalent to resetting the N-bit register to this value. Note that in the Hopfield model, since the synapses are quadratic in the spins, there is always a symmetry between the memory and its NOT for one stored pattern, e.g., $s_i = 1 \to s_i = -1 \ \forall i$, if the stored pattern all spins up as we chose in the present case. Both are minima for the dynamic. However, when a pattern is presented, the system recovers the one that is closed in the Hamming distance to the stored pattern.

The deterministic update law Equation (6) can be made probabilistic, introducing a fictitious temperature $T = 1/k\beta$ and, thus, thermal noise:

$$\text{Prob}[s_i(t+1) = +1] = f[h_i(t)] \,, \tag{11}$$

where the activation function f is the Fermi function

$$f(h) = \frac{1}{1 + \exp(-2\beta h)} \,. \tag{12}$$

The deterministic behavior is recovered in the limit $\beta \to \infty$. The main difference with respect to deterministic neurons, which are always active or dormant according to the sign of h is that stochastic neuron activities fluctuate due to thermal noise and we can define a mean activity for a single neuron:

$$\langle s_i \rangle = (+1) f(h_i) + (-1) f(-h_i) \,, \tag{13}$$

where $\langle \ldots \rangle$ denotes the thermal average. Now we note that, for the long-range Ising model, the mean field approximation $\langle f(h_i) \rangle \to f(\langle h_i \rangle)$ is exact [37], and we thus obtain the deterministic equation:

$$\langle s_i \rangle = \tanh\left(\frac{\beta J}{N} \sum_{j \neq i} \langle s_j \rangle\right) \,. \tag{14}$$

Defining the mean magnetization as $m \equiv (1/N) \sum_i <s_i>$, we can rewrite Equation (14) as

$$m = \tanh(\beta J m) \,, \tag{15}$$

where we considered the thermodynamic limit $N \to \infty$. We can now apply the known results for the mean field Ising model. The self-consistency Equation (15) has only one solution for $\beta J < 1$, which corresponds to zero magnetization, $m = 0$. When $\beta J > 1$, Equation (15) admits three solutions $m = 0$ and $m = \pm m_0(\beta)$, but only the second two solutions are stable against small fluctuations; we thus have a magnetization $m \neq 0$. The condition $\beta J = 1$ gives the critical temperature $T_c = J/k$: for $T > T_c$, the network is disordered and remembering is not possible, while for $T < T_c$, the network exhibits a partial magnetization $m \neq 0$, which goes $m \to 1$ for $T \to 0$. Partial erasure is, thus, possible.

Remembering for stochastic neurons is equivalent to a reset operation with errors. For $T \geq T_c$, individual neurons fluctuate freely, and we are in the disordered phase. When T

goes below T_c, neurons become partially frozen in the stored pattern configuration and $m(T)$ will tell us what is the average rate of errors in the reset process at this temperature. In this procedure, all work performed by lowering the temperature goes into lowering the entropy of the system. In fact, as T goes infinitesimally below T_C, the Landau function [24] bifurcates into two minima, creating a new order and a new configuration space for the network. Note, however, that if the erasure processes is performed in a finite amount of time, in this case, the system will dissipate a finite amount of heat [38,39].

Following the standard treatment for the mean field Ising model (which in the present case is an exact solution), we expand the spin variables s_i around their mean value m as $s_i = m + \delta s_i$, with $\delta s_i \equiv (s_i - m)$. At the lowest order, the energy functional becomes

$$E = \frac{JNm^2}{2} - Jm \sum_i s_i, \qquad (16)$$

where we omitted an irrelevant constant. At this order in δs_i, the partition function is

$$Z = \sum_{\text{conf.}} e^{-\beta E} = e^{-\beta J N m^2/2} [2\cosh(\beta J m)]^N. \qquad (17)$$

We thus obtain for the entropy the expression

$$\begin{aligned} S &= \frac{\partial}{\partial T}(kT \ln Z) \\ &= kN[\ln(2\cosh(\beta m J)) - \beta m J \tanh(\beta m J)]. \end{aligned} \qquad (18)$$

At $T = T_c$, $m = 0$, the system is disordered, and the entropy takes the maximum value $S = kN\ln 2$, while at $T = 0$, $m = 1$ and $S = 0$, the system is ordered and the remembering is perfect. The entropy variation between the disordered state and the state with partial remembering $0 < m(T) < 1$ is

$$\begin{aligned} \frac{-\Delta S}{kN} &= \frac{1}{kN}(S_{T_c} - S_T) \\ &= \ln 2 - \ln(2\cosh(\frac{mT_c}{T})) + \frac{mT_c}{T}\tanh(\frac{mT_c}{T}). \end{aligned} \qquad (19)$$

Equation (19) represents the heat dissipated per bit during the simulated annealing erasure procedure, and, thus, the Landauer bound for stochastic neurons described by the Hopfield model at temperature T. Perfect remembering, $T = 0$ and $m = 1$, gives back the original bound $\ln(2)$. Higher temperature corresponds to erasure with errors, in our case, due to thermal fluctuations in the fictitious temperature and, when T reaches T_C and m becomes 0, the system has a phase transition to a disordered state, and remembering is not possible anymore. In the Landauer erasure, this corresponds to resetting to an unknown state, i.e., setting the probability error $p = 1/2$ in Equation (1).

The previous analysis tell us that the error probability p in the Landauer erasure is represented by the stochastic updating rules for the Hopfield network Equation (11). According to Equation (11), the probability that a neuron flips due to thermal noise is

$$\text{Prob}[s_i(t+1) = -s_i(t)] = \frac{\exp[-\beta h_i(t)s_i(t)]}{2\cosh[\beta h_i(t)s_i(t)]}, \qquad (20)$$

so the probability that it flips from the desired value +1, since we are resetting to a memory register with all bits +1, to the wrong value -1 is

$$p = \text{Prob}[+1 \to -1] \equiv \frac{1}{2}(1 - m) = \frac{\exp(-\beta J m)}{2\cosh(\beta J m)}. \qquad (21)$$

The maximum error probability $p = 1/2$ corresponds to $m = 0$, the maximally disordered state of the network reached at $T = T_C$, while $p = 0$ corresponds to the perfect order for the network with order parameter $m = 1$ at $T = 0$. Inserting Equation (21) into Equation (19), we obtain for the entropy difference, and thus for the dissipated heat, exactly the information-theoretic expression Equation (1):

$$\frac{-\Delta S}{kN} = \ln 2 + p \ln(p) + (1-p) \ln(1-p) \,. \tag{22}$$

When $p = 0$, the Landauer bound is saturated, and the entropy difference between the increasingly disordered state of the model and its perfectly ordered $T = 0$ state reaches the exact value

$$\Delta S = kN \ln(2) \,. \tag{23}$$

Once we reach the value $m = 0$ for the order parameter, which describes the broken symmetry phase, we reach the maximum entropy for the network and we cannot keep disordering the system without violating the Landauer bound and, thus, the second law of thermodynamics. The phase transition, which takes place at T_C, thus corresponds to the saturation of the Landauer limit. The generalized Landauer theorem states, thus, that the sum of the entropy loss per bit and the one-bit error entropy cannot be lower than the bound $k\ln(2)$, and it is exactly equal to this bound when the procedure is efficient. When this bound is saturated by the error entropy, resetting (remembering here) is no longer possible, and a phase transition occurs.

The Hopfield model has a discrete Z_2 symmetry corresponding to a spin $1/2$. The generalization to higher-order spins with a classical $Z_{(2n+1)}$ symmetry, with $n = 1/2, 1, 3/2 \ldots$ is, however, straightforward. In the case of a $Z_{(2n+1)}$ symmetry, Equation (23) becomes

$$-\Delta S = (S(T_C) - S(0)) = kN \ln(2n+1) \,. \tag{24}$$

In the more general case of a continuous phase transition of a system of N elementary components with D degrees of freedom each, which undergoes a continuous phase transition to a partially ordered phase below a critical temperature, we have only d degrees of freedom, which survive in the partially ordered phase, while the others are frozen. The phase transition is characterized by a complex vector of ordered parameters whose norm η rises from 0 in the disordered phase to 1 at zero temperature. The ration between the original degrees of freedom D and the one in the partially ordered phase d can be written as

$$D/d = q^n \,, \tag{25}$$

with n being an integer larger than one if D/d is a prime power and q a prime number. If D/d is not a prime power, we have $n = 1$ and $q = D/d$. If we take, for example, the simple case $q = 2$, the phase transition can be seen as the formal "resetting" of dN bits to their standard value, with error probability $p(T) = (1 - \eta(T))/2$. The entropy change during a generic phase transition is, thus, again given by Equation (22) with $N \to dN$. Otherwise, the Landauer bound would be violated in the ordering process. For $q = 3$, we have trits instead of bits, and the generalization to other values of q is straightforward.

3. Analog Computing Systems

In analog computing systems, information is encoded in a continuous variable. To compute the entropy change during the erasure of information encoded in a continuous variable, we will use the relation between the Landauer principle and entropy change during continuous phase transitions [23]. We will again assume that the erasure is efficient.

We study the 3-dimensional ferromagnetic classic Heisenberg model, which undergoes a phase transition with spontaneous symmetry breaking of $O(3) \to O(2)$ [24], which is described by the Hamiltonian

$$\mathcal{H} = -\frac{J}{2} \sum_{\langle i,j \rangle} s_i \cdot s_j - H \sum_i s_i \,, \tag{26}$$

where $\langle i, j \rangle$, which denotes the sum over nearest neighbors spin, with i that goes from 1 to the number N of spins and $|s|^2 = 1$. In this case, the spin orientation, that encodes analog information, can take all values on a sphere of unit radius and we have, thus, a continuum of possible values; for the Ising spins, the orientation is binary, up or down.

Since the model is ferromagnetic, we have $J > 0$. H is a constant external magnetic field in the $\hat{z}$ direction. The ferromagnetic Heisenberg model undergoes a continuous phase transition [24], characterized by an order parameter m, the mean magnetization. For $T \geq T_C$, the system is disordered, while for $T < T_C$, the phase becomes partially ordered and m reaches the value 1 at $T = 0$. As in the case of discrete symmetry, lowering the temperature is akin to an erasure process, and m plays the role of the error probability in the reset operation [20].

Following what we did in the previous section, we identify the Shannon entropy of the erasure process in the analog computing system with the entropy variation during the transition from from $T = T_C$ to $T = 0$. The entropy variation

$$-\frac{\Delta S}{kN} = \frac{(S(T_C) - S(0))}{kN}, \tag{27}$$

gives, thus, the Landauer bound for an analog computing system [23].

We use again the mean field approximation; the mean field Hamiltonian for the Heisenberg model is [24]

$$\mathcal{H}_{\text{mf}} = -J \sum_{<i,j>} s_i H_{\text{eff}} + \frac{JNm^2}{2},$$
$$H_{\text{eff}} = (Jm + H), \tag{28}$$

where m is the mean magnetization: $m \equiv (1/N) \sum_i \langle s_i \rangle$. The effective magnetic field is the sum of the average magnetic field, generated by all other spins, plus the external magnetic field H. As usual, we will take the limit $H \to 0$, obtaining, thus, the partition function:

$$Z = \exp\left[\beta \frac{JN3m^2}{2}\right] \int d^3s \delta(s^2 - 1) \exp\left[\beta J \sum_{i=1}^{N} m \cos\theta_i\right], \tag{29}$$

where θ_i is the angle between the spin and the $\hat{z}$ direction and $\beta = (kT)^{-1}$. From Equation (29), we derive the free energy

$$\frac{F}{N} = \frac{Jm^2 3}{2} - \frac{1}{\beta} \ln\left[\frac{4\pi \sinh \beta m J}{\beta m J}\right], \tag{30}$$

and from the free energy, the entropy

$$\frac{S}{kN} = \ln\left[\frac{4\pi \sinh \beta m J}{\beta m J}\right] - \beta m J L(\beta m J), \tag{31}$$

where $L(x) = \coth x - 1/x$ is the Langevin function.

Let us now consider the limits for $T = T_C$ and $T = 0$ of Equation (36). When $T \to T_C$, $m \to 0$, and the entropy reaches its maximal value, the logarithm of the volume of the configuration space, namely, the area of a sphere of unitary radius:

$$\frac{S(T_C)}{kN} = \ln(4\pi). \tag{32}$$

When $T \to 0$ and $m \to 1$, which corresponds to the perfect reset, the entropy becomes negative and divergent, contrary to the third law of thermodynamics:

$$\frac{S(T \to 0)}{kN} \to -\infty. \tag{33}$$

This problem is common for various classical systems. One textbook example is the classical harmonic oscillator [40], and, in general, the way to cure this problem is to consider the classical system as the limit of its quantum counterpart.

In the mean field approximation, the quantum ferromagnetic Heisenberg model describes a system of quantum, non-interacting spins s_i with $(2s + 1)$ components in an external magnetic field H_{eff}. The mean field Hamiltonian for the quantum Heisenberg model is [41]:

$$\mathcal{H} = -H_{\text{eff}} \sum_{i=1}^{N} s_i \,. \tag{34}$$

It describes non-interacting $(2s+1)$ components spins in an external magnetic field H_{eff}, which, again, is the sum of the average magnetic field generated by all other spins plus an external magnetic field H. The partition function is

$$Z = \left[\sum_{n=-s}^{s} \exp \beta H_{\text{eff}} n \right]^{N}, \tag{35}$$

while the entropy, in the limit in which the external magnetic field $H \to 0$, is

$$\frac{S}{kN} = \ln \left[\frac{\sinh(1+\frac{1}{2s})\beta m J s}{\sinh \frac{\beta m J s}{2s}} \right] - \beta m J s B_s(\beta m J) \,, \tag{36}$$

where $B_s(\beta m J)$ is the Brillouin function defined as $B_n(x) = \frac{2n+1}{2n} \coth\left(\frac{2n+1}{2n} x\right) - \frac{1}{2n} \coth\left(\frac{1}{2n} x\right)$. In the limit $T \to 0$, the entropy Equation (36) goes to zero, $\frac{S(T=0)}{kN} = 0$, in agreement with the third law of thermodynamics.

The classical limit of the quantum Heisenberg model [42–44] is obtained by properly distributing the $(2s+1)$ values of the quantum spin on the classical sphere of area $4\pi r^2$ with r that is the dimension of an action and is equal to 1 in our case. If we call $s_{\max}$ the highest weight of the representation in the quantum case, we can define the spin density as [42]

$$\Delta(2s_{\max}+1) \to 4\pi \text{ for } s_{\max} \to \infty, \Delta \to 0 \,. \tag{37}$$

To ensure the existence of the infinite spin limit [42], we need, however, to rescale the spin as $s \to s/s_{\max}$. The minimum state volume Δ represents the minimum area in the unitary sphere occupied by a spin. This minimum volume is given by the Heisenberg principle:

$$\Delta = \frac{1}{2}\hbar^2 s_{\max} \,; \hbar s_{\max} \to s_{\text{clas}} \text{ for } s_{\max} \to \infty, \hbar \to 0, \tag{38}$$

with s_{class}, which has the dimensions of an action, and $s_{\text{class}} = 1$ in our case. Correspondingly, we define the regularized entropy as

$$\frac{S}{kN} = \ln \frac{4\pi}{(2s_{\max}+1)} \left[\frac{\sinh(1+\frac{1}{2s_{\max}})\beta m J}{\sinh \frac{\beta m J}{2s_{\max}}} \right] \\ - \beta m J B_{s_{\max}}(\beta m J) \,. \tag{39}$$

The classical limit corresponds to $s_{\max} \to \infty$. When $T = T_C$, the entropy is, as before,

$$\frac{S(T=T_C)}{kN} = \ln(4\pi) \,, \tag{40}$$

while at $T = 0$, we obtain

$$\frac{S(T \to 0)}{kN} = \ln\left(\frac{4\pi}{2s_{\max}+1}\right) = \ln \frac{1}{2}\hbar^2 s_{\max} = \ln \frac{1}{2}\hbar \,, \tag{41}$$

where we use Equations (37) and (38) (note that in the last term of Equation (41), $\hbar$ is divided by a constant that has the dimension of an action and that it is equal to one). This result tells us that if we want to avoid the entropy divergence, we cannot actually send $\hbar \to 0$. In fact, the limit $\hbar \to 0$ corresponds to a classical distribution concentrated in regions smaller than the minimum area allowed by the Heisenberg principle. Δ is the factor $p_0(M)$ in Equation (4), and its presence is due to the fact that the continuous Shannon entropy must be regularized in order to make it invariant upon a change of coordinates.

Using Equations (40) and (41), we obtain for the entropy variation

$$-\frac{\Delta S}{kN} = \frac{S(T_C) - S(T=0)}{kN} =$$
$$= \ln(4\pi s_{\text{clas}}^2) - \ln\frac{1}{2}\hbar^2 s_{\max} = \ln\frac{8\pi s_{\text{clas}}}{\hbar}. \quad (42)$$

For the Heisenberg model, we have $s_{\text{class}} = 1$, and we thus obtain

$$-\frac{\Delta S}{kN} = \frac{S(T_C) - S(T=0)}{kN} = \ln\frac{8\pi}{\hbar}, \quad (43)$$

(note that the quantity inside the logarithm is dimensionless since $s_{\text{class}} = 1$ has the dimensions of an action). Entropy variation Equation (43) represents the analog generalization of the Landauer bound: the entropy change during the erasure process performed by resetting a continuous variable, the spin s, to a standard value is given by the available configuration volume (the area 4π in this case) measured in units of the minimum quantum of configuration volume Δ. This implies that, both for digital or analog information, physical systems can encode only a finite countable amount of information [28,45,46], and that information can be manipulated only with finite precision: infinite precision, namely the realization of a truly analog computing system, is forbidden by the laws of physics.

The maximum number of possible logic states that we can associate with the Heisenberg model is

$$N_l = \text{int}\left(\frac{8\pi}{\hbar}\right), \quad (44)$$

(int(a) is the integer part of number a), while for a generic angular momentum L, it is

$$N_l = \text{int}\left(\frac{8\pi L}{\hbar}\right), \quad (45)$$

to which we can associate a finite number of bits:

$$n = \log_2(N_l). \quad (46)$$

For the case of a cube of $5 \times 5 \times 5 = 125$ atoms [47], with an angular momentum per atom of the order of $L \approx \hbar$, for which the interactions between the momenta are such that they behave like a single classical momentum, we have $N_l = 3140$. From Equation (46), we obtain a number $n \approx 11.6$ of bits that can be stored. Under the same assumption, in a system of magnetic nano-dots with a 20 nm side, containing approximately 200 million atoms, we can store up to $n = 27.6$ bits. If we want to perform with this system a perfect Landauer reset, the amount of heat to be dissipated is readily provided by Equation (42): $Q \geq 19.11kT$, approximately 30 times what we would have for a binary system reset.

We now want to consider the more general case of the symmetry breaking pattern $O(n) \to O(n-1)$. Within the mean field approximation, this generalization is straightforward. From Equation (29), substituting $d^3s \to d^n s$, we have

$$Z = \exp\left[\beta\frac{JN3m^2}{2}\right]\int d^n s\delta(s^2-1)\exp\left[\beta J\sum_{i=1}^N m\cos\theta_i\right], \quad (47)$$

and for the entropy

$$\frac{S}{kN} = \ln\left[2^{\frac{n}{2}}\pi^{\frac{n}{2}}\frac{I_{\frac{n}{2}-1}(\beta mJ)}{(\beta mJ)^{\frac{n}{2}}}\right] - \beta mJ\frac{I_{\frac{n}{2}}(\beta mJ)}{I_{\frac{n}{2}-1}(\beta mJ)}, \quad (48)$$

with $I_\nu(z)$, the modified Bessel functions of the first kind.

The entropy difference between the perfectly ordered state at $T=0$ and the completely disordered one, at $T = T_C$, $m = 0$, which gives the Landauer bound for the erasure of a $O(n)$ spin s is

$$-\frac{\Delta S}{kN} = \frac{S(T_C) - S(0)}{kN}, \quad (49)$$

with
$$\frac{S(T_C)}{kN} = \ln S_{n-1}, \quad S_{n-1} = \frac{2\pi^{\frac{n}{2}}}{\Gamma\left(\frac{n}{2}\right)}, \tag{50}$$

where S_{n-1} is the area of the $(n-1)$-sphere of unit radius and $\Gamma(x)$ is the Euler gamma function. As for the Heisenberg model, the limit $T \to 0$ is singular, and the entropy is negative and logarithmically divergent: $(S(T \to 0)/kN) \to -\infty$.

The regularization of the entropy in this case is, however, more complicated since, contrary to the $O(3)$ Heisenberg model, the analytical results are not known [48] for the $O(n)$-symmetric quantum Heisenberg model, not even in the mean field. Additionally, the definition of the classical limit is not clear. Extending to this case the results obtained for the $O(3)$ case, given by Equation (50), we conjecture that for the $O(n)$-symmetric case, the entropy change during the erasure process will be given by the available configuration volume, the area of the n-sphere, measured in units of the minimum quantum of the configuration volume that in this case will be $\propto \hbar^{n-2}$. In the case of the $SU(n)$-symmetric (restricted to symmetric representations) Heisenberg model, the possibility of having a positive classical entropy was proposed by Lieb and Solovey [49] using a coherent states approach.

Funding: This research received no external funding.

Institutional Review Board Statement: Not applicable.

Data Availability Statement: Not applicable.

Conflicts of Interest: The author declares no conflict of interest.

References

1. Landauer, R. Irreversibility and heat generation in the computing process. *IBM J. Res. Dev.* **1961**, *5*, 183–191. [CrossRef]
2. Landauer, R. Information Is Physical. *Phys. Today* **1991**, *44*, 23–29. [CrossRef]
3. Landauer, R. The Physical Nature of Information. *Phys. Lett. A* **1996**, *217*, 188–193. [CrossRef]
4. Szilard, L. Uber die Entropieverminderung in einem thermodynamischen System bei Eingriffen intelligenter Wesen. *Z. Phys.* **1929**, *53*, 840–856. [CrossRef]
5. Bennet, C.H. The thermodynamics of computation—A review. *Int. J. Theor. Phys.* **1982**, *21*, 905–940. [CrossRef]
6. Brillouin, L. Maxwell's Demon Cannot Operate: Information and entropy. I. *J. Appl. Phys.* **1951**, *22*, 334–337. [CrossRef]
7. Brillouin, L. Physical Entropy and Information. II. *J. Appl. Phys.* **1951**, *22*, 338–343. [CrossRef]
8. Zivieri, R. Magnetic Skyrmions as Information Entropy Carriers. *IEEE Trans. Magn.* **2022**, *58*, 1500105. [CrossRef]
9. Zivieri, R. From Thermodynamics to Information: Landauer's Limit and Negentropy Principle Applied to Magnetic Skyrmions. *Front. Phys.* **2022**, *10*, 769904. [CrossRef]
10. Berut, A.; Arakelyan, A.; Petrosyan, A.; Cilberto, S.; Dillenschneider, R.; Lutz, E. Experimental verification of Landauer's principle linking information and thermodynamics. *Nature* **2012**, *483*, 187–189. [CrossRef]
11. Roland, E.; Martinez, I.A.; Parrondo, J.M.R.; Petrov, D. Universal features in the energetics of symmetry breaking. *Nat. Phys.* **2014**, *10*, 457.
12. Jun, Y.; Gavrilov, M.; Bechhoefer, J. High-Precision Test of Landauer's Principle in a Feedback Trap. *Phys. Rev. Lett.* **2014**, *113*, 190601. [CrossRef] [PubMed]
13. Hong, J.H.; Lambson, B.; Dhuey, S.; Bokor, J. Experimental test of Landauer's principle in single-bit operations on nanomagnetic memory bits. *Sci. Adv.* **2016**, *2*, e1501492. [CrossRef]
14. Maroney, O.J.E. Generalising Landauer's principle. *Phys. Rev. E* **2009**, *79*, 031105. [CrossRef] [PubMed]
15. Kish, L.B.; Granqvist, C.G. Energy requirement of control: Comments on Szilard's engine and Maxwell's demon. *Europhys. Lett.* **2012**, *98*, 68001. [CrossRef]
16. Norton, J.D. All shook up: Fluctuations, Maxwell's demon and the thermodynamics of computation. *Entropy* **2013**, *15*, 4432–4483. [CrossRef]
17. Sagawa, T. Thermodynamic and logical reversibilities revisited. *J. Stat. Mech.* **2014**, *2014*, 03025. [CrossRef]
18. Chiuchiu, D.; Diamantini, M.C.; Gammaitoni, L. Conditional entropy and Landauer principle. *Europhys. Lett.* **2015**, *111*, 40004. [CrossRef]
19. Parrondo, J.M.; Horowitz, J.M.; Sagawa, T. Thermodynamics of information. *Nat. Phys.* **2015**, *11*, 131–139. [CrossRef]
20. Gammaitoni, L. Beating the Landauer's limit by trading energy with uncertainty. *arXiv* **2011**, arXiv:1111.2937v1.
21. Sagawa, T.; Ueda, M. Nonequilibrium thermodynamics of feedback control. *Phys. Rev. E* **2012**, *85*, 021104. [CrossRef]

22. Sagawa, T.; Ueda, M. Minimal energy cost for thermodynamic information processing: Measurement and information erasure. *Phys. Rev. Lett.* **2009**, *102*, 250602. [CrossRef]
23. Diamantini, M.C.; Trugenberger, C.A. Generalized Landauer bound as a universal thermodynamic entropy in continuous phase transitions. *Phys. Rev. E* **2014**, *89*, 052138. [CrossRef]
24. Negele, J.W.; Orland, H. *Quantum Many-Particle Systems*; Addison-Wesley: Boston, MA, USA, 1998.
25. Müller, B.; Reinhardt, J. *Neural Networks*; Springer: Berlin, Germany, 1990.
26. Hopfield, J.J. Neural networks and physical systems with emergent collective computational abilities. *Proc. Nat. Acad. Sci. USA* **1982**, *79*, 2554. [CrossRef]
27. Diamantini, M.C.; Gammaitoni, L.; Trugenberger, C.A. Landauer bound for analog computing systems. *Phys. Rev. E* **2016**, *94*, 012139. [CrossRef]
28. Ihara, S. *Information Theory for Continuous Systems*; World Scientific: Singapore, 1993.
29. Shannon, C.E. *The Mathematical Theory of Communication*; University of Illinois Press: Champaign, IL, USA, 1949.
30. Jaynes, E.T. *Information Theory and Statistical Mechanics*; Brandeis University Summer Institute Lectures in Theoretical Physics; Brandeis University: Waltham, MA, USA, 1963.
31. Jaynes, E.T. Information Theory and Statistical Mechanics I. *Phys. Rev.* **1957**, *106*, 620–630. [CrossRef]
32. Jaynes, E.T. Information Theory and Statistical Mechanics II. *Phys. Rev.* **1957**, *108*, 171–190. [CrossRef]
33. Ash, R. *Information Theory*; Interscience Publication: New York, NY, USA, 1965.
34. Wehrl, A. On the relation between classical and quantum-mechanical entropy. *Rep. Math. Phys.* **1979**, *16*, 353–358. [CrossRef]
35. Chiuchiu, D.; Lopez-Suarez, M.; Neri, I.; Diamantini, M.C.; Gammaitoni, L. Cost of remembering a bit of information. *Phys. Rev. A* **2018**, *97*, 052108. [CrossRef]
36. Mezard, M.; Parisi, G.; Virasoro, M.A. *Spin Glass Theory and Beyond*; World Scientific: Singapore, 1987.
37. Zinn-Justin, J. *Quantum Field Theory and Critical Phenomena*; Oxford University Press: Oxford, UK, 1989.
38. Proesmans, K.; Ehrich, J.; Bechhoefer, J. Finite-time Landauer principle. *Phys. Rev. Lett.* **2020**, *125*, 100602. [CrossRef]
39. Van Vu, T.; Saito, K. Finite-time quantum Landauer principle and quantum coherence. *Phys. Rev. Lett.* **2022**, *128*, 010602. [CrossRef] [PubMed]
40. Hängi, P.; Ingold, G.L. Quantum Brownian motion and the Third Law of thermodynamics. *Acta Phys. Pol. B* **2006**, *37*, 1537.
41. Pathria, R.K. *Statistical Mechanics*; Pergamon Press: Oxford, UK, 1972.
42. Fisher, M.E. Magnetism in one-dimensional systems—The Heisenberg model for infinite spin. *Am. J. Phys.* **1964**, *32*, 343–346. [CrossRef]
43. Millard, K.; Leff, H.S. Infinite-Spin Limit of the Quantum Heisenberg Model. *J. Math. Phys.* **1971**, *12*, 1000. [CrossRef]
44. Lieb, E.H. The classical limit of quantum spin systems. *Commun. Math. Phys.* **1973**, *31*, 327–340. [CrossRef]
45. Bekenstein, J.D. Entropy content and information flow in systems with limited energy. *Phys. Rev. D* **1984**, *30*, 1669. [CrossRef]
46. Loydd, S. Ultimate physical limits to computation. *Nature* **2000**, *406*, 1047. [CrossRef]
47. Feynman, R.P. There's plenty of room at the bottom [data storage]. *J. Microelectromech. Syst.* **1992**, *1*, 60–66. [CrossRef]
48. Berdnikov, B.A. *Quantum Magnets with an SO(n) Symmetry*; MIT: Cambridge, MA, USA, 1998; and reference therein.
49. Lieb, E.H.; Solovej, J.P. Proof of the Wehrl-type Entropy Conjecture for Symmmetric SU(N) Coherent States. *Commun. Math. Phys.* **2016**, *348*, 567–578. [CrossRef]

Disclaimer/Publisher's Note: The statements, opinions and data contained in all publications are solely those of the individual author(s) and contributor(s) and not of MDPI and/or the editor(s). MDPI and/or the editor(s) disclaim responsibility for any injury to people or property resulting from any ideas, methods, instructions or products referred to in the content.

Article

Dissipation during the Gating Cycle of the Bacterial Mechanosensitive Ion Channel Approaches the Landauer Limit

Uğur Çetiner [1,*,†], Oren Raz [2], Madolyn Britt [1] and Sergei Sukharev [1]

[1] Maryland Biophysics Program, Institute for Physical Science and Technology, Department of Biology, University of Maryland, College Park, MD 20742, USA
[2] Department of Physics of Complex Systems, Faculty of Physics, Weizmann Institute of Science, Rehovot 7610001, Israel
* Correspondence: ugur_cetiner@hms.harvard.edu
[†] Current address: Department of Systems Biology, Harvard Medical School, Boston, MA 02115, USA.

Abstract: The Landauer principle sets a thermodynamic bound of $k_B T \ln 2$ on the energetic cost of erasing each bit of information. It holds for any memory device, regardless of its physical implementation. It was recently shown that carefully built artificial devices can attain this bound. In contrast, biological computation-like processes, e.g., DNA replication, transcription and translation use an order of magnitude more than their Landauer minimum. Here, we show that reaching the Landauer bound is nevertheless possible with biological devices. This is achieved using a mechanosensitive channel of small conductance (MscS) from *E. coli* as a memory bit. MscS is a fast-acting osmolyte release valve adjusting turgor pressure inside the cell. Our patch-clamp experiments and data analysis demonstrate that under a slow switching regime, the heat dissipation in the course of tension-driven gating transitions in MscS closely approaches its Landauer limit. We discuss the biological implications of this physical trait.

Keywords: Landauer's principle; heat dissipation; MscS

1. Introduction

Any computation performed on a physical system is subject to fundamental limitations imposed by the laws of physics. For example, the uncertainty principle implies that to perform an elementary logical operation faster than some Δt, at least an average amount of energy $E \geq \pi \hbar / 2 \Delta t$ must be consumed [1]. This bound can be understood intuitively as a consequence of the fact that there is a fundamental limit on the maximum number of different states that a physical system can traverse per unit of time, as first demonstrated by Margolus and Levitin [2]. Another important bound on computation, which is the main focus of this work, is set by the laws of thermodynamics. According to Landauer's principle [3], at least $k_B T \ln 2$ of heat dissipation must accompany any one-bit erasing process. Here, k_B is Boltzmann's constant and T is the ambient temperature. Equality can be achieved for quasi-static (reversible) erasure protocols. The heat released into the environment during the erasure of information assures that the total increase in the entropy of the system and bath together is a non-negative quantity. Importantly, this bound applies to any non-reversible erasing process of a memory, regardless of the physical system that was used to implement it. Therefore, Landauer's principle demonstrates the interplay between physics and information. In recent decades, Landauer's principle was generalized to include: a probabilistic erasure process [4,5]; other types of thermodynamic resources [6]; entropically unbalanced bits [7]; a unified view on the cost of erasing and measuring a bit [8,9]; N state bit [10]; optimal erasure at finite time [11,12]; and others [13].

The existence of a fundamental bound does not imply that the bound can be attained. Indeed, current computer memory devices dissipate about 6 orders of magnitude more energy than the minimum amount required by the bound. Similarly, estimations of the energy dissipated in biological computations such as DNA and gene replications show that these are performed with about an order of magnitude more dissipation than required by

Landauer's bound [14]. Recently, however, it was demonstrated that carefully built artificial systems can actually operate very close to Landauer's bound. This was achieved with several types of systems: a single colloidal particle in an optical [15,16] or feedback [17–19] traps, nanomagnetic bits [20–22], superconducting flux bit [23] and even quantum systems [24,25]. Based on these results, it is natural to ask whether there are any biological memory-erasing processes that operate close to Landauer's limit.

Out of many biological systems, the bacterial mechanosensitive ion channels of small and large conductance, MscS and MscL, appear to be the most tractable systems controlled by tension in the surrounding membrane [26–28]. MscL is essentially a two-state (closed↔open) whereas MscS shows inactivating behavior (inactivated↔closed↔open), but under certain tension protocols it can be treated as a two-state channel [29]. They function as osmolyte release valves when bacteria face changing environmental osmotic conditions, such as with drastic dilution in the rain. While the large-conductance MscL channel opens by extreme near-lytic tensions and acts as an emergency valve, the small-conductance MscS channel opens at moderate tensions and appears to be active throughout the normal bacterial lifecycle [27,30–32].

In this work, we present a framework for the analysis of heat dissipation in membrane channels gated by tension. We employ the patch-clamp technique applied to the native *E. coli* membrane to record discrete single-molecule opening and closing events in MscS under specially designed tension stimuli and extract the dissipated heat that accompanies gating transitions. The state of the ion channel, which can be either "open" or "closed", encodes a single bit of information. Setting the experimental conditions such that the channel occupies these two states with equal probability introduces the maximum degree of randomness. Changing the biasing tension that re-distributes the channel population to one particular state is equivalent to "erasing the memory" stored in the initially randomized population. We extract the heat dissipated during the "restore to open" process imposed with different rates and show that this system dissipates substantially at high transition rates, but under slower driving protocols, MscS gating closely approaches its Landauer limit. We discuss the physiological importance of this physical trait, which predicts the activation of MscS with minimal dissipation under moderate osmotic shocks experienced by bacteria.

2. Experimental and Theoretical Setup

To measure the dissipated heat during the erasure of a single bit, Landauer suggested the use of a "restore to one" protocol [3], which results in the bit occupying a single state—the "one" state—regardless of the initial state of the bit. He then argued that the heat dissipated in applying this protocol, averaged over the two initial states of the bit, must be at least $k_B T \ln 2$.

To record gating (closed↔open) transitions in MscS channels, a standard patch-clamp technique was applied to giant *E. coli* spheroplasts [33–35]. Approaching the surface of a spheroplast with a polished glass pipette with a tip diameter of ~1.5 μm and applying gentle suction forms a contact between the glass and membrane with a Giga-Ohm resistance (Giga-seal). This tight seal isolates the patch membrane under the pipette both electrically and mechanically. Excision of the patch from the spheroplast provides electrical access to both sides of the membrane, which now separates the "pipette" and "bath" aqueous solutions (Figure 1 left). Under constant voltage of 30 mV across the patch and applying stronger suction (−60–150 mm Hg), which stretches the membrane, we can see the activation of mechanosensitive channels observed as the increase in the patch (DC) current. Tension in the membrane (γ), the main activating stimulus, is related to the applied pressure (p) through the radius of curvature of the patch (r) according to the law of Laplace $\gamma = pr/2$ (see the Materials and Methods for the details of tension calibration). Pressure ramps applied to multi-channel patches activate multiple (~100) channels, and these "population currents" directly reflect the mean open probability (P_{open}) in the population when normalized to the current level at saturating pressures. The analysis of channel population responses to ramps allows us to determine the threshold, the level of saturation and the midpoint ($p_{0.5}$ or $\gamma_{0.5}$), which is the condition of equipartitioning between the closed and open states.

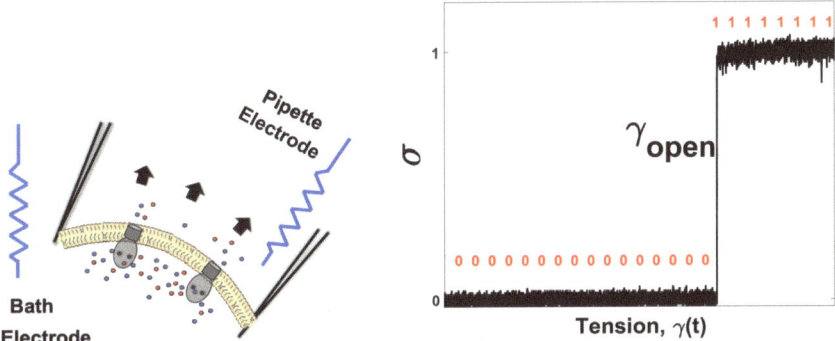

Figure 1. (**Left**) Schematic description of the experimental apparatus. The Giga-ohm resistance of the piece of *E. coli*'s inner membrane with naturally embedded mechanosensitive ion channels (MscS) seals the micro-pipette, and provides electrical isolation between its inner and outer sides. Application of suction to the glass pipette stretches the curved membrane according to Laplace's law. This tension can change the state of the MscS channels, generating detectable conducting pathways between the two electrodes. (**Right**) The state of the channel (σ) as a function of the membrane tension (γ). A single channel event is shown. The state of the channel can be monitored with a high temporal resolution. The transition from the closed (0) state to the open state (1) occurs at γ_{open}.

With a higher amplification, these molecular activation events can be monitored with pico-ampere precision, which allows us to track the distribution of channels between the open and closed states at a single-channel resolution [36]. To achieve this resolution and discern transitions in individual channels, we switched to a special vector in which *mscS* expression was controlled by a tight promotor. This allowed us to reduce the channel population to 10-20 channels per patch and observe individual molecular activation events (see, for example, Figure 2B).

In this setting, we implemented the "restore to one" protocol on MscS ion channels, where the one-bit information is stored in the "open" and "closed" states of a single MscS ion channel (Figure 2A). In a typical experiment, after seal formation and patch excision, a linear ramp of negative pressure (suction) from zero to the saturating level is applied to the patch with simultaneous current recording. This step determines the activation pressure midpoint ($p_{0.5}$) at which the population is equally distributed between the closed and open conformations, i.e., the state of highest uncertainty. In the following "bit erasure" protocol, the pressure is quickly ramped to $p_{0.5}$, the population is allowed to equilibrate for 3 s and then the pressure is ramped with different rates to a higher level, where all channels uniformly assume the open conformation (state of highest certainty). The recorded traces with easily discernable single-channel steps are analyzed with the "edge detection" protocol (An Edge Detector program (http://cismm.web.unc.edu/resources/tutorials/edge-detector-1d-tutorial/, accessed on 19 May 2020, see Figure 4) was employed to detect the single channel events.) as described below.

At room temperature, the minimal dissipated heat set by Landauer's bound, $k_B T \ln 2$, is extremely low—about 10^{-21} joules. This makes any direct measurement of the heat absorbed by the environment, e.g., by measuring its thermal expansion or temperature raising, highly challenging. Fortunately, the recent theory of stochastic thermodynamics [37] suggests a way to measure the dissipated heat by watching the behavior of the thermal system itself, rather than measuring the environment. This method was used in measuring the saturation of Landauer's bound in artificial systems [15–21]. The usage of stochastic thermodynamics was already successfully demonstrated on MscS ion channels in a different context [38].

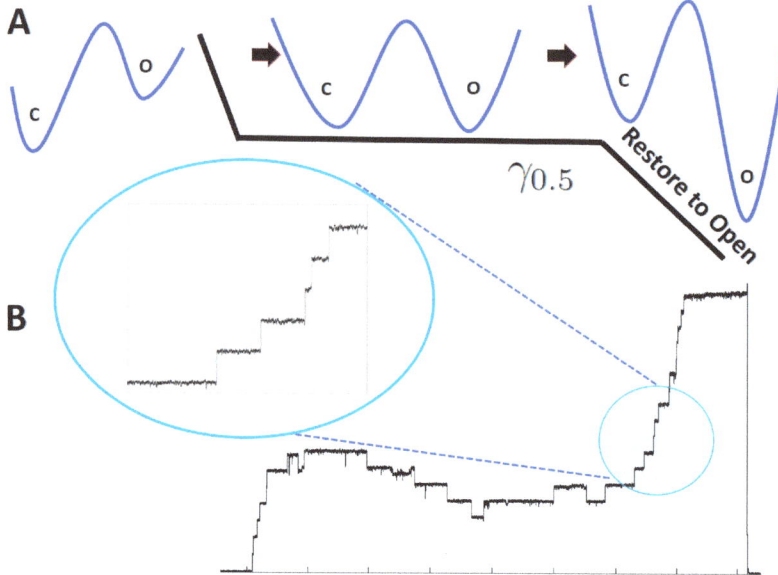

Figure 2. (**A**): Restore to open protocol. When unperturbed, the channels naturally occupy the low energy configuration, which is the closed state. In the first part of the protocol, the tension was quickly (∼ 0.25 s) increased to the midpoint tension $\gamma_{0.5}$ (1.9 $k_B T$/nm^2) [39] at which the probability of finding a channel in the open or closed state was 0.5. The tension was kept fixed at $\gamma_{0.5}$ for 3 s to let the channels thermalize at this specific tension value. In the final setup, the tension was increased from $\gamma_{0.5}$ to $\gamma_\tau = \gamma_{max}$ (3 $k_B T$/nm^2) in 0.25, 1, 5 and 10 s. Regardless of the initial state of the channels, at the end of the final step, all channels were forced to be in the open state. (**B**): An experimental trace obtained from the restore to open protocol. In the final step, the tension was increased from $\gamma_{0.5}$ to γ_τ in 1 s. The inset shows the single-channel gating events at a higher magnification during the restore to one operation.

To discuss heat dissipation in the MscS ion channel, we model it as a two-state system ("open" and "closed"), and introduce a state variable, $\sigma = 0$ for a closed channel and $\sigma = 1$ for an open one. For a system with N such channels, we denote with $\bar{\sigma}$ the average over the states of the different channels. In contrast to σ, which can take only 0 and 1 as its value, $\bar{\sigma}$ can take any value between 0 and 1 with an accuracy N^{-1}. Let ϵ_{closed} and ϵ_{open} denote the energies of the closed and open states of the ion channel itself. The total energy of the ion channels and the membrane is a function of the tension γ and the state variable σ, and is given by [38,40,41]:

$$H(\bar{\sigma}, \gamma) = N\big[(1-\bar{\sigma})\epsilon_{\text{closed}} + \bar{\sigma}\epsilon_{\text{open}}\big] - \gamma A(\bar{\sigma}), \tag{1}$$

The additional term $\gamma A(\bar{\sigma}) = N\gamma\bar{\sigma}\Delta A$ represents the decrease in the energy of the membrane that occurs when the channels open in response to the applied tension, γ. Here, ΔA is the area difference between the closed and open state of the channel. Thus, in the presence of external tension on the membrane, states with larger areas become favorable [28,29]. The energy and area difference between the closed and open states of a single MscS channel were already measured in previous publications [29,38], and are given by: $\Delta\epsilon \equiv \epsilon_{\text{open}} - \epsilon_{\text{closed}} = 22\ k_B T$ and $\Delta A = 12$ nm^2 (for more details, see Section 5.2). In what follows, we used the standard assumption that ΔA and $\Delta\epsilon$ are the same for all MscS channels.

Based on the above energy in the system, the total change in energy can be expressed as follows [42]:

$$dH(\bar{\sigma}, \gamma) = \left[\left(\frac{\partial H}{\partial \gamma}\right)_{\bar{\sigma}} d\gamma + \left(\frac{\partial H}{\partial \bar{\sigma}}\right)_{\gamma} d\bar{\sigma} \right]. \quad (2)$$

The first term on the square brackets of Equation (2) is the change in energy resulting from some external force changing the tension, which is therefore associated with work. The second term is the variation of the energy resulting from the change in the internal configuration of the system, namely due to redistribution between states. To conserve the total energy, this energetic change requires an exchange of energy with the surrounding thermal bath, and is therefore associated with heat. With these interpretations, the total heat and work associated with a realization of the experimental protocol can be written as:

$$W \equiv \int_0^\tau \dot{\gamma} \frac{\partial H}{\partial \gamma} dt = -\Delta A N \int_0^\tau \dot{\gamma} \bar{\sigma} dt \quad (3)$$

$$Q \equiv \int_0^\tau \dot{\bar{\sigma}} \frac{\partial H}{\partial \bar{\sigma}} dt = N \int_0^\tau (\epsilon_{\text{open}} - \epsilon_{\text{closed}} - \gamma \Delta A) \dot{\bar{\sigma}} dt \quad (4)$$

where τ is the protocol's duration. In our experiments, the tension γ is changed linearly with time; therefore, we can write the work integral in the following form:

$$W = -N\Delta A \int_0^{\gamma_\tau} \bar{\sigma} d\gamma, \quad (5)$$

which can be interpreted as $N\Delta A$ times minus the area under the $\bar{\sigma}(\gamma)$ graph. The above definitions of heat and work imply the $N \to \infty$ limit, to make sense of $\bar{\sigma}$. The tools of stochastic thermodynamics enable us to extend these definitions to small systems with even a single channel, where σ can take only discrete values of 0 or 1, and changes abruptly between them. In this case, the work in Equation (5) can be directly used. To calculate the heat, however, we note that in this case $\sigma(t)$, shown in Figure 1, can be approximated with the Heaviside step function:

$$\sigma(t) = \theta(t - t_{\text{open}}). \quad (6)$$

Exploiting the relations between the Heaviside step function and the Dirac delta function, we can write the heat integral in a particular realization:

$$\begin{aligned} Q_{\text{realization}} &= \int_0^\tau \dot{\bar{\sigma}} \frac{\partial H}{\partial \bar{\sigma}} dt = \int_0^{\gamma_\tau} \frac{\partial H}{\partial \bar{\sigma}} \sum_{\text{Transitions}} \delta(\gamma - \gamma_{\text{trans.}}) d\gamma \\ &= \sum_{\text{Transitions}} (\Delta \epsilon - \gamma_{\text{trans.}} \Delta A) \end{aligned} \quad (7)$$

Alternatively, the heat can be expressed as the difference between the total change in energy and the work.

$$\begin{aligned} Q &= \Delta H - W = [\epsilon_{\text{open}} - \epsilon_{\text{closed}} - \gamma_\tau \Delta A] - [-\Delta A(\gamma_\tau - \gamma_{\text{trans.}})] \\ &= [\epsilon_{\text{open}} - \epsilon_{\text{closed}} - \gamma_{\text{trans.}} \Delta A], \end{aligned} \quad (8)$$

where we expressed $\dot{\bar{\sigma}}$ as a sum of delta functions located at the transition tensions $\gamma_{\text{trans.}}$ in this specific realization, and $\Delta \epsilon$ and ΔA represent the changes corresponding to the specific transition, which can be both the opening or closing of a channel. As the channels are independent, this definition also gives a heat value for each gating event. Stochastic thermodynamics assures [37] that the average of the heat calculated by Equation (7) over many realizations converges to the correct ensemble average of the heat dissipation. Note that Equation (7) with a minus sign corresponds to the heat released by the system into the environment: the difference between the intrinsic transition energy in the channel molecule (which is constant) and the work that is performed on the molecule by external tension during the transition (which is proportional to applied tension) gives us the dissipated heat. By construction, the above definitions of heat and work recover both the first and second laws of thermodynamics [38]. With the above interpretation, heat and work can be associated with every realization of the protocol. It is important to note, however, that they do not have the same value at every single realization, and they may fluctuate from one realization to the next. Therefore, averaging over many trajectories is required to obtain a reliable estimate for the dissipated heat.

3. Results

In a typical experimental setup, the MscS channels naturally reside in the closed state when no pressure is applied to the system. Therefore, in the first stage of the experiment, we increased the membrane tension by applying suction pressure on the micro-pipette, to the midpoint tension value $\gamma_{0.5}$ at which probabilities of finding the channel in the closed or open states are equal, $P_{\text{Open}} = P_{\text{Closed}} = 0.5$ (this ramping is performed during 0.25 s). We then let the system thermalize at this tension value ($\gamma_{0.5}$) by keeping the pressure fixed for 3 s. The system's entropy at this stage can be calculated as: $S_{\text{Initial}} = -k_B \sum_i P_i \ln P_i = k_B \ln 2$ (see Figure 2A).

In the second stage of the experiment, we increased the membrane tension to $3\,k_B T \text{nm}^2$ at which $P_{\text{Open}} = 1$. This was performed at various ramping rates. This protocol mimics Landauer's "restore to one" operation, which deletes a single bit of information. To see why, note that the channels are *restored* to the open state from an initial configuration where the closed and open states are equally likely to be occupied. Since the channels are forced to the open configuration regardless of their initial status, this protocol is equivalent to the "restore to open". The entropy of the system after this stage is given by: $S_{\text{Final}} = -k_B \sum_i P_i \ln P_i = 0$. Therefore, the change in the entropy of the system is $\Delta S = S_{\text{Final}} - S_{\text{Initial}} = -k_B \ln 2$. This operation corresponds to deleting a single bit of information. Formally, the system has to get back to the same tension value. However, this does not make any difference since we can always release the tension instantaneously without changing the work or heat. To compensate for the system's entropy decrease, the heat released into the environment must be at least $k_B T \ln 2$, otherwise, the total entropy of the system and the bath decreases, leading to a violation of the second law of thermodynamic.

We repeated the above experiments many times and gathered ~200 single-channel events for each erasure protocol. In each realization, we monitored the heat released into the environment using Equation (7) and the known values of $\Delta \epsilon$ and ΔA. These were plotted as a function of the rate at which the tension was changed from $\gamma_{0.5}$ to γ_τ in Figure 3. As expected, the averaged dissipated heat decreases with the protocol duration. At the slowest experimental erasure protocol achievable (see Section 4), we reach very close to the Landauer limit of $k_B T \ln 2$, much closer than any other biological system reported so far.

To further verify our results, we simulated a Markovian model of MscS gating using our experimental protocol (restore to open) as the input driving force in the simulation using QUBexpress software The software is available at https://qub.mandelics.com (accessed on 19 May 2020). The parameters used in the simulation and details of the two-state Markov model of MscS are given in Section 5. Since in the simulations the erasure protocols can be made arbitrarily slow, we obtained the heat distribution as a function of longer erasure protocols (Figure 2, red data points). The simulation results are in good agreement with the experimental measurements at short protocols, and for longer protocols, they in fact attain the $k_B T \ln 2$ bound.

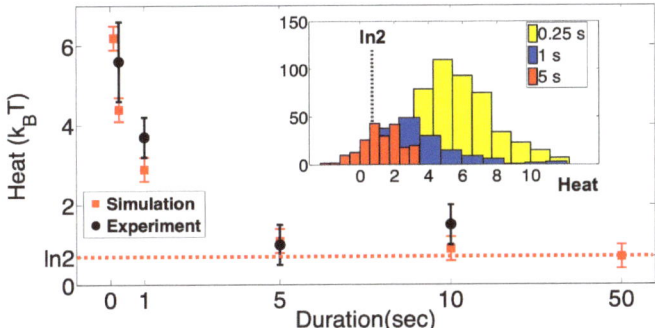

Figure 3. The average dissipated heat as a function of the "restore to open" operation rate. As the channels are restored to the open state slower and slower (the duration increases), the average heat dissipated decreases, but it is always above Landauer's limit of $ln2$. Under sustained mechanical stimuli, the MscS channels inactivate wherein they enter a non-conductive and tension-insensitive state. Therefore, the slowest experimentally achievable erasure duration was limited to 10 s after which the channels display significant inactivation. A Markov model of two-state MscS has been also simulated using QUBexpress software with different rates of the "restore to open" protocol (red data points). The simulation results not only agree with the experimental counterpart but also attain the same limit of $ln2$. The simulation parameters are provided in Section 5. The inset shows the histograms of heat distributions from which the averages are obtained.

4. Discussion

Living systems are inherently dissipative, especially as they execute multiple steps of chemical energy conversion, pump metabolites, produce mechanical work or maintain constant temperature. The question that the researchers studying *structural information content and cellular computation* try to address is not about the total energy balance and dissipation, but rather about the energy consumption by the "cellular switchboard" itself that turns the cellular processes on and off, replicating information and thus making decisions. Previous analyses based on the generalized Landauer bound [14] have suggested that protein synthesis, which is an RNA-guided non-random polymerization of amino acids, takes about an order of magnitude more energy than the amount of information stored in the sequence requires. Synthesis of DNA on a DNA template, according to estimations [14], consumes about two orders of magnitude more energy than the Landauer bound predicts. The problem with these systems is that the energy provided by the splitting of deoxyribonucleotide triphosphates (dNTPs) is strictly coupled with each polymer extension step, which makes this chemical energy component inseparable from the purely entropic change of information content.

In this work, we studied the mechanosensitive ion channel of small conductance (MscS) from *E. coli* acting as a tension-operated membrane valve requiring no chemical energy input. MscS evolved to release excess osmolyte from cells in response to osmotic water influx that causes the cell envelope to swell and stretch. Opening the entire MS channel population during strong shock massively dissipates internal ions and osmolytes that can amount to up to 15% of cellular dry weight [27,43]. This undoubtedly inflicts substantial energy and metabolite loss on the cell that is trying to evade lysis at any cost. However, as our results show, the operation of MscS itself in a slow (nearly equilibrium) regime costs that minimum, exactly as the Landauer limit predicts.

Our experimental conditions allowed us to treat MscS as a two-state memory device. By applying tension to the patch membrane, we forced the population of channels to change its state occupancy, from which we measured the thermodynamic cost of deleting a single bit of information. The heat dissipated during the bit-erasing transition to the singular open state was measured as the average difference between the intrinsic transition energy in the channel molecule and the work that is performed on the molecule by external tension.

The dissipated heat measured with a short "restore to open" time (0.25 s) exceeded $5\,k_BT$, whereas at slow ramps it approached $\ln 2\,k_BT$, corresponding to the Landauer bound.

The practical requirements we had to satisfy in our experiments were as follows. (i) Because MscS channels tend to inactivate when exposed to moderate tension ($\gamma_{0.5}$) for a prolonged period of time, the time for the state restoration protocol cannot be arbitrarily slow. In order to stay in the two-state regime, we used a short (0.5 s) pressure ramp to $\gamma_{0.5}$, a 3-s equilibration, and a variable duration "erasure ramp" that was limited to 10 s. The non-inactivating mechanosensitive ion channel of large conductance MscL would also be a good system for dissipation analysis, but it gates at near-lytic tensions where membrane patches become unstable [27]. For this reason, MscL was not used. (ii) The MscS expression level had to be carefully adjusted through the use of a tight-promoter expression system such that the number of channels per patch (10–20) was suitable for the edge detection analysis of individual transitions. With all these precautions, a small degree of adaptation and inactivation were still observed (expected to be around 10% for a 3 s holding time at $\gamma_{0.5}$), which gave rise to a non-monotonic current response shown in Figure 2.

It is important to note that for finite-time erasure processes, the Landauer bound takes the form $\ln 2 + C/\tau$, where τ is the erasing time and C is a system-dependent constant [15,17,44,45]. However, depending on the intrinsic relaxation time scale of the experimental setup, it is possible to obtain effective quasi-static erasure processes, which may explain why the energetic cost of erasing the bit of information encoded in the ion channel is as low as the theoretic bound. We think that from a biological point of view, this trait seems natural. Under hyperosmotic conditions, bacteria accumulate ions and organic osmolytes to maintain a positive turgor pressure inside the cytoplasm. Moreover, bacteria maintain relatively high voltage across the cytoplasmic membrane (150–200 mV) as a part of electrochemical potential driving ATP synthesis [46,47]. The thermodynamic and kinetic stability of the closed state are therefore critical because thermally-driven random opening events would produce deleterious leakage and uncoupling of bacterial energetics. Thus, evolution has perfected the energy gap ($\sim 22\,k_BT$) between the end states and the height of the separating barrier such that thermal energy does not produce spurious openings at rest during the lifespan of bacteria. However, in the event of a sudden osmotic down-shock such as during a rainstorm, cellular osmolytes are quickly released through mechanosensitive ion channels in order to reduce the turgor pressure. The low-threshold MscS and the high-threshold MscL channels are responsible for the bulk of osmolyte exchange in E. coli, but each channel is specialized in handling different magnitudes of osmotic shocks. The 3–nS MscL is an emergency valve that opens abruptly at near-lytic tensions ($\sim 3.5\,k_BT/\text{nm}^2$) and jettisons the osmolytes non-selectively. The 1–nS MscS, on the other hand, operates at moderate tensions ($\sim 2\,k_BT/\text{nm}^2$), and effectively counteracts small osmotic shocks. These channels evolved to defend bacteria under different osmotic conditions, e.g., emergency vs non-emergency situations, and they perform more efficiently under certain timescales [29].

Stopped-flow experiments revealed that the characteristic time scales of bacterial swelling in response to an abrupt dilution vary from seconds at low shocks (100–300 mOsm downshifts) to 100 milliseconds at stronger (600–1000 mOsm) shocks [27]. Such strong osmotic down-shock experiments yield the typical timescales at which an emergency valve operates in nature. MscS populations residing in the cytoplasmic membrane of a bacterium are usually able to meet the kinetic requirement, i.e., opening and helping to reduce the internal turgor pressure by quickly releasing the excessive osmotic gradient before water influx rips open the cell. However, MscS, not being a true emergency valve, is somewhat inefficient when it is forced to open under timescales of 30–50 ms that correspond to super-threshold tensions in the cytoplasmic membrane generated by fast dilution in vivo. This dissipation at higher tensions (and rates) is a "tax" imposed by a relatively high transition barrier providing a "safety curb" that precludes spurious openings at low tensions. However, under moderate osmotic shock conditions, when tension buildup in the cytoplasmic membrane occurs within a time span of a few seconds, MscS performs a smooth action in a non-dissipative manner, which seems to be consistent with the in vivo role of MscS in the overall osmotic fitness of E. coli.

5. Materials and Methods

5.1. Preparation of Giant Spheroplasts and Patch Clamp

The giant spheroplasts of E. coli were prepared following the protocol described in [36]. A total of 3 mL of the colony-derived culture was transferred into 27 mL of LB containing 0.06 mg/mL cephalexin, which selectively blocks septation. After 1.5–2 h of shaking in the presence of cephalexin, 100–250 µm long filaments formed. Toward the end of the filamentous growth stage, induction with 0.001% L-Arabinose was conducted for 0–20 min, which gave 1–15 channels per patch. The filaments were transferred into a hypertonic buffer containing 1 M sucrose and subjected to digestion by lysozyme (0.2 mg/mL) in the presence of 5 mM EDTA. As a result, filaments collapsed into spheres of 3–7 µm in diameter in 7–10 min. The reaction was terminated by adding 20 mM Mg^{2+}. Spheroplasts were separated from the rest of the reaction mixture by sedimentation through a one-step sucrose gradient. Borosilicate glass (Drummond 2-000-100) pipets 1–1.3 µm in diameter were used to form tight seals with the inner membrane. The MS channel activities were recorded via inside-out excised patch clamp method after expressing them in MJF641. The pipette solution had 200 mM KCl, 50 mM $MgCl_2$, 5 mM $CaCl_2$, 5 mM HEPES. The bath solution was the same as the pipette solution with 400 mM sucrose added. Both pipette and bath solution had a pH of 7.4. Traces were recorded using Clampex 10.3 software (MDS Analytical Technologies). Mechanical stimuli were delivered using a high-speed pressure clamp apparatus (HSPC-1; ALA Scientific Instruments).

Tension Calibration

The pressure (p) was converted to the tension (γ) using the following relation: $\gamma = (p/p_{0.5})\gamma_{0.5}$ assuming the radius of curvature of the patch does not change in the range of pressures where the channels were active $p > 40$ mmHg) and the constant of proportionality between tension and pressure is $\gamma_{0.5}/p_{0.5}$ [26,28,39]. The midpoint tension, $\gamma_{0.5}$ of MscS was taken to be 7.85 mN/m [39]. $p_{0.5}$ represents the pressure value at which half of the population is in the open state and was determined from the averages of 5–10 traces obtained by using 1-s triangular ramp protocols at the beginning of each experiment (1 $k_B T/nm^2 = 4.114$ mN/m).

5.2. Two-State Markov Model

In the context of discrete-space continuous-time Markov processes, k_{xy} represents the transition rate, probability per unit time, to make a transition from state y to state x and is described by the Arrhenius-type relation: $k_{xy} = k_{xy}^0 \exp(\beta\gamma\Delta A_{yB})$ where k_{xy}^0 is the intrinsic rate (frequency) of the system's attempts to overcome the barrier between states x and y in the absence of the tension and ΔA_{yB} is the expansion area from state y to the barrier, γ is the applied tension and $\beta = 1/k_B T$. Equivalently, it is easy to show that $k_{oc}/k_{co} = e^{-\beta(\epsilon_{open}-\epsilon_{closed})}e^{\gamma\Delta A}$. The following parameters were used for the two-state model of MscS: $k_{co}^0 = 9897\ s^{-1}$, $k_{oc}^0 = 4e-6\ s^{-1}$, $|\Delta A_{cB}| = 7$ and $|\Delta A_{oB}| = 5$, $\Delta A = 12$.

$$C \underset{k_{CO}}{\overset{k_{OC}}{\rightleftarrows}} O$$

These parameters have been determined by an independent set of experiments. Typically, in patch-clamp experiments, k_{xy} is measured at various tension values (γ). By plotting the rate as a function of tension ($\ln(k_{xy})$ vs. γ) on a semi-logarithmic scale, the slope can provide an estimate of ΔA_{yB}, while the y intercept can suggest the intrinsic closing rate in the absence of tension [29]. This is because $\ln(k_{xy})$ can be expressed as $\ln(k_{co}^0) + \beta\gamma\Delta A_{yB}$. In more recent studies, the estimation of $\Delta\epsilon$ has been achieved through the utilization of the Crooks fluctuation theorem and Jarzynski equality, as demonstrated in [38].

5.3. Edge Detection

Experimental traces (current vs. time) are analyzed to detect single-channel events through the use of an edge detector program, as illustrated in Figure 4.

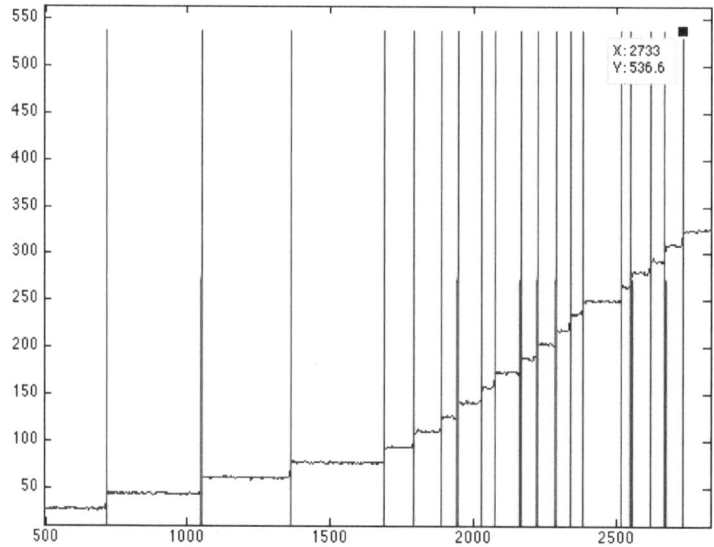

Figure 4. An Edge detector program (http://cismm.web.unc.edu/resources/tutorials/edge-detector-1d-tutorial/ (accessed on 19 May 2020)) was employed to detect the single channel events.

Author Contributions: Conceptualization, U.Ç. and O.R.; Methodology, U.Ç. and S.S.; Formal analysis, U.Ç. and O.R.; Investigation, U.Ç., O.R., M.B. and S.S.; Resources, S.S.; Data curation, U.Ç. and M.B.; Writing—original draft, U.Ç., O.R. and S.S.; Writing—review & editing, S.S.; Visualization, U.Ç. and O.R.; Supervision, U.Ç., O.R. and S.S.; Project administration, S.S.; Funding acquisition, S.S. All authors have read and agreed to the published version of the manuscript.

Funding: This work was supported by NIH R01AI135015 grant to S.S. U.Ç. was supported by the U.S. Department of Education GAANN Mathematics in Biology Fellowship. O.R. is the incumbent of the Shlomo and Michla Tomarin career development chair, and is supported by the Abramson Family Center for Young Scientists and by the Israel Science Foundation, Grant No. 950/19.

Institutional Review Board Statement: Not applicable.

Informed Consent Statement: Not applicable.

Data Availability Statement: Data available upon request.

Acknowledgments: This research was performed while UC was a PhD student in the Maryland Biophysics program. UC thanks Stephanie Sansbury for cloning MscS into tightly-regulated pBAD for expression system.

Conflicts of Interest: The funders had no role in the design of the study; in the collection, analyses, or interpretation of data; in the writing of the manuscript; or in the decision to publish the results.

References

1. Lloyd, S. Ultimate physical limits to computation. *Nature* **2000**, *406*, 1047. [CrossRef] [PubMed]
2. Margolus, N.; Levitin, L.B. The maximum speed of dynamical evolution. *Phys. D Nonlinear Phenom.* **1998**, *120*, 188–195. [CrossRef]
3. Landauer, R. Irreversibility and heat generation in the computing process. *IBM J. Res. Dev.* **1961**, *5*, 183–191. [CrossRef]
4. Maroney, O.J. Generalizing Landauer's principle. *Phys. Rev. E* **2009**, *79*, 031105. [CrossRef]
5. Gammaitoni, L. Beating the Landauer's limit by trading energy with uncertainty. *arXiv* **2011**, arXiv:1111.2937.
6. Vaccaro, J.A.; Barnett, S.M. Information erasure without an energy cost. *Proc. R. Soc. A Math. Phys. Eng. Sci.* **2011**, *467*, 1770–1778. [CrossRef]

7. Sagawa, T. Thermodynamic and logical reversibilities revisited. *J. Stat. Mech. Theory Exp.* **2014**, *2014*, P03025. [CrossRef]
8. Sagawa, T.; Ueda, M. Minimal Energy Cost for Thermodynamic Information Processing: Measurement and Information Erasure. *Phys. Rev. Lett.* **2009**, *102*, 250602. [CrossRef]
9. Boyd, A.B.; Crutchfield, J.P. Maxwell Demon Dynamics: Deterministic Chaos, the Szilard Map, and the Intelligence of Thermodynamic Systems. *Phys. Rev. Lett.* **2016**, *116*, 190601. [CrossRef]
10. Bormashenko, E. Generalization of the Landauer Principle for Computing Devices Based on Many-Valued Logic. *Entropy* **2019**, *21*, 1150. [CrossRef]
11. Proesmans, K.; Ehrich, J.; Bechhoefer, J. Optimal finite-time bit erasure under full control. *Phys. Rev. E* **2020**, *102*, 032105. [CrossRef] [PubMed]
12. Proesmans, K.; Ehrich, J.; Bechhoefer, J. Finite-time Landauer principle. *Phys. Rev. Lett.* **2020**, *125*, 100602. [CrossRef] [PubMed]
13. Wolpert, D.H. The stochastic thermodynamics of computation. *J. Phys. A: Math. Theor.* **2019**, *52*, 193001. [CrossRef]
14. Kempes, C.P.; Wolpert, D.; Cohen, Z.; Pérez-Mercader, J. The thermodynamic efficiency of computations made in cells across the range of life. *Philos. Trans. R. Soc. A Math. Phys. Eng. Sci.* **2017**, *375*, 20160343. [CrossRef] [PubMed]
15. Bérut, A.; Arakelyan, A.; Petrosyan, A.; Ciliberto, S.; Dillenschneider, R.; Lutz, E. Experimental verification of Landauer's principle linking information and thermodynamics. *Nature* **2012**, *483*, 187. [CrossRef]
16. Bérut, A.; Petrosyan, A.; Ciliberto, S. Information and thermodynamics: Experimental verification of Landauer's Erasure principle. *J. Stat. Mech. Theory Exp.* **2015**, *2015*, P06015. [CrossRef]
17. Jun, Y.; Gavrilov, M.; Bechhoefer, J. High-precision test of Landauer's principle in a feedback trap. *Phys. Rev. Lett.* **2014**, *113*, 190601. [CrossRef]
18. Gavrilov, M.; Bechhoefer, J. Erasure without Work in an Asymmetric Double-Well Potential. *Phys. Rev. Lett.* **2016**, *117*, 200601. [CrossRef]
19. Gavrilov, M.; Chétrite, R.; Bechhoefer, J. Direct measurement of weakly nonequilibrium system entropy is consistent with Gibbs–Shannon form. *Proc. Natl. Acad. Sci. USA* **2017**, *114*, 11097–11102. [CrossRef]
20. Hong, J.; Lambson, B.; Dhuey, S.; Bokor, J. Experimental test of Landauer's principle in single-bit operations on nanomagnetic memory bits. *Sci. Adv.* **2016**, *2*, e1501492. [CrossRef]
21. Martini, L.; Pancaldi, M.; Madami, M.; Vavassori, P.; Gubbiotti, G.; Tacchi, S.; Hartmann, F.; Emmerling, M.; Höfling, S.; Worschech, L.; et al. Experimental and theoretical analysis of Landauer erasure in nano-magnetic switches of different sizes. *Nano Energy* **2016**, *19*, 108–116. [CrossRef]
22. Gaudenzi, R.; Burzurí, E.; Maegawa, S.; van der Zant, H.; Luis, F. Quantum Landauer erasure with a molecular nanomagnet. *Nat. Phys.* **2018**, *14*, 565–568. [CrossRef]
23. Saira, O.P.; Matheny, M.H.; Katti, R.; Fon, W.; Wimsatt, G.; Crutchfield, J.P.; Han, S.; Roukes, M.L. Nonequilibrium thermodynamics of erasure with superconducting flux logic. *Phys. Rev. Res.* **2020**, *2*, 013249. [CrossRef]
24. Peterson, J.P.; Sarthour, R.S.; Souza, A.M.; Oliveira, I.S.; Goold, J.; Modi, K.; Soares-Pinto, D.O.; Céleri, L.C. Experimental demonstration of information to energy conversion in a quantum system at the Landauer limit. *Proc. R. Soc. A Math. Phys. Eng. Sci.* **2016**, *472*, 20150813. [CrossRef]
25. Yan, L.; Xiong, T.; Rehan, K.; Zhou, F.; Liang, D.; Chen, L.; Zhang, J.; Yang, W.; Ma, Z.; Feng, M. Single-atom demonstration of the quantum Landauer principle. *Phys. Rev. Lett.* **2018**, *120*, 210601. [CrossRef] [PubMed]
26. Moe, P.; Blount, P. Assessment of potential stimuli for mechano-dependent gating of MscL: Effects of pressure, tension, and lipid headgroups. *Biochemistry* **2005**, *44*, 12239–12244. [CrossRef]
27. Çetiner, U.; Rowe, I.; Schams, A.; Mayhew, C.; Rubin, D.; Anishkin, A.; Sukharev, S. Tension-activated channels in the mechanism of osmotic fitness in *Pseudomonas aeruginosa*. *J. Gen. Physiol.* **2017**, *149*, 595–609. [CrossRef]
28. Sukharev, S.I.; Sigurdson, W.J.; Kung, C.; Sachs, F. Energetic and spatial parameters for gating of the bacterial large conductance mechanosensitive channel, MscL. *J. Gen. Physiol.* **1999**, *113*, 525–540. [CrossRef]
29. Çetiner, U.; Anishkin, A.; Sukharev, S. Spatiotemporal relationships defining the adaptive gating of the bacterial mechanosensitive channel MscS. *Eur. Biophys. J.* **2018**, *47*, 663–677. [CrossRef]
30. Levina, N.; Tötemeyer, S.; Stokes, N.R.; Louis, P.; Jones, M.A.; Booth, I.R. Protection of Escherichia coli cells against extreme turgor by activation of MscS and MscL mechanosensitive channels: Identification of genes required for MscS activity. *EMBO J.* **1999**, *18*, 1730–1737. [CrossRef]
31. Kung, C.; Martinac, B.; Sukharev, S. Mechanosensitive channels in microbes. *Annu. Rev. Microbiol.* **2010**, *64*, 313–329. [CrossRef] [PubMed]
32. Sukharev, S.; Martinac, B.; Arshavsky, V.; Kung, C. Two types of mechanosensitive channels in the Escherichia coli cell envelope: Solubilization and functional reconstitution. *Biophys. J.* **1993**, *65*, 177–183. [CrossRef] [PubMed]
33. Neher, E.; Sakmann, B. Single-channel currents recorded from membrane of denervated frog muscle fibres. *Nature* **1976**, *260*, 799. [CrossRef] [PubMed]
34. Hamill, O.P.; Marty, A.; Neher, E.; Sakmann, B.; Sigworth, F. Improved patch-clamp techniques for high-resolution current recording from cells and cell-free membrane patches. *Pflügers Arch.* **1981**, *391*, 85–100. [CrossRef] [PubMed]
35. Sakmann, B.; Neher, E. Patch clamp techniques for studying ionic channels in excitable membranes. *Annu. Rev. Physiol.* **1984**, *46*, 455–472. [CrossRef] [PubMed]
36. Martinac, B.; Buechner, M.; Delcour, A.H.; Adler, J.; Kung, C. Pressure-sensitive ion channel in *Escherichia coli*. *Proc. Natl. Acad. Sci. USA* **1987**, *84*, 2297–2301. [CrossRef]
37. Seifert, U. Stochastic thermodynamics, fluctuation theorems and molecular machines. *Rep. Prog. Phys.* **2012**, *75*, 126001. [CrossRef]

38. Çetiner, U.; Raz, O.; Sukharev, S.; Jarzynski, C. Recovery of Equilibrium Free Energy from Nonequilibrium Thermodynamics with Mechanosensitive Ion Channels in *E. coli*. *Phys. Rev. Lett.* **2020**, *124*, 228101. [CrossRef]
39. Belyy, V.; Kamaraju, K.; Akitake, B.; Anishkin, A.; Sukharev, S. Adaptive behavior of bacterial mechanosensitive channels is coupled to membrane mechanics. *J. Gen. Physiol.* **2010**, *135*, 641–652. [CrossRef]
40. Phillips, R.; Ursell, T.; Wiggins, P.; Sens, P. Emerging roles for lipids in shaping membrane-protein function. *Nature* **2009**, *459*, 379. [CrossRef]
41. Phillips, R.; Theriot, J.; Kondev, J.; Garcia, H. *Physical Biology of the Cell*; Garland Science: New York, NY, USA, 2012.
42. Bustamante, C.; Liphardt, J.; Ritort, F. The nonequilibrium thermodynamics of small systems. *arXiv* **2005**, arXiv:cond-mat/0511629v1.
43. Moller, E.; Britt, M.; Schams, A.; Cetuk, H.; Anishkin, A.; Sukharev, S. Mechanosensitive channel MscS is critical for termination of the bacterial hypoosmotic permeability response. *J. Gen. Physiol.* **2023**, *155*, e202213168. [CrossRef] [PubMed]
44. Lee, J.S.; Lee, S.; Kwon, H.; Park, H. Speed limit for a highly irreversible process and tight finite-time Landauer's bound. *Phys. Rev. Lett.* **2022**, *129*, 120603. [CrossRef] [PubMed]
45. Van Vu, T.; Saito, K. Thermodynamic unification of optimal transport: Thermodynamic uncertainty relation, minimum dissipation, and thermodynamic speed limits. *Phys. Rev. X* **2023**, *13*, 011013. [CrossRef]
46. Kashket, E.R. The proton motive force in bacteria: A critical assessment of methods. *Annu. Rev. Microbiol.* **1985**, *39*, 219–242. [CrossRef] [PubMed]
47. Krulwich, T.A.; Sachs, G.; Padan, E. Molecular aspects of bacterial pH sensing and homeostasis. *Nat. Rev. Microbiol.* **2011**, *9*, 330. [CrossRef] [PubMed]

Disclaimer/Publisher's Note: The statements, opinions and data contained in all publications are solely those of the individual author(s) and contributor(s) and not of MDPI and/or the editor(s). MDPI and/or the editor(s) disclaim responsibility for any injury to people or property resulting from any ideas, methods, instructions or products referred to in the content.

Article

Thermodynamical versus Logical Irreversibility: A Concrete Objection to Landauer's Principle

Didier Lairez

Laboratoire des Solides Irradiés, École Polytechnique, CEA, CNRS, IPP, 91128 Palaiseau, France; didier.lairez@polytechnique.edu

Abstract: Landauer's principle states that the logical irreversibility of an operation, such as erasing one bit, whatever its physical implementation, necessarily implies its thermodynamical irreversibility. In this paper, a very simple counterexample of physical implementation (that uses a two-to-one relation between logic and thermodynamic states) is given that allows one bit to be erased in a thermodynamical quasistatic manner (i.e., one that may tend to be reversible if slowed down enough).

Keywords: thermodynamics; information theory; Landauer's eraser

1. Introduction

Entropy was originally defined by Clausius [1] as the state quantity that accounts for heat exchanges and their irreversible features. The state of a system is defined by a set of parameters, the state quantities, such as internal energy, temperature, volume, pressure, quantity of matter, etc., which make it possible to describe the system, i.e., to construct a representation of the system as it appears to our senses (there is nothing else we can access). After Shannon [2], entropy was revealed as the state quantity that quantifies the complexity of this representation considered as a random variable, that is to say, the quantity of information required in unit of bits to encode this representation in the memory of a computer.

The link between information (complexity) and thermodynamics (energy) is neither a metaphor (a figure of speech) nor an analogy (a comparison based on resemblance) nor an interpretation (a personal way to explain something). In all these cases, it would be questionable. However, here, it is absolutely valid and comes from mathematics. Gibbs' entropy (that of statistical mechanics) is a special case of Shannon's entropy (the other name for the quantity of information) and the former is directly derived from Clausius' entropy (for a derivation, see [3]). Hence, the connection. The mathematical relations between the "three entropies" leaves no space for interpretation.

The connection between energy and information makes it possible to understand the functioning of strange machines such as that of Maxwell's demon [4] and its variations. By acquiring and processing information about the velocities or positions of gas particles, the demon (in the 21st century let us say a computer) is able to establish either a temperature or a pressure difference which, in turn, could produce work. Without a connection between information and energy, the demon's machinery would either violate the second law of thermodynamics or (more likely) require an energy compensation of unknown origin.

The link between information and energy that comes from Shannon's information theory is purely mathematical. It has its advantages (rigor) and its disadvantages (abstraction). To overcome the latter, Landauer [5,6], followed by Bennett [7,8], tried to establish this link by using an entirely different method to that of Shannon. Their idea is basically the following. Information, say a set of bits, has necessarily a physical support. So that to be stored and processed, the logical values 0 or 1 of one given bit should "necessarily" (the quotation marks emphasize that it is this precise point which is questioned in this paper) be mapped by a one-to-one relation to the states that can be adopted by a thermodynamical system with a two-minimum (bistable) potential. This one-to-one mapping, known as Launder's principle, automatically associates information processing with thermodynamics laws. A first corollary is that logical (information) and Clausius entropies behave in the same way, a second is that logical irreversibility (such as erasing one bit of information) implies thermodynamical irreversibility.

Landauer's principle is actually a conjecture that has been demonstrated in the particular case of a one-to-one physical implementation of a bit. Common objections to this conjecture are mainly conceptual [8]. For example, what exactly "erasing a bit" means has been discussed and the Landauer–Bennett conception has been questioned. The starting point that one bit requires a physical medium to exist has also been questioned [9]. However, this objection is more philosophical than scientific. It deals with the meaning of "existence". Personally, I am a materialist who thinks that even abstractions need physical support, at least in the form of our brain thinking them. However, this question ultimately boils down to discussing whether or not something exists outside of our perception. As interesting as it is, this question is not the responsibility of science, whose theories are founded and validated by experiments [10].

The purpose of this paper is to propose a concrete (as opposed to conceptual) objection that comes as close as possible to the requirements of what an ERASE operation should be according to Landauer. Establishing Landauer's conjecture as a principle presupposes its generality that can be accepted until proven otherwise. In other words, whereas it is not possible to definitely prove that it is true, it is possible to prove it is false by finding a counterexample. This is the concern of this paper that presents a bistable bit linked (by a two-to-one surjective relation) to a monostable thermodynamical potential. This two-to-one implementation allows logical irreversibility to occur in a thermodynamical quasistatic manner, which may, therefore, tend to be reversible if slowed down sufficiently.

2. Irreversibility

2.1. Logical Irreversibility

Logical operations take one or more bit-values as input and produce a single bit-value as output. They are logically irreversible if the probability of a given output value differs from that of the input. Reversible logical operations preserve the quantity of information, whereas irreversible operations do not. In the case where the initial value of one given bit is known, the operation RESET TO 0 [5] (equivalent to ERASE [7]) is logically irreversible because two possible initial values (0 or 1) lead to a single result (0). Once the operation has been performed, the information on the initial value of the bit is lost.

Note that erasing a set of bits decreases (or leaves constant) their statistical entropy, e.g., a set of bits with random equiprobable values and maximum entropy has zero entropy once all values are reset to 0. So that associating the corresponding logical irreversibility to thermodynamical irreversibility is not straightforward as the latter is most easily associated with an increase in the entropy of the system (one can think for instance of spontaneous processes that occur at constant internal energy).

2.2. Thermodynamical Irreversibility

Consider a system that can be found in two different states, say A and B. In thermodynamics, a process which would consist in bringing the system from A to B (A→B) is said to be reversible (or irreversible) if there is a restore process (B→A) that allows the system to be returned to its initial state, and such that at the end of the whole cycle (A→B→A) the net quantity of heat Q produced by the system and dissipated into the surroundings is zero (or strictly negative, sign with respect to the system). In most cases, heat is not the quantity we are interested in. Rather, it would be its complement

$$E_{\text{cost}} = -Q, \quad (1)$$

that is, the sum of all other forms of energy supplied to the system.

First, note that whether a process is reversible or irreversible is not an inherent property of states A and B, but a property of the path that is taken. In reality, no thermodynamical process is exactly reversible, perpetual motion does not exist, and a cycle is always accompanied with the dissipation of energy in the form of a net quantity of heat passing from the system to its surroundings. This is formalized by the second law of thermodynamics which has never been faulted and will not be by this paper either.

To illustrate this point (see Figure 1), let us consider a unit amount of gas in contact with a temperature reservoir at temperature T. A typical example of a reversible cycle is that of the isothermal expansion/compression from volume V to $2V$ by the means of a piston. If the temperature of the gas is effectively kept constant throughout the process, so is its internal energy. Due to the conservation principle of energy, at every moment the gas provides mechanical work dW but draws exactly the same quantity of heat dQ from the environment. At the end of the expansion stage: $Q = -W = T\ln(2V) - T\ln(V) = T\ln 2$ (where T is expressed in joules). The cycle is closed by a restore process that involves exactly the same amount of heat and work but with opposite signs. So that $E_{cost} = 0$. This is an ideal reversible situation that is never reached.

There are two fundamentally different categories of irreversible processes (therefore, two categories of process altogether). Consider the above expansion with a piston. From a general rule in physics there exists an unavoidable delay between cause (expansion) and effect (thermalization), which here implies the inequality $T\ln 2 \geq Q$.

The second law of thermodynamics is twofold: (1) it identifies $\ln 2$ (in this example) as being the difference ΔS of a state quantity, namely, the entropy S of the system that only depends on A and B, but not on the process; (2) it tells us that $T\Delta S \geq Q$ (in all cases), so that:

$$T\Delta S = T\ln 2 \geq Q, \qquad (2)$$

where the equality holds for an infinitely slow process allowing an infinitely small delay. The second law of thermodynamics says absolutely nothing more than that.

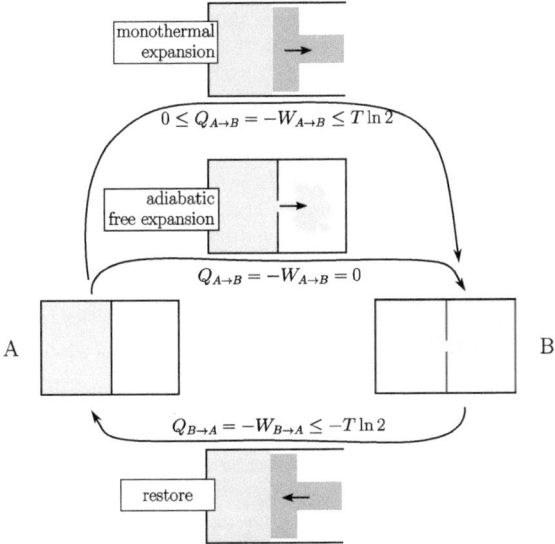

Figure 1. Expansion of a unit amount of gas from volume V (state A) to $2V$ (state B) at the same temperature T (in joules). (1) Monothermal expansion with a piston (top): the gas produces work W and pumps heat Q. (2) Adiabatic free expansion (middle): no heat and no work are exchanged with the surroundings. In both cases the cycle is closed using the same restoring process (bottom). In the first case, the net energy cost $E_{cost} = -Q$ of a cycle can be as small as desired (quasistatic, Equation (3)). In the second case, it has a lower limit of $T\ln 2$ (Equation (4)).

Note that the equality in Equation (2) gives us the only way to measure ΔS, in particular by using an infinitely slow process (i.e., reversible) to go back to the initial state (B→A). In our case, this corresponds to the compression of a piston from B to A that requires mechanical work and provides heat to the surroundings (ideally both with the same absolute value as for the expansion but with opposite sign). Using this restore process, the energy cost at the end of the cycle (A→B→A) is:

$$E_{\text{cost}} \geq 0 \tag{3}$$

which means that there is no conceptual impossibility for this energy cost to be as small as desired by slowing down the process, which is then said to be quasistatic. Processes belonging to this first category can be considered as potentially reversible. This includes all those which experience only friction and always remain under control.

Another class of thermodynamic processes are those that are inherently irreversible because they are out of control. An example is the adiabatic free expansion (see Figure 1) of a gas without a piston: no heat and no work are exchanged with the surroundings (it is adiabatic and there is no piston to capture the work). However, something happens because work has to be done (this time with a piston) to restore the system to its initial state. This restoring process is the same as in the previous category, so that the energy balance of such a cycle is:

$$E_{\text{cost}} \geq T \ln 2, \tag{4}$$

which means that $T \ln 2$ (the entropy difference between A and B expressed in temperature units) is a lower limit for E_{cost} that can never be bypassed.

A point which deserves to be underlined in order to avoid a misinterpretation of what follows, is that the assertion that a process belongs to one category or another is not a violation of the second law of thermodynamics. The two categories are both consistent with it.

Landauer's principle claims that all physical implementations of the operation RESET TO 0 (or ERASE) correspond to processes that belong to the second category (inherently irreversible like the adiabatic free expansion). The aim of this paper is to provide a counterexample that belongs to the first (potentially reversible if slowed down enough, like the monothermal expansion).

3. Erasers

3.1. Landauer's Eraser (One-to-One Implementation)

For some reasons (that are not challenged in this paper), Landauer [5] considers that the two logical states of a bit, 0 and 1, cannot be physically implemented with the two states A (volume V) and B (volume $2V$) of the previous section. A correct physical implementation must fulfill two conditions (see [5] p. 184):

(1) states 0 and 1 must be stable;
(2) the operation RESET TO 0 must correspond to the same physical process whatever the initial state.

Next, Landauer claims (here is the very point challenged in this paper) that the only possible way to fulfill these two conditions is to realize a one-to-one mapping between the two bit-values and two stable thermodynamical states separated by an energy barrier, such as a particle in a bistable potential.

Note that as is, the bistable potential seems to be not convenient to fulfill the second condition, because there is nothing to do to RESET TO 0 in case the initial state is already at 0, while an energy barrier must be crossed otherwise. To overcome this problem, Landauer imagines the following functional procedure that follows three stages (Figure 2):

(1) lower the energy barrier down to a value smaller than the thermal energy T, leaving the system to a "standard" (S) state (Consider a single particle in a diathermal box in contact with a temperature reservoir. Even if this particle is alone, its temperature is

well defined by the multiple collisions with the wall of the box. Let us assign bit value 0 when the particle is in the left side and bit value 1 when the particle is in the right side. The logical states are stable and well defined only when a barrier exists (higher than thermal energy) between the two sides. The S-state corresponds to the situation where the barrier is removed);

(2) apply a small energy bias in the desired direction in order to drive the particle into the desired state;

(3) put up the barrier and remove the bias.

The point is that during the first stage, the probability density of the particle leaks from its initial potential well to fill both [7]. This leakage occurs in an out-of-control and irreversible thermodynamical manner, because putting up the barrier at the end of this stage would not necessarily return the particle back to its initial well. Like free expansion, stage 1 occurs without energy exchange with the surroundings, contrary to the rest of the procedure that can be quasistatic, amounts to an isothermal compression, and dissipates at least $T \ln 2$ (as heat) to the surroundings. In the rest of the argument, Bennett [7] proves that the initial logical state can be restored to the initial value (0 or 1) by a WRITE operation that can be performed in a quasistatic manner. So that the whole cycle (ERASE then RESTORE) costs at least $T \ln 2$ (as in Equation (4)). It follows that this physical implementation of the irreversible logical operation RESET TO 0 is a process of the second category, that is to say, thermodynamically intrinsically irreversible (Equation (4)).

The direct physical implementations of a bit by using a bistable potential has been experimentally achieved. Berut et al. [11] trapped a colloidal particle with a double-beam optical tweezer. Hong et al. [12] directly worked on magnetic memory at the nanoscale. This type of experience is unquestionably very difficult and the state of the art. The authors actually measure a lower energy bound equal to $T \ln 2$ to move the bit from one state to the other. So that the irreversible and out-of-control "leakage" invoked by Bennet to erase one bit seems unavoidable. However, Landauer's principle is stronger than that. It states that it is unavoidable whatever the physical implementation.

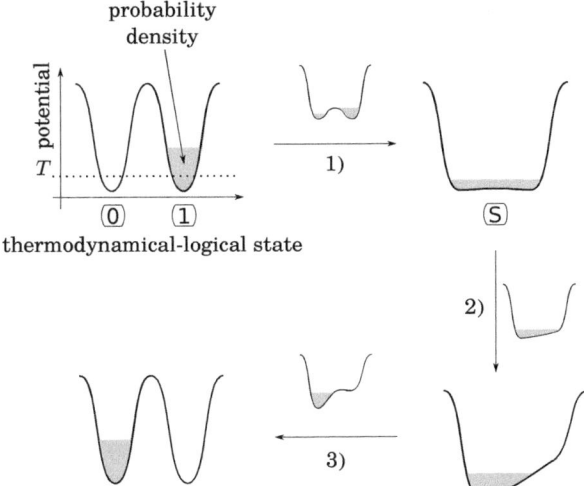

Figure 2. Landauer's functional procedure to physically implement the RESET TO 0 (ERASE) logical operation by the means of a thermodynamical bistable potential with a tunable barrier and a bias. Here, the bit is initially set to 1 but the same procedure would apply if the was were set to 0.

3.2. Counterexample (Two-to-One Implementation)

The counterexample I propose is based on the fact that the irreversible leakage from one potential well to the other of Landauer's eraser cannot occur if there is only one potential well: that is to say, two logical states corresponding to one single thermodynamical state. It remains to find a physical implementation allowing this.

Let us fill a diathermal gas container below a piston at atmospheric pressure while the piston is at the position of maximum expansion. Then, close the container. This thermodynamical system is monostable when the piston is up (Figure 3). Let us link the piston to a connecting rod, a crankshaft, and a pulley of radius 1. A frequency divider is obtained with a belt and another pulley of radius 2 equipped with a crank, so that to the single stable position of the piston there correspond two stable positions of the crank (up and down in Figure 3 if the belt is initially closed while the two pulley angles are zero). The two crank positions define a bit whose thermodynamics depends on: (1) the expansion/compression of the gas; (2) the friction of the transmission. As both can be quasistatic, operations on this bit are too.

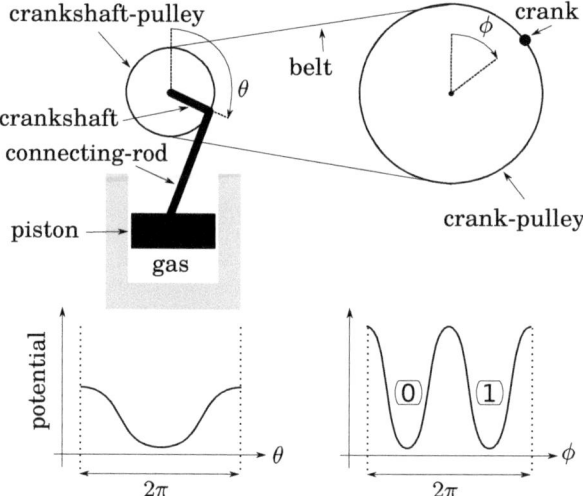

Figure 3. Two-to-one implementation of a bit: quasistatic isothermal compression/expansion of a gas is performed with a transmission of gear ratio 2 (crank–pulley/crankshaft–pulley). The two stable positions of the crank (to which are assigned bit values 0 and 1) correspond to a single stable position of the piston.

Before investigating bit operations, note that (1) due to conservation of energy, the height of energy barriers for the crank (logical barrier) increases linearly with the gear ratio crank/crankshaft, whereas that of the piston is constant (thermodynamical barrier); (2) the gear ratio can vary continuously by using a so-called "continuously variable transmission" mechanism, say, for instance, a conical pulley for the crank. So that there is no conceptual impossibility for this variation to be performed as slowly as desired in a fully controlled and quasistatic manner. It follows that, while the bit is initially at an equilibrium position (either 0 or 1), the gear ratio can be decreased enough so that the logical barrier becomes smaller than the thermal energy T (see Figure 4). Then, due to fluctuations of pressure below the piston, the position of the crank can fluctuate in any position between 0 and 2π, leading to an undetermined bit value. We, thus, obtain a soft potential well (standard bit-state S), as in the papers of Landauer and Bennett [5,7].

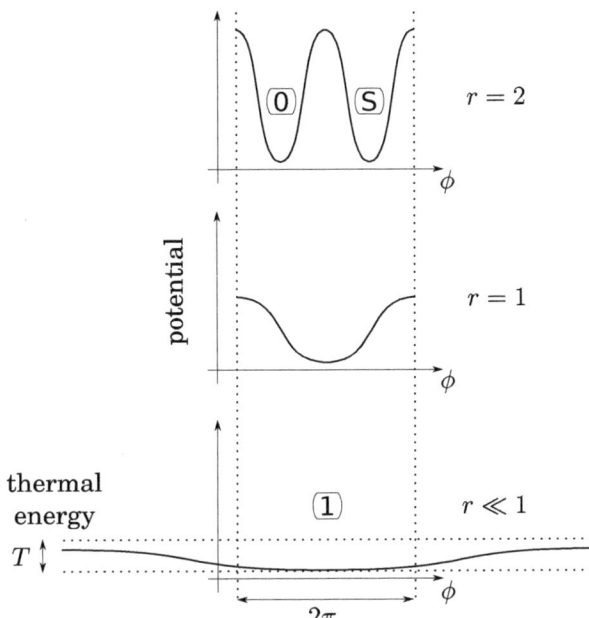

Figure 4. The gear ratio r can be small enough so that thermal fluctuations of the gas below the piston permit the crank-angle (ϕ) to be in any position. This soft potential well determines a third state (S for "standard") for a virgin bit.

The RESET TO 0 operation can be performed by the following sequence which is copied from that of Landauer–Bennett:

(1) put the gear ratio to a small enough value so that the bit is in the S-state;
(2) set the crank to the desired position 0 (by applying in a quasistatic manner a force similar to the bias in the Landauer–Bennett implementation);
(3) put the gear ratio back to 2.

This sequence is analogous to that of Landauer–Bennett (so that the bit is erased), but there is a major difference due to the two-to-one implementation. In the S-state, the crank can move without modifying the position of the piston. The bit position (logic) and piston position (thermodynamic) are practically uncoupled. Another way to say the same thing is that at the end of the first stage putting up the energy barrier does not necessarily return the system to the same logical state (logical irreversibility), but necessarily leaves the system to the same thermodynamical state (thermodynamical reversibility) because there is only one potential well.

As the other stages of the sequence do not involve rotation, the overall operation is performed without any change in the thermodynamical state, nor energy dissipation (except that of the friction of the transmission, that can be as small as desired). Note that Shenker [13] (Figure 5 in his paper) proposed another mechanism allowing the coupling/uncoupling logic and thermodynamic parts. However, the discontinuous procedure for the operation does not permit it to be quasistatic, as explained by Bennett [8].

The bit implementation proposed here avoids this issue. So, although it is logically irreversible, the procedure with this implementation may be thermodynamically quasistatic. This procedure fulfills the two conditions stated by Landauer (1—two stable bit-states, 2—the same procedure whatever the initial bit-state) and obeys the same sequence as that of Landauer (1—lower the barrier; 2—apply a bias; 3—raise the barrier). So that if these criteria are correct, this two-to-one implementation is also correct from a computational point of view. This implementation permits the bit to really be erased, at least as much as that of Landauer, but this time in a quasistatic manner, allowing E_{cost} to be down to the $T\ln 2$ limit, provided the operation is performed slowly enough. Here, "slowly enough" is in comparison with the rate of thermalization of the gas below the piston (including the heat transfer through the container wall) and fundamentally means "allowing E_{cost} to be smaller than $T\ln 2$". The characteristic fluctuations rate (or the relaxation rate) of the system (here the gas) could be viewed as a practical lower-boundary limitation for the rate of the process. However. actually it is not, for two reasons: (1) the height the energy barrier can be (in principle) is as high as desired (it only depends on the ratio of the pressures between the two extreme positions of the piston); (2) in the S-state the bias value can be increased as much as desired (in principle) as the process is slowed down.

Note that the above physical implementation, here exposed for binary logic, could be easily extended to multivalued logic [14] by increasing the maximum value of the gear ratio r. For instance, $r = 3$ would allow three logical states, etc.

4. Maxwell's Demon, Szilard's Engine, and Ratchets

Maxwell was far ahead of his time and was the first to understand the link between energy and information. He imagined [4] a gas in an insulating container separated in two parts along the x-axis by a thermally insulating wall having a small door. A demon is able to measure the velocity component v_x of molecules and open the door, allowing faster molecules to go from A to B while slower ones can only go from B to A. This results in a decrease in the entropy of the system or equivalently in a temperature difference between the two compartments, which can eventually be used for running a thermodynamic cycle and producing work.

A simplified version of this device is due to Szilard [15], the system is made of a single "gas" particle submitted to thermal motion in a box divided into two parts (say left and right). The demon puts a wall on the middle, then measures where the particle is, places a piston on the opposite side, and removes the wall so that the pressure can produce work on the piston. Today, Szilard's engine is no longer a curiosity. It is at the basis of some experimental realizations of Feynman's ratchet [16] at a molecular level [17–19] with potential interesting applications.

How can these machines work in accordance with the second law of thermodynamics? Landauer's principle is often presented as the key point for their understanding. Let us examine this.

4.1. Energy, Entropy, and Information

Energy is a strange physical quantity. It is a universally used concept, but there is no definition of what exactly energy is. Actually, energy is an abstraction only defined by a conservation principle. This is explained by Feynman in his physics lessons [20]. In thermodynamics, this conservation principle originates from the experiments of Joule [21], who produced heat (in calorie) by providing mechanical work (in Nm) and observed that both quantities are proportional, so that by using the same unit (joule) one can introduce a quantity (namely the internal energy) that is constant for an isolated system. Then, each time this principle of conservation seems to be violated, it suffices, to conserve it, to declare that a new form of energy has been discovered.

The introduction of the concept of entropy with the second law of thermodynamics is quite similar. This law can be stated as: (1) there exists a form of internal energy proportional to the temperature T and to a state-quantity S named entropy such that $T\Delta S$ is the heat exchanged for a reversible process; (2) the entropy of the state of a system cannot decrease at no cost in energy. Each time this law seems to be violated, it suffices, to preserve it, to declare that we have missed something in performing the energy balance.

Maxwell is also the person who wrote, well before Shannon's theory of information, "The idea of dissipation of energy depends on the extent of our knowledge" [22]. So, it is clear that in his mind the missing term in the energy balance lies in the knowledge (or information) necessary for the demon to operate. Information is a new form of energy.

After Shannon, things become clearer. The link between entropy and probabilities was made by Boltzmann, Planck, and Gibbs [23–25], leading to the equality: $S = \sum_i p_i \ln(1/p_i)$, where p_i is the probability for the system to adopt the microstate i. Then, Shannon [2] demonstrated that this quantity is also the average number of bits required to encode and store a representation of the microstate of the system (i.e., the minimum requirement to treat this information). The link between information and energy is made and Maxwell's demon machine has no more mystery. Except we do not know exactly where inside the demon the energy dissipation is happening. If we want to be more precise, as a demon does not exist, we must first specify what we are going to replace it with. We must enter into the details of the physical implementation of the ratchet. However, before this, let us first note that there is absolutely no reason for the "location" of the dissipation to be universal. So that with regard to what a theory should be, i.e., not an explanation but rather an economy of thought [10,26], it is not certain that we gain much by doing this.

4.2. Landauer–Bennett vs. "Shannon Only" Interpretations

Following Bennett [7], Szilard's demon is replaced by a Turing machine and the measure is a COPY of the particle position (left or right) to one bit (0 or 1) of the memory buffer of the machine to the state on which the rest of the process depends. To run cyclically, the COPY operation is actually an OVERWRITE, that can be split into ERASE (i.e., RESET TO 0) then WRITE. Hence, the answer: the expansion of the gas produces mechanical work equal (at best) to $T \ln 2$, but the ERASE costs (at least) the same quantity (Equation (4)). In Bennett's mind, the place where dissipation occurs is then well identified (ERASE operation). Landauer's principle claims the generality of this. Two objections can be made to this reasoning.

The first objection is that splitting OWERWRITE is not necessary. The overwriting can be performed directly according to the same mechanism as in Figure 2 (i.e., independent of the initial state) but with a final state which depends on the measurement and which is not always equal to 0. For a cyclic process, overwriting the previous measurement by the last one does not change the entropy of the system because both measurements have the same probability distribution. In this case, OVERWRITE is logically and thermodynamically (statistically) reversible, even in the framework of Landauer's physical implementation. Introducing an irreversible ERASE operation is artificial.

Note that this objection is different to that of Earman and Norton [27] who attempt to replace ERASE by reversible operations. The authors introduce a conditional operation (IF) that is equally logically irreversible, as explained by Bennett ([8] p. 505) in his refutation.

The second objection directly comes from the counterexample given in this paper: the reasoning falls down if ERASE can be achieved in a quasistatic manner as is shown here.

Understanding of Szilard's engine in the framework of Shannon's information theory is different. Because the phase space of the gas is discrete and finite, a given microstate corresponds to a given value of an integer random variable with a finite support. The gas is a random source of information that can be encoded by using a number of bits per word (per microstate) equal to the Shannon's entropy (namely, the quantity of information or the uncertainty about the source). As Shannon's entropy of microstates distribution is the same as Gibbs' entropy, that is the same as Clausius' entropy, it follows that reducing the uncertainty in the source by a factor of 2 (making the economy of one bit) has necessarily an energy cost at least equal to $T \ln 2$ (according to the second law used here, exactly as it was also in Landauer's eraser approach). This is exactly what is performed when Szilard's demon puts up the wall prior to any measurement. However, this should be seen as part of a cycle with an arbitrary beginning and end. So that the cost has not to be paid immediately but either by the rest of the process necessary to close the loop or its equivalent belonging to the previous cycle. This solution *à la* Shannon does not enter in the detailed mechanism of the demon's black-box, thus leaving the space for specific implementations. It is free of any physical support for information because the entropy of the source (the emitter) does not depend on the presence or absence of a receiver (the physical support). For instance, Brillouin [28] outlines that the demon needs light to see where the particle is (measurement) and that the energy needed for this light emission will prevent violation of the second law.

What we know from Shannon, is that $T \ln 2$ must we paid somewhere for Szilard's engine to work, but that this cost can be everywhere in the demon and is not necessarily due to an ERASE operation: (1) because ERASE is not unavoidable; (2) because ERASE can be performed in a thermodynamical quasistatic manner.

5. Concluding Remark on Computing Power Limits

Computing requires ERASE operations. As a consequence, Launder's eraser energy cost ($T \ln 2$) is often considered as an absolute quantity that limits the computing power. The bit-implementation given in this paper shows that this idea is not correct: logical irreversibility does not necessarily imply thermodynamical irreversibility.

The question is not whether a computer can be built by using such a mechanical implementation (clearly it should not), but rather whether other two-to-one implementations would allow the same result. This cannot be excluded, in particular in cases where the information is not processed by computers but by biological systems. Launder's principle that involves a one-to-one implementation is likely very (may be the most) common, but it is not general (the counterexample demonstrates this). Szilard's engines need at least $T \ln 2$ per cycle to work in agreement with the second law whatever way the engines are physically implemented. However, computing is not only dedicated to these engines. Following Landauer [6], there are no unavoidable energy consumption requirements per step in a computer provided reversible computation is performed. This article shows that this assertion can be extended to irreversible computation.

Funding: This research received no external funding.

Conflicts of Interest: The author declares no conflict of interest.

References

1. Clausius, R. *The Mechanical Theory of Heat*; Macmillan & Co.: London, UK, 1879.
2. Shannon, C.E. A mathematical theory of communication. *Bell Syst. Tech. J.* **1948**, *27*, 379–423. [CrossRef]
3. Lairez, D. A short derivation of Boltzmann distribution and Gibbs entropy formula from the fundamental postulate. *arXiv* **2022**. [CrossRef]
4. Maxwell, J.C. *Theory of Heat*, 3rd ed.; Longmans, Green and Co.: London, UK, 1872.
5. Landauer, R. Irreversibility and Heat Generation in the Computing Process. *IBM J. Res. Dev.* **1961**, *5*, 183–191. [CrossRef]
6. Landauer, R. Information is Physical. *Phys. Today* **1991**, *44*, 23–29. [CrossRef]
7. Bennett, C.H. The thermodynamics of computation—A review. *Int. J. Theor. Phys.* **1982**, *21*, 905–940. [CrossRef]
8. Bennett, C.H. Notes on Landauer's principle, reversible computation, and Maxwell's Demon. *Stud. Hist. Philos. Sci. Part B Stud. Hist. Philos. Mod. Phys.* **2003**, *34*, 501–510. [CrossRef]
9. Vopson, M.M. The mass-energy-information equivalence principle. *AIP Adv.* **2019**, *9*, 095206. [CrossRef]
10. Einstein, A. On the method of theoretical physics. *Philos. Sci.* **1934**, *1*, 163–169. [CrossRef]
11. Bérut, A.; Arakelyan, A.; Petrosyan, A.; Ciliberto, S.; Dillenschneider, R.; Lutz, E. Experimental verification of Landauer's principle linking information and thermodynamics. *Nature* **2012**, *483*, 187–189. [CrossRef]
12. Hong, J.; Lambson, B.; Dhuey, S.; Bokor, J. Experimental test of Landauer's principle in single-bit operations on nanomagnetic memory bits. *Sci. Adv.* **2016**, *2*, e1501492. [CrossRef]
13. Shenker, O.R. Logic and Entropy. 2000. Available online: http://philsci-archive.pitt.edu/115/ (accessed on 28 July 2023).
14. Bormashenko, E. Generalization of the Landauer principle for computing devices based on many-valued logic. *Entropy* **2019**, *21*, 1150. [CrossRef]
15. Szilard, L. On the decrease of entropy in a thermodynamic system by the intervention of intelligent beings. *Behav. Sci.* **1964**, *9*, 301–310. [CrossRef]
16. Feynman, R. *The Feynman Lectures on Physics: Ratchet and Pawl*: Addison-Wesley, Reading, MA, USA, 1963; Volume I, Chapter 46. Available online: https://www.feynmanlectures.caltech.edu/I_46.html (accessed on 28 July 2023).
17. Toyabe, S.; Sagawa, T.; Ueda, M.; Muneyuki, E.; Sano, M. Experimental demonstration of information-to-energy conversion and validation of the generalized Jarzynski equality. *Nat. Phys.* **2010**, *6*, 988–992. [CrossRef]

18. Koski, J.; Kutvonen, A.; Khaymovich, I.; Ala-Nissila, T.; Pekola, J. On-Chip Maxwell's Demon as an Information-Powered Refrigerator. *Phys. Rev. Lett.* **2015**, *115*, 260602. [CrossRef]
19. Bang, J.; Pan, R.; Hoang, T.M.; Ahn, J.; Jarzynski, C.; Quan, H.T.; Li, T. Experimental realization of Feynman's ratchet. *New J. Phys.* **2018**, *20*, 103032. [CrossRef]
20. Feynman, R.P.; Leighton, R.B.; Sands, M. *The Feynman Lectures on Physics*; Addison-Wesley: Reading, MA, USA, 1966; Chapter 4.
21. Joule, J. On the mechanical equivalent of heat. *Philos. Trans. R. Soc. Lond.* **1850**, *140*, 61–82. [CrossRef]
22. Maxwell, J.C. Diffusion. *Encycl. Br. Reprod. Sci. Pap.* **1878**, *2*, 625–646. [CrossRef]
23. Boltzmann, L. *Lectures on Gas Theory*; Dover: New York, NY, USA, 1964.
24. Planck, M. *The Theory of Heat Radiation*; P. Blakiston's Son: Philadelphia, PA, USA, 1914.
25. Gibbs, J. *Elementary Principles in Statistical Mechanics*; Charles Scribner's Sons: New York, NY, USA, 1902.
26. Duhem, P. *The Aim and Structure of Physical Theory*; Princeton University Press: Princeton, NJ, USA, 2021. [CrossRef]
27. Earman, J.; Norton, J.D. EXORCIST XIV: The Wrath of Maxwell's Demon. Part II. From Szilard to Landauer and Beyond. *Stud. Hist. Philos. Sci. Part B Stud. Hist. Philos. Mod. Phys.* **1999**, *30*, 1–40. [CrossRef]
28. Brillouin, L. Maxwell's Demon Cannot Operate: Information and Entropy. I. *J. Appl. Phys.* **1951**, *22*, 334–337. [CrossRef]

Disclaimer/Publisher's Note: The statements, opinions and data contained in all publications are solely those of the individual author(s) and contributor(s) and not of MDPI and/or the editor(s). MDPI and/or the editor(s) disclaim responsibility for any injury to people or property resulting from any ideas, methods, instructions or products referred to in the content.

Article

On the Precise Link between Energy and Information

Cameron Witkowski [1,*,†], Stephen Brown [1] and Kevin Truong [1,2]

1. Edward S. Rogers, Sr. Department of Electrical and Computer Engineering, University of Toronto, 10 King's College Circle, Toronto, ON M5S 3G4, Canada; prof.brown@utoronto.ca (S.B.); kevin.truong@utoronto.ca (K.T.)
2. Institute of Biomedical Engineering, University of Toronto, 164 College Street, Toronto, ON M5S 3G9, Canada
* Correspondence: cameron.witkowski@mail.utoronto.ca; Tel.: +1-905-809-1696
† Current address: Division of Engineering Science, University of Toronto, 6 King's College Road, Toronto, ON M5S 3H5, Canada.

Abstract: We present a modified version of the Szilard engine, demonstrating that an explicit measurement procedure is entirely unnecessary for its operation. By considering our modified engine, we are able to provide a new interpretation of Landauer's original argument for the cost of erasure. From this view, we demonstrate that a reset operation is strictly impossible in a dynamical system with only conservative forces. Then, we prove that approaching a reset yields an unavoidable instability at the reset point. Finally, we present an original proof of Landauer's principle that is completely independent from the Second Law of thermodynamics.

Keywords: Maxwell's Demon; Landauer's principle; Szilard's engine; erasure; cost; energy; information; measurement

1. Introduction

Since the inception of thermodynamics, a delicate tension between physics and information has been unfolding. On the one hand, it is generally believed that knowledge of a system's evolution will not, by itself, change that evolution. Simultaneously, what an observer can do with a system (i.e., extract work or decrease entropy) does depend upon the knowledge they possess. Since the Second Law of thermodynamics, roughly speaking, requires that the thermodynamic entropy of a closed system can only increase, a paradox emerges: can an intelligent being circumvent the laws of thermodynamics?

The first recognition of this paradox was by Maxwell, who described how the entropy of a gas could be decreased by "the intelligence of a very observant and neat-fingered being" [1]. In a thought experiment, Maxwell imagined this being opening and closing a massless shutter between two vessels of gas at equilibrium. With knowledge of the paths and velocities of all the molecules, the intelligent being can selectively let fast-moving molecules pass to one side and slow-moving molecules to the other. As a temperature difference grows between the two vessels, the entropy of the system decreases. This intelligent being became known as Maxwell's Demon.

Since the Second Law of thermodynamics forbids such decreases of entropy in closed systems, there must be a way of accounting for the Demon's information about the system. Such was the thought of Leo Szilard, who in 1929 created an engine that permits easier analysis of the connection between information and thermodynamics [2]. A depiction of Szilard's engine is presented in Figure 1.

In contrast to the Maxwell's Demon thought experiment, Szilard's engine contains only one particle in a closed vessel kept at temperature T_b. A movable partition is inserted in the centre of the vessel, creating two sub-chambers, which we take here to be equal volumes $V_l = V_r = \frac{1}{2} V_{total}$. The partition also confines the particle to one side of the vessel. Several assumptions are made in the analysis of the Szilard engine:

1. The partition can be inserted or removed from the chamber at a fixed position with zero energy cost.
2. When the partition is removed from the chamber, it can be slid left and right with zero energy cost.
3. The heat bath at temperature T is infinitely large.
4. The practical difficulties (i.e., constructing a particular mechanical assembly) of extracting work from a single particle may be ignored.
5. During expansion, the partition can be moved slowly enough to be considered quasi-static, so nonequilibrium and transitory effects may be ignored.
6. The pulleys exert no force in equilibrium other than to redirect the tension of the string.

To justify assumptions 1 and 2, one may note that when the partition is not in contact with the particle, the partition may be moved by conservative forces alone (i.e., any kinetic energy transferred to the partition may be recovered when slowing it to a halt). Assumptions 3–5 are, strictly speaking, idealizations. Assumption 6 is weaker than assuming that the pulleys are massless and frictionless (typical for dynamics problems), and is hardly a step from their real behavior. Szilard made assumptions 1–5 either implicitly or explicitly, and here we add assumption 6 for our analysis [2].

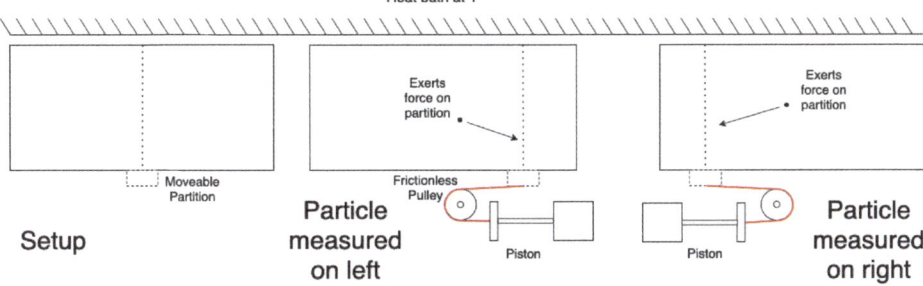

Figure 1. A depiction of the classic Szilard engine.

Following Szilard, we start with the partition at the midpoint of the chamber. If the piston is positioned correctly, then work can be extracted from this engine by a quasi-static isothermal expansion. For a single particle, this work is given in Joules by:

$$W = \int_{V_i}^{V_f} P \, dV \tag{1}$$

$$= \int_{V_i}^{V_f} \frac{NkT}{V} \, dV \tag{2}$$

$$= NkT \ln \frac{V_f}{V_i} \tag{3}$$

$$= (1)kT \ln \frac{V_{total}}{\frac{1}{2} V_{total}} \tag{4}$$

$$= kT \ln 2 \tag{5}$$

where N is the number of particles (in this case 1), k is the Boltzmann constant, and T is the temperature in degrees Kelvin. It may seem dubious to use thermodynamic quantities to describe a single particle. However, this is justified if we imagine time-averaging the particle's behavior, as is common practice in such idealizations [3].

In order to position the piston correctly, however, a measurement must be made to determine which side of the partition the particle occupies. Thus, Szilard argued, we must associate $k \ln 2$ units of entropy with the measurement, in order to account for the work we are able to extract as a result. Szilard writes:

> If we do not wish to admit that the Second Law has been violated, we must conclude that the intervention which establishes the coupling between y and x, the measurement of x by y, must be accompanied by a production of entropy [2].

Since these words were put down in 1929, the story has remained much the same. The only major change was made by Landauer, who suggested that the *erasure* of information was specifically what generated heat. In particular, Landauer wrote that the energy cost we must pay when erasing this measurement equals or surpasses $kT \ln 2$ [4]. Thus, the cost of erasing our measurement ultimately saves the Second Law from the Demon's wiles. Notably, realizations of the Szilard engine have been confirmed in experiment [5].

Surprisingly, the question of whether measurement is necessary at all to operate Szilard's engine seems completely absent from the literature. This consideration does not appear to have crossed Szilard's mind, or the minds of any subsequent authors. While we would be delighted to find out we overlooked an analysis somewhere, our search through the literature did not reveal any previous discussion of this question. We present our modified engine to demonstrate one way the engine could work without us measuring.

2. Modified Szilard Engine

In Figure 2, the modified Szilard engine is shown. The only difference between the setups in Figures 1 and 2 is the positioning of the piston and the use of a second pulley. Importantly, the piston does not have to be moved to a different location to extract work from the engine in Figure 2, regardless of the side the particle is on. Thus, since the side the particle is on does not matter to the action of the engine, the measurement is superfluous.

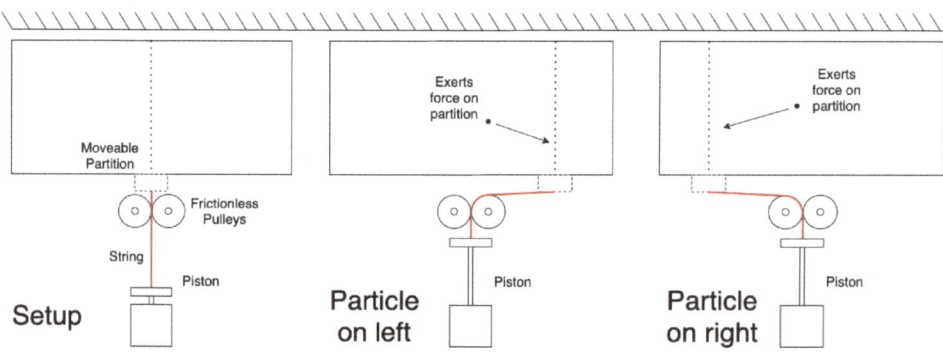

Figure 2. Our modified Szilard engine.

2.1. Work Extraction Protocol

The most likely objection to our modified engine in Figure 2 is that work cannot actually be extracted by it; work can only be extracted in a directed manner. Since the modified engine does not allow for knowledge of which way the partition should move, no sort of directed expansion is possible. Note, however, that the necessity of directing the expansion (thus the necessity of measuring) is exactly what is under question to begin with. We cannot assume a priori that this is impossible simply because it is unfamiliar.

To shed some more light on the analysis of work extraction, consider the following common description of quasi-static compression and expansion. Imagine a pile of sand placed on top of a piston against which gas is compressed. By adding a single grain of sand to the pile, the gas compresses slightly and reaches a new equilibrium. Grain-by-grain, the gas can be compressed to any desired amount. Likewise, grains can be removed one-by-one and the pile of sand will rise to find a new equilibrium. Assuming a constant temperature, the work performed on the sand during this compression or expansion is given as:

$$W = \int_{x_i}^{x_f} F \cdot dx \quad (6)$$

$$= \int_{x_i}^{x_f} -m(x)g \cdot dx \quad (7)$$

$$= \int_{x_i}^{x_f} P(x)A \cdot dx \quad (8)$$

$$= \int_{V_i}^{V_f} \frac{NkT}{V} dV \quad (9)$$

$$= NkT \ln \frac{V_f}{V_i} \quad (10)$$

where x is the piston's displacement, F is the force on the gas, and m(x) is the mass of the sand pile as a function of displacement. In Equation (8), since the system is in equilibrium, we may use $P(x)A = -m(x)g$. In Equation (9), we use the fact that $A \cdot dx$ is a change in volume dV. Unsurprisingly, the final expression in Equation (10) is equivalent to Equation (3). Thus, as long as we may remove grains of sand one-by-one from a piston, we may extract work in a quasi-static manner.

Can grains of sand be placed on the piston in Figure 2 as easily as they could for Szilard's engine? Upon close inspection, we see nothing that would prevent this. Sure, the gravitational force from a single grain is orders of magnitude greater than the average pressure from a single particle, but the same challenge is faced by Szilard's engine. For both cases, in principle, nothing prevents the design of a piston with enough mechanical advantage that the average force exerted by the particle will reach equilibrium with the gravitational force of a reasonably sized pile of sand. Moreover, we made assumption 4 to secure us against such practical challenges. Thus, we conclude that work can be extracted by quasi-static expansion of the engine shown in Figure 2.

To be fully explicit about the cycle we imagine for Figure 2, we specify the following four steps, beginning with the partition at the midpoint of the chamber:

1. 'Grains of sand' are placed on the piston.
2. The partition is inserted into the chamber (with no energy cost, per assumption 1).
3. 'Grains of sand' are removed yielding a quasi-static expansion.
4. The partition is removed from the chamber and brought back to the midpoint (with no energy cost, per assumption 2).

The attentive reader should immediately be suspicious of these four steps. If carried out exactly as written, we would have extracted a definite quantity of work while spending no energy in a complete engine cycle. Clearly, such a situation would violate the Second Law, and the Kelvin statement in particular. Without question, something is amiss. As we expose what that is in the next few sections, we will discover exactly where the cost of erasure comes from, and illuminate the precise link between energy and information.

2.2. Considering Information

At this point, it is natural to wonder what happened to the information. It seems to have played no role thus far—and precisely characterizing its role was our motivation from the start. Is it encoded in the engine somehow?

Upon closer inspection, we find that the position of the partition (or equivalently, the position of the string), carries the information about the particle's original position. Let x represent the (horizontal) position of the partition, with the starting position being $x = 0$, and the positive direction being to the right. After one expansion, if the particle started on the left, then we will have $x > 0$, and if the particle started on the right, then we will have $x < 0$. Thus, the sign of x, taking two possible values, can be treated as a bit of memory that stores the measurement of the particle's initial side.

The reader may feel some unease with interpreting the partition's position as a 'measurement', for this is certainly an unfamiliar way of thinking about measurement. However, consider Szilard's description of measurement in his 1929 paper:

> For brevity we shall talk about a "measurement", if we succeed in coupling the value of a parameter y_s (for instance the position coordinate of a pointer of a measuring instrument) at one moment with the simultaneous value of a fluctuating parameter x_s of the system, in such a way that, from the value y_s, we can draw conclusions about the value that x_s had at the moment of the "measurement". (The s subscripts were added to distinguish Szilard's notation from ours.) [2]

We contend this description accords exactly with the common intuition of what a measurement is: a coupling between one variable and another, such that the one informs an observer of the other. Thus, by letting $y_s = \text{sign}(x)$, and letting x_s represent the original side of the particle, the value of x_s can be concluded from the value of y_s. Thus, the description justifies the interpretation of the partition's location as representing a measurement.

At face value, this reinterpretation seems to offer little value, as it appears we are in the same position as with Szilard's original engine. Namely, our work extraction protocol generates information, which must be accounted for in the analysis. However, we are in fact at a great advantage since now informational concepts are on the same playing field as the dynamics; we can analyze this information strictly using the tools of physics. In doing so, we will find a better reason for the link between energy and information than simply not wanting to admit that the Second Law has been violated.

3. Landauer's Original Argument

Landauer's principle states that the act of erasing one bit of information necessarily carries an energy cost of $kT \ln 2$. With our modified engine, we are now in a position to fully explain the reason for this cost, pinpoint its source, and demonstrate its generality. However, before turning attention to the reset operation (step 4) of our modified engine in Figure 2, it will be most helpful to remind ourselves of Landauer's argument for why erasure is necessarily dissipative. He considers a single particle in a bistable potential well, then asks whether we can reset the particle to the ONE state with a single time-varying force. He writes:

> Since the system is conservative, its whole history can be reversed in time, and we will still have a system satisfying the laws of motion. In the time-reversed system we then have the possibility that for a single initial condition (position in the ONE state, zero velocity) we can end up in at least two places: the ZERO state or the ONE state. This, however, is impossible. The laws of mechanics are completely deterministic and a trajectory is determined by an initial position and velocity. (An initially unstable position can, in a sense, constitute an exception. We can roll away from the unstable point in one of at least two directions. Our initial point ONE is, however, a point of stable equilibrium.) Reverting to the original direction of time development, we see then that it is not possible to invent a single F(t) which causes the particle to arrive at ONE regardless of its initial state [4].

Landauer's first point is that for a conservative system, the history can be reversed in time. A classical mechanical system is conservative if there exists a potential function V such that

$$F(x,t) = -\nabla V(x) \tag{11}$$

where F is the net force vector, x is position, and t is time [6]. In such a system, Newton's equations are time reversal invariant since the forces depend only on position and not time. Thus, $F(x, v, t) = F(x, -v, -t)$. Recognizing this fact is critical to the rest of the argument.

The dynamics of such a system are described by the second order ordinary differential equation:

$$\ddot{x} = -\frac{\nabla V(x)}{m} \qquad (12)$$

where m is the mass. (Equation (12) and the following arguments are written for a one-dimensional system for the sake of simplicity, although extending them to multiple dimensions would be relatively straightforward. In addition, the arguments can be made mutatis mutandis in general coordinates using Lagrangian mechanics, also neglected for simplicity). With such dynamics in mind, Landauer then states that, in the time-reversed system, for a single initial condition, we can end up in two places, which is impossible. This fact can be seen as a direct consequence of the Existence and Uniqueness Theorem for Ordinary Differential Equations, also known as the Picard–Lindelöf Theorem [7].

Theorem 1 (The Existence and Uniqueness Theorem; Picard–Lindelöf). *Let $R \subseteq \mathbb{R} \times \mathbb{R}^n$ be a closed rectangle with $(t_0, \mathbf{x}_0) \in R$. Let $f : R \to \mathbb{R}^n$ be continuous in t and Lipschitz continuous in $\mathbf{x}$. Then, there exists some $\varepsilon > 0$ such that the initial value problem*

$$\dot{\mathbf{x}}(t) = f(t, \mathbf{x}(t)), \quad \mathbf{x}(t_0) = \mathbf{x}_0 \qquad (13)$$

has a unique solution, $x(t)$ on the interval $[t_0 - \varepsilon, t_0 + \varepsilon]$.

To apply the theorem to the dynamics in Equation (12), we set

$$\mathbf{x} = \begin{bmatrix} x \\ v \end{bmatrix} = \begin{bmatrix} x \\ \dot{x} \end{bmatrix} \qquad (14)$$

$$f(t, \mathbf{x}(t)) = \begin{bmatrix} v(t) \\ -\nabla V(x)/m \end{bmatrix} \qquad (15)$$

then it follows that, so long as $\nabla V(x)$ is Lipschitz continuous, then a unique solution $\mathbf{x}(t)$ is guaranteed to exist on some interval including t_0. If we set $t = t_0$ at the moment of reset, then the reverse dynamics of the reset operation will yield two nonunique solutions to the same initial value problem. Thus, if we allow reset under conservative dynamics, we violate the Existence and Uniqueness Theorem. This is another crucial fact to recognize for the argument.

Landauer then notes that an unstable equilibrium constitutes an exception in some sense. This point is actually quite nuanced, and we will treat it comprehensively in the following analysis. For now, we simply mention that it will play an instrumental role in proving the cost-of-erasure bound, and will constitute the precise location where this cost is paid.

Finally, again considering the possibility of a reset operation, Landauer writes "if, however, we permit the potential well to be lossy, this becomes easy" [4]. Here, lossy may be taken as a synonym for nonconservative. Thus, the seeds of a rigorous argument are laid: a reset operation is not possible under conservative dynamics due to the Existence and Uniqueness Theorem, and therefore, it must involve nonconservative dynamics resulting in an energy cost.

What remains is to explicitly demonstrate that the cost of erasing one bit has a particular lower bound, namely $kT \ln 2$. Landauer's approach was to include this bit in the thermodynamical state space and conclude that its erasure decreased the system's entropy by $k \ln 2$, thus generating $kT \ln 2$ J of heat. While satisfying to some, the validity and generality of his conclusions remain highly controversial to this day [8–13]. In Section 5, we will prove this lower bound directly by mechanical and statistical considerations alone, providing what we hope is a satisfying and definitive conclusion to this controversy.

4. Reset Operations with Conservative Forces

We now shift our gaze to step 4 of our modified Szilard's engine cycle: removing the partition from the chamber and returning it to the midpoint. At the end of step 3, the partition can be in one of two places: the right side of the chamber, or the left side. In step 4, we hope to bring the partition back to the midpoint regardless of which side it was on. Thus, if we look closely at step 4, we should expect to catch the act of erasure on full display, ready to be subjected to our scrutiny.

4.1. Approaching Reset

In Section 3, we demonstrated that a reset operation under conservative dynamics is strictly impossible. In this section, we are going to try anyway, to see exactly what happens when we get close. In particular, we will take the limit as we approach a reset operation, with the constraint that we dissipate zero energy.

If we dissipate zero energy, we may not use any dissipative forces to return the partition to the midpoint. Instead, we may only use conservative forces, which can be expressed as the gradient of a potential function, defined by Equation (11). The challenge is thus: can we invent some potential function, $V(x)$, such that when the partition is subjected to this $V(x)$, the forces that are induced will return the partition to the midpoint, regardless of whether it started on the right or left? Consider the potential function in Figure 3, where we present one attempt at such a function.

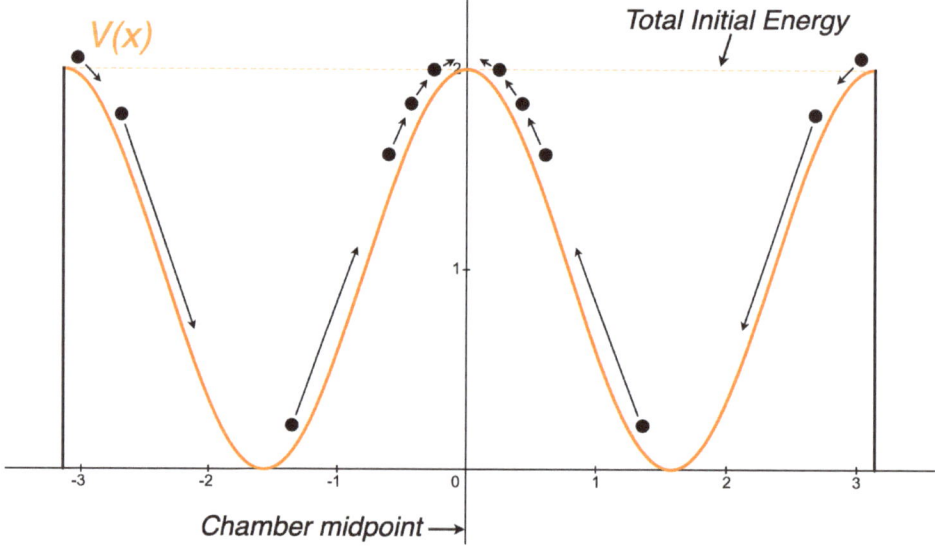

Figure 3. A potential energy function, $V(x)$, one might use to attempt a reset procedure using conservative forces.

The ball represents the partition. The arrows showcase how the partition would be brought back to the midpoint if it started on the left and the right. We find that when the partition comes to rest at $x = 0$, it will be at an unstable equilibrium point. We now see in greater detail why reset in a conservative system is impossible. If the partition starts exactly at $x = 0$, then it will stay at $x = 0$ as long as there are no disturbances. If the partition starts anywhere else, it will never come to rest at $x = 0$. This can be seen as another consequence of the time reversal invariance property and the Existence and Uniqueness Theorem, presented in Section 3.

The presence of an unstable equilibrium at $x = 0$ is no coincidence and will play an important role. It turns out that every system approaching a reset operation with conservative forces will result in an unstable equilibrium at the reset point. We present proof of this fact next.

4.2. General Proof of Instability

First, we define a parameter h that measures how close we are to executing a reset. To be precise, consider two trajectories $x_1(t)$ and $x_2(t)$, and some equilibrium point x_e, which we will treat as our reset state. We characterize these trajectories as follows:

$$||x_1(0) - x_2(0)|| > 0 \tag{16}$$

$$\left\| \begin{bmatrix} x_1(\tau) \\ v_1(\tau) \end{bmatrix} - \begin{bmatrix} x_e \\ 0 \end{bmatrix} \right\| \leq h \tag{17}$$

$$\left\| \begin{bmatrix} x_2(\tau) \\ v_2(\tau) \end{bmatrix} - \begin{bmatrix} x_e \\ 0 \end{bmatrix} \right\| \leq h \tag{18}$$

$$\nabla V(x_e) = 0 \tag{19}$$

where $\tau > 0$ is some elapsed time. Equation (16) says that the two trajectories start in different places, while Equations (17) and (18) specify how close our trajectories are to being 'merged,' and Equation (19) is simply the equilibrium condition. We take $x_1(0)$ and $x_2(0)$ as given, meaning the starting points do not vary with h. Our goal is to investigate what happens as $h \to 0$. We will prove that, for any conservative system under these conditions, the reset state is an unstable equilibrium. To begin, we turn to Lyapunov for a rigorous definition of stability [14].

Definition 1 (Lyapunov Stability). *Consider an autonomous dynamical system given by*

$$\dot{\mathbf{x}} = f(\mathbf{x}(t)), \quad \mathbf{x}(0) = \mathbf{x}_0, \tag{20}$$

where $\mathbf{x}(t) \in \mathcal{D} \subseteq \mathbb{R}^n$ denotes the system state vector, $\mathcal{D}$ is an open set containing the origin, and $f : \mathcal{D} \to \mathbb{R}^n$ is a continuous vector field on $\mathcal{D}$. Suppose f has an equilibrium at x_e such that $f(\mathbf{x}_e) = 0$.

This equilibrium is said to be Lyapunov stable, if, for every $\varepsilon > 0$, there exists a $\delta > 0$ such that, if $\|\mathbf{x}(0) - \mathbf{x}_e\| < \delta$, then for every $t \geq 0$ we have $\|\mathbf{x}(t) - \mathbf{x}_e\| < \varepsilon$.

Definition 2 (Instability). *The equilibrium point $\mathbf{x}_e$ is defined to be unstable if it is not Lyapunov stable.*

We write out our conservative system from Equation (12) as follows:

$$\mathbf{x}(t) = \begin{bmatrix} x(t) \\ v(t) \end{bmatrix} \tag{21}$$

$$f(\mathbf{x}(t)) = \begin{bmatrix} v(t) \\ -\nabla V(x)/m \end{bmatrix} \tag{22}$$

$$\dot{\mathbf{x}}(t) = \begin{bmatrix} \dot{x}(t) \\ \dot{v}(t) \end{bmatrix} = f(\mathbf{x}(t)) \tag{23}$$

where $v = \dot{x}$ is the velocity.

Theorem 2 (Instability of Conservative Reset). *Let $x_1(t)$ and $x_2(t)$ be trajectories of a conservative system and let x_e be a point. If $x_1(t)$, $x_2(t)$, and x_e satisfy Equations (16)–(19), then in the limit as $h \to 0$, x_e is an unstable equilibrium.*

Proof. We must show that it is not the case that for every $\varepsilon > 0$, there exists a $\delta > 0$ such that, if $||\mathbf{x}(0) - \mathbf{x}_e|| < \delta$, then for every $t \geq 0$ we have $||\mathbf{x}(t) - \mathbf{x}_e|| < \varepsilon$. Equivalently, we will show that there exists an $\varepsilon > 0$ such that for every $\delta > 0$, there exists a $t \geq 0$ and $\mathbf{x}(0)$ satisfying $||\mathbf{x}(0) - \mathbf{x}_e|| < \delta$ such that $||\mathbf{x}(t) - \mathbf{x}_e|| \geq \varepsilon$.

Let $\mathbf{x}_1(t) = \begin{bmatrix} x_1(t) \\ v_1(t) \end{bmatrix}$, $\mathbf{x}_2(t) = \begin{bmatrix} x_2(t) \\ v_2(t) \end{bmatrix}$, and $\mathbf{x}_e = \begin{bmatrix} x_e \\ 0 \end{bmatrix}$. We then set

$$\varepsilon = \max\left(||\mathbf{x}_1(0) - \mathbf{x}_e||, ||\mathbf{x}_2(0) - \mathbf{x}_e||\right) \quad (24)$$

We may have that $\mathbf{x}_1(0) = \mathbf{x}_e$ or $\mathbf{x}_2(0) = \mathbf{x}_e$, but these two conditions cannot both be true, as this would violate Equation (16). Thus, our selection for ε always yields $\varepsilon > 0$. Consider the reverse dynamics.

Case 1: if $||\mathbf{x}_1(0) - \mathbf{x}_e|| > 0$ then set $\mathbf{x}(0) = \begin{bmatrix} x_1(\tau) \\ -v_1(\tau) \end{bmatrix}$. Then, $\mathbf{x}(\tau) = \mathbf{x}_1(0)$ and $\lim_{h \to 0} ||\mathbf{x}(0) - \mathbf{x}_e|| \leq \lim_{h \to 0} h < \delta$ for all $\delta > 0$. Thus, for every $\delta > 0$ there exists a $t \geq 0$ such that

$$||\mathbf{x}(t) - \mathbf{x}_e|| \geq \max\left(||\mathbf{x}_1(0) - \mathbf{x}_e||, ||\mathbf{x}_2(0) - \mathbf{x}_e||\right) = \varepsilon \quad (25)$$

Case 2: if $||\mathbf{x}_2(0) - \mathbf{x}_e|| > 0$, then set $\mathbf{x}(0) = \begin{bmatrix} x_2(\tau) \\ -v_2(\tau) \end{bmatrix}$. Then, $\mathbf{x}(\tau) = \mathbf{x}_2(0)$ and $\lim_{h \to 0} ||\mathbf{x}(0) - \mathbf{x}_e|| \leq \lim_{h \to 0} h < \delta$ for all $\delta > 0$. Thus, for every $\delta > 0$ there exists a $t \geq 0$ such that

$$||\mathbf{x}(t) - \mathbf{x}_e|| \geq \max\left(||\mathbf{x}_1(0) - \mathbf{x}_e||, ||\mathbf{x}_2(0) - \mathbf{x}_e||\right) = \varepsilon \quad (26)$$

□

Thus, we have demonstrated that any equilibrium point at which two trajectories merge in a conservative classical mechanical system is necessarily unstable. (Note that, in a nonconservative system, the preceding argument fails, for the time-reversal property plays a necessary role in setting $\mathbf{x}(0)$.) This result can easily be generalized to trajectories that merge (anywhere) away from equilibrium, simply by viewing the trajectories in the proper inertial or noninertial frame of reference (such that the merge point is an equilibrium in that frame). Moreover, we did not require any assumption that either $\mathbf{x}_1(0) \neq \mathbf{x}_e$ or $\mathbf{x}_2(0) \neq \mathbf{x}_e$. As a result, even though the reset state in Figure 3 is distinct, our proof covers the case of 'reset to ONE', which Landauer originally discussed [4]. To conclude, without any loss of generality, we can view Figure 3 as stereotypical of any scheme to erase information without spending energy.

5. Proof of Landauer's Principle

In Section 4.2, we showed that performing a reset operation with only conservative forces is not only impossible, but to even approach it we create an unavoidable instability at the reset point. Fortunately, we can overcome both these difficulties if we are just willing to spend a little energy. To determine how much energy we need to spend, consider Figure 4 below, which we will analyze in detail.

The system in Figure 4 is no longer conservative: we have placed a friction force, labelled 'Brake,' at the $x = 0$ location to dissipate some small quantity of energy and ensure the partition does not spontaneously slide away. Our intention with the brake is to 'trap' the partition at the reset point. The quantity of energy we dissipate is labelled by ϵ.

Our ultimate question is: what is the minimum value of ϵ such that we can reliably perform a reset? At first glance it appears that our brake will have this desired effect for any $\epsilon > 0$. In other words, we can 'trap' the partition at $x = 0$ as long as we dissipate nonzero energy; we imagine that once the partition falls into our trap, it simply will not have the energy to spontaneously jump back out.

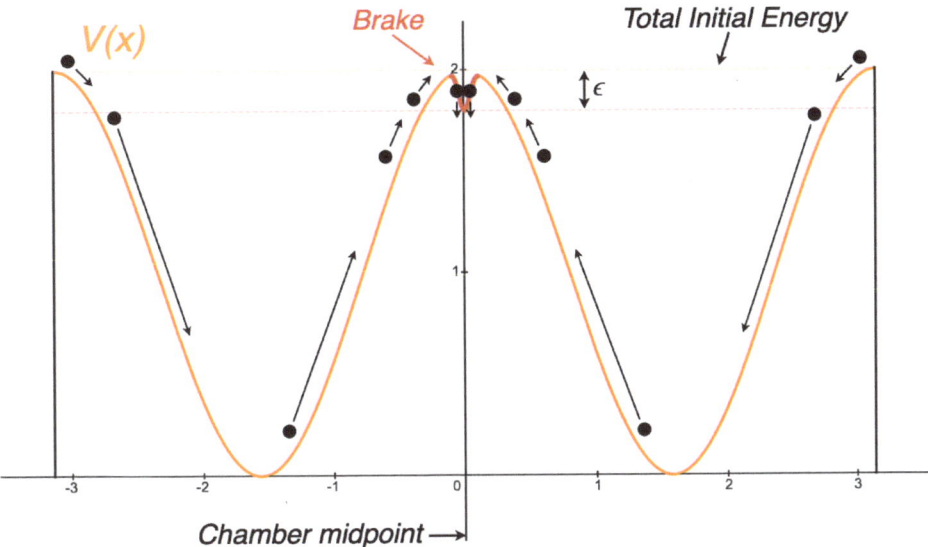

Figure 4. An energy landscape one might implement to perform a reset with minimal energy loss.

This conclusion is compelling, and it would be true if the partition was at absolute zero. If the partition has any significant thermal energy, however, it will constantly be undergoing vibrations. We immediately see that if we make ϵ too small, the partition may actually vibrate out of our trap. Fortunately for Landauer's principle, these vibrations place a lower limit on ϵ, meaning it cannot be arbitrarily close to zero. In our system, the chamber is in thermal contact with a heat bath at temperature T. Thus, unless we pretend there are other energy sources or sinks, we should find the partition at temperature T also.

When we consider the possibility of the partition vibrating out of our trap in the context of our engine cycle for Figure 2, we face a startling and beautiful realization: the entire engine cycle could work in reverse. In particular, consider the following alternate steps, recalling that the partition starts at the midpoint:

1. The partition jumps away from the midpoint and comes to rest at either the right or left of the chamber, then is inserted into the chamber.
2. 'Grains of sand' are placed on the piston, yielding a quasi-static compression.
3. The partition is removed from the chamber.
4. The grains of sand are removed from the piston.

Thus, we see that for a given value of ϵ, there will be some probability of the forward cycle and some probability of the reverse cycle. Fundamentally, this means that the measurement that was made may instead be unmade, and the work carried out on the sand (by the gas) may instead be conducted on the gas (by the sand). Here, we are reminded of the ratchet and pawl thought experiment, beautifully analyzed by Feynman [15]. The ratchet and pawl appear more likely to proceed in one direction than another but are ultimately found to be in equilibrium. We will prove Landauer's principle by a similar approach to the argument Feynman makes.

Let $\mathcal{X}$ denote an autonomous physical system in contact with a heat bath at temperature T. Let x_L, x_R, and x_e be memoryless states of $\mathcal{X}$, representing the ZERO, ONE, and RESET states. Let $x(t)$ represent the system's trajectory through these states over time. Additionally, let E_L, E_R, and E_e represent the energy of states x_L, x_R, and x_e, respectively, with $E_L = E_R$. Finally, define $E_L - E_e = E_R - E_e = \epsilon$ to be the energy cost of reset. We define these terms in full generality, applying to any system, though it may be helpful to imagine x_L corresponding to the partition at the left, x_R to the partition at the right, and x_e to the partition at the midpoint.

Consider some time interval $[t_i, t_f]$. Let

$$P(x(t_f) = x_e \mid x(t_i) = x_L) = P(x(t_f) = x_e \mid x(t_i) = x_R) = p \in (0,1) \quad (27)$$
$$P(x(t_f) = x_L \mid x(t_i) = x_e) = P(x(t_f) = x_R \mid x(t_i) = x_L) = q \in (0,1) \quad (28)$$
$$P(x(t_f) = x_L \mid x(t_i) = x_L) = P(x(t_f) = x_R \mid x(t_i) = x_R) = r \in (0,1) \quad (29)$$

These transition relations are represented graphically in Figure 5.

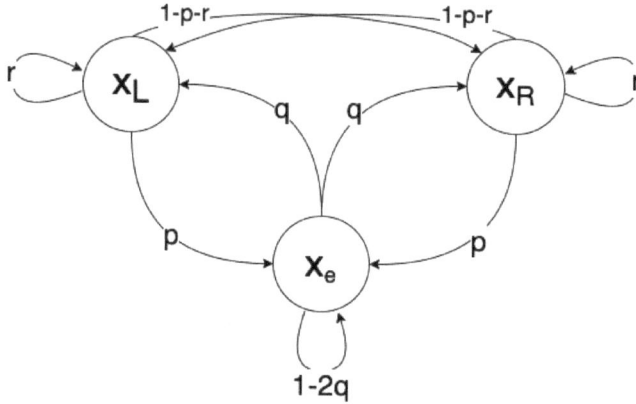

Figure 5. A graphical representation of the transition probabilities described by Equations (27)–(29).

To perform a reset, we should want the probability that the system goes *into* the reset state to be greater than the probability that it *leaves* the reset state. Observe that if the system is in x_L or x_R, the probability that it will move to x_e (performing the reset) is p. On the other hand, if the system is in x_e, the probability that it will move to x_L or x_R (undoing the reset) is $2q$. We say $\mathcal{X}$ implements a reset if the former case is more probable than the latter. Precisely, $\mathcal{X}$ implements a reset if

$$p > 2q \quad (30)$$

When applied to our engine cycle, this constraint would enforce that the forward cycle is more likely than the reverse.

Theorem 3 (Landauer's Principle). *If $\mathcal{X}$ implements a reset, then $\epsilon > kT \ln 2$.*

Proof. Since x_L, x_R, and x_e are memoryless states and $\mathcal{X}$ is autonomous, the transition probabilities described by Equations (27)–(29) generate a Markov Chain. Since $p \in (0,1)$, $q \in (0,1)$, and $r \in (0,1)$, it is easily verified that this chain is aperiodic and irreducible, and thus has a stationary distribution. Let $P(x_L)$, $P(x_R)$, and $P(x_e)$ be the probabilities of each state in the stationary distribution, which we can also consider as a statistical ensemble.

For the stationary distribution, we will have:

$$P(x_e)(2q) = P(x_L)(p) + P(x_R)(p) \quad (31)$$
$$P(x_L)(p) + P(x_L)(1-p-r) = P(x_e)(q) + P(x_R)(1-p-r) \quad (32)$$
$$P(x_R)(p) + P(x_R)(1-p-r) = P(x_e)(q) + P(x_L)(1-p-r) \quad (33)$$

Subtracting Equation (33) from (32), we obtain

$$(P(x_L) - P(x_R))(1 - r) = (P(x_R) - P(x_L))(1 - p - r) \tag{34}$$
$$(P(x_L) - P(x_R))(p) = 0 \tag{35}$$
$$P(x_L) = P(x_R) \tag{36}$$

Applying Equations (36)–(31), we obtain

$$P(x_e)(2q) = 2P(x_L)(p) \tag{37}$$
$$P(x_e)q = P(x_L)p \tag{38}$$

Now, recalling we must have $p > 2q$ if $\mathcal{X}$ implements a reset, we obtain

$$P(x_e)q > P(x_L)(2q) \tag{39}$$
$$P(x_e) > 2P(x_L) \tag{40}$$

Equation (40) was the key relation we needed from the analysis of the Markov Chain. Now, we will seek to write the stationary probability of states in terms of their energy. First, observe that the expected energy of the statistical ensemble is given by:

$$\langle E \rangle = P(x_L)E_L + P(x_R)E_R + P(x_e)E_e \tag{41}$$

If the distribution over states is stationary, the energy of the statistical ensemble will be constant. Then, there can be no net flow of thermal energy between $\mathcal{X}$ and the heat bath. Thus, the stationary distribution is in thermal equilibrium with the heat bath.

Since the stationary distribution is a statistical ensemble in thermal equilibrium with a heat bath, it is exactly the canonical ensemble [16]. The probability distribution over states as a function of energy (measured in Joules) is thus given by:

$$P(x_i) = \frac{e^{-\frac{1}{kT}E_i}}{\sum_j e^{-\frac{1}{kT}E_j}} \tag{42}$$

where k is Boltzmann's constant, and T is the temperature in Kelvin. We then continue from Equation (40):

$$\frac{e^{-\frac{1}{kT}E_e}}{\sum_j e^{-\frac{1}{kT}E_j}} > 2 \frac{e^{-\frac{1}{kT}E_L}}{\sum_j e^{-\frac{1}{kT}E_j}} \tag{43}$$
$$e^{-\frac{1}{kT}E_e} > 2e^{-\frac{1}{kT}E_L} \tag{44}$$
$$e^{\frac{1}{kT}(E_L - E_e)} > 2 \tag{45}$$
$$e^{\frac{\epsilon}{kT}} > 2 \tag{46}$$
$$\frac{\epsilon}{kT} > \ln 2 \tag{47}$$
$$\epsilon > kT \ln 2 \tag{48}$$

□

6. Discussion

The result in Equation (48) is quite general. It is not limited to particles in boxes but applies to any autonomous system in contact with a heat bath. Naturally, it is trivial to extend the argument for the cost of erasure to any other logically irreversible function or 'merging of computational paths.' Moreover, for systems of multiple bits, the bound scales exactly as expected. For instance, imagine the engine in Figure 2 was divided into four quadrants rather than two chambers, thus generating a 'measurement' of two bits rather than one. An isothermal expansion to four times the volume, by the same calculations as

Equations (1)–(5), gives $W = kT \ln 4$. The two bits would occupy four states that merge into one; thus, Equation (30) would become $p > 4q$. With this, it is easy to recompute the bound as $\epsilon > kT \ln 4 = 2kT \ln 2$. By extension, the cost to erase n bits has a lower bound of $nkT \ln 2$. These results dovetail nicely with considerations of many-valued logic, where the Landauer bound remains the same [17].

Interestingly, the case of equality ($\epsilon = kT \ln 2$) corresponds to the reset process having equal likelihood of working forward or backward. In the context of our engine from Figure 2, the forward cycle will be equally as likely as the backward cycle. This result should not be surprising since a nearly identical consideration is used to demonstrate that the ratchet and pawl cannot produce work at equilibrium [15].

With regard to the heat generated by erasure, we may now observe exactly where it comes from. In the reset scheme of Figure 4, for instance, we see that the mechanical energy of the partition had to be dissipated. In general, the source of heat will depend on the memory device used, but it will be whatever form of energy facilitated the switch to the reset state; this energy must be spent or else the same energy could facilitate a switch back.

We may gain a deeper intuition of this idea by the following analogy with regard to the reverse dynamics. Imagine balancing on a nearly unstable equilibrium, such as that of Figure 4 with $\epsilon = kT \ln 2$. If we stay perfectly atop, our total energy will not change. In the presence of thermal vibrations, however, eventually, a disturbance will push us along one trajectory or another. This 'push' is actually a small quantity of heat that (by starting our motion) is converted to mechanical energy, in accordance with the conservation of energy. As a result, we can view the entire backward cycle as an isothermal compression used to cool the partition. Each cycle the engine operates in reverse, $kT \ln 2$ work is performed on the particle, and $kT \ln 2$ heat is removed from the partition. In the forward direction then, we see in great detail why the mechanical energy must be converted to heat.

7. Conclusions

In conclusion, we offer a definitive exorcism of Maxwell's Demon by clarifying the necessity of measurement in Szilard's engine and presenting a proof of Landauer's principle. Remarkably, our proof is entirely independent of the Second Law. Nowhere did we require any assumption that the Second Law is true or that it holds for our engine. Instead, we compute the energy cost of erasure directly by mechanical and statistical means alone. Our result instills greater confidence in the Second Law, as it sheds light on independent reasons why perpetual motion machines are impossible even for Maxwell's Demon.

We summarize our conclusions as follows. We showed that an explicit measurement procedure is unnecessary to operate Szilard's engine if we instead interpret the partition's location as bearing information. This reinterpretation shed light on how information can be analyzed strictly using the tools of physics—dynamical systems theory in particular. Using these tools, it follows that a reset operation in a conservative system is strictly impossible due to the Existence and Uniqueness Theorem for ordinary differential equations. Worse, to even approach a reset operation produces an unavoidable instability (in the sense of Lyapunov) at the reset point. Practically, thermal vibrations at this instability allow the reset operation to proceed in reverse, which becomes more likely as ϵ decreases. We showed that when a reset operation is more likely to proceed forward than backwards, we must have $\epsilon > kT \ln 2$. Finally, to the question of whether an intelligent being can circumvent the Second Law by gathering and exploiting information, we answer no.

Author Contributions: Conceptualization, C.W.; formal analysis, C.W.; investigation, C.W.; writing, C.W.; supervision, S.B. and K.T. All authors have read and agreed to the published version of the manuscript.

Funding: This work was supported by the Natural Sciences and Engineering Research Council of Canada [#RGPIN-2020-07118 to S.B., #RGPIN-2019-04183 to K.T.] and the Canadian Institutes of Health Research [#PJT-156317 to K.T.].

Institutional Review Board Statement: Not applicable.

Data Availability Statement: No new data were created or analyzed in this study. Data sharing is not applicable to this article.

Acknowledgments: This work has greatly benefited from the insightful and fruitful discussions with Artemy Kolchinsky, whose valuable input was instrumental to gaining an appreciation for the current wisdom in informational physics and the Szilard engine. Artemy also brought to light the 'grains of sand' metaphor used throughout the paper. Immense gratitude is extended to Saiyam Patel for sanity checking the initial concerns with Szilard's engine, and for employing his discerning mind to thoroughly vet the proofs presented in this paper. Sincere appreciation extends to Frank Kschischang, who graciously served as a soundboard for several preliminary ideas on the subject, offering his wisdom and expertise. Lastly, heartfelt thanks go to Simone Descary, whose unwavering support and encouragement have been a cornerstone of this endeavor.

Conflicts of Interest: The authors declare no conflicts of interest.

Abbreviation

The following abbreviation is used in this manuscript:

DOAJ   Directory of open access journals

References

1. Knott, C.G. Quote from undated letter from Maxwell to Tait. In *Life and Scientific Work of Peter Guthrie Tait*; Cambridge University Press: Cambridge, UK, 1911; p. 215.
2. Szilard, L. On the decrease of entropy in a thermodynamic system by the intervention of intelligent beings. *Behav. Sci.* **1964**, *9*, 301–310. [CrossRef] [PubMed]
3. Bormashenko, E.; Shkorbatov, A.; Gendelman, O. The Carnot engine based on the small thermodynamic system: Its efficiency and the ergodic hypothesis. *Am. J. Phys.* **2007**, *75*, 911–915. [CrossRef]
4. Landauer, R. Irreversibility and Heat Generation in the Computing Process. *IBM J. Res. Dev.* **1961**, *5*, 183–191. [CrossRef]
5. Toyabe, S.; Sagawa, T.; Ueda, M.; Muneyuki, E.; Sano, M. Experimental demonstration of information-to-energy conversion and validation of the generalized Jarzynski equality. *Nat. Phys.* **2010**, *6*, 988–992. [CrossRef]
6. Arnol'd, V.I. *Mathematical Methods of Classical Mechanics*; Springer Science & Business Media: Berlin, Germany, 2013; Volume 60, p. 22.
7. Coddington, E.A.; Levinson, N. *Theory of Ordinary Differential Equations*; McGraw-Hill Book Company, Inc.: New York, NY, USA, 1955.
8. Earman, J.; Norton, J.D. EXORCIST XIV: The wrath of Maxwell's demon. Part I. From Maxwell to Szilard. In *Studies In History and Philosophy of Science Part B: Studies In History and Philosophy of Modern Physics*; Elsevier: Amsterdam, The Netherlands, 1998; Volume 29, pp. 435–471.
9. Earman, J.; Norton, J.D. EXORCIST XIV: The wrath of Maxwell's demon. Part II. From Szilard to Landauer and beyond. In *Studies in History and Philosophy of Science Part B: Studies in History and Philosophy of Modern Physics*; Elsevier: Amsterdam, The Netherlands, 1999; Volume 30, pp. 1–40.
10. Norton, J.D. Waiting for Landauer. In *Studies in History and Philosophy of Science Part B: Studies in History and Philosophy of Modern Physics*; Elsevier: Amsterdam, The Netherlands, 2011; Volume 42, pp. 184–198.
11. Ladyman, J.; Robertson, K. Landauer defended: Reply to Norton. In *Studies in History and Philosophy of Science Part B: Studies in History and Philosophy of Modern Physics*; Elsevier: Amsterdam, The Netherlands, 2013; Volume 44, pp. 263–271.
12. Bormashenko, E. The Landauer principle: Re-formulation of the second thermodynamics law or a step to great unification? *Entropy* **2019**, *21*, 918.
13. Robertson, K.; Prunkl, C. Is thermodynamics subjective? In *Philosophy of Science*; Cambridge University Press: Cambridge, UK, 2023; Volume 90, pp. 1320–1330.
14. Lyapunov, A.M. Stability of motion: General problem. *Int. J. Control* **1992**, *55*, 540–541. [CrossRef]
15. Feynman, R.P. *Feynman Lectures on Physics*; California Institute of Technology: Pasadena, CA, USA, 1967; Chapter 46.
16. Gibbs, J.W. *Elementary Principles of Statistical Mechanics*; Charles Scribner's Sons: New York, NY, USA, 1902.
17. Bormashenko, E. Generalization of the Landauer Principle for computing devices based on many-valued logic. *Entropy* **2019**, *21*, 1150. [CrossRef]

Disclaimer/Publisher's Note: The statements, opinions and data contained in all publications are solely those of the individual author(s) and contributor(s) and not of MDPI and/or the editor(s). MDPI and/or the editor(s) disclaim responsibility for any injury to people or property resulting from any ideas, methods, instructions or products referred to in the content.

Article

Events as Elements of Physical Observation: Experimental Evidence

J. Gerhard Müller

Department of Applied Sciences and Mechatronics, Munich University of Applied Sciences, D-80335 Munich, Germany; gerhard.mueller@hm.edu

Abstract: It is argued that all physical knowledge ultimately stems from observation and that the simplest possible observation is that an event has happened at a certain space–time location $\vec{X} = (\vec{x}, t)$. Considering historic experiments, which have been groundbreaking in the evolution of our modern ideas of matter on the atomic, nuclear, and elementary particle scales, it is shown that such experiments produce as outputs streams of macroscopically observable events which accumulate in the course of time into spatio-temporal patterns of events whose forms allow decisions to be taken concerning conceivable alternatives of explanation. Working towards elucidating the physical and informational characteristics of those elementary observations, we show that these represent hugely amplified images of the initiating micro-events and that the resulting macro-images have a cognitive value of 1 bit and a physical value of $W_{obs} = E_{obs}\tau_{obs} \gg h$. In this latter equation, E_{obs} stands for the energy spent in turning the initiating micro-events into macroscopically observable events, τ_{obs} for the lifetimes during which the generated events remain macroscopically observable, and h for Planck's constant. The relative value $G_{obs} = W_{obs}/h$ finally represents a measure of amplification that was gained in the observation process.

Keywords: physical measurement; information gain; event generation; physical action; energy dissipation; space–time expansion

1. Introduction

In this paper, we are concerned with the problem of gaining information about nature by performing physical experiments. In order to introduce this subject, we sketch in Section 2 three historic experiments which were ground-breaking in the evolution of theories which form the background of our current understanding of matter on the atomic, nuclear, and elementary particle scales. These are the Rutherford scattering experiments of Geiger and Marsden [1], which proved the nuclear nature of atoms [2,3]; the double-slit experiments performed with photons and all kinds of corpuscular matter, which proved the dual nature of matter [4–7]; and the cloud, bubble, and streaming chamber experiments [8–10] in high-energy physics, which led to the discovery of the standard model of elementary particles [11]. In the past, these experiments were conceived and carried out with the aim of producing macroscopically observable phenomena which allow conceivable alternatives of explanation to be distinguished that had been discussed at their times of invention.

Regarding these key experiments as questions posed to nature, it is interesting to note that all questions are answered in the form of transient effects which are localized in space and time, and which accumulate over time into spatio-temporal patterns of events which allow decisions to be taken concerning conceivable alternatives of explanation. Turning to those elementary observations, it is clear that the events of observation need to involve a great deal of amplification to turn them into macroscopic images of those initiating events between matter and experimental equipment that had occurred on the microscale. A second relevant observation is that the events of observation are meaningless in the sense that they do not yield any information other than that that an event has happened or not at a certain space–time location $\vec{X} = (\vec{x}, t)$. As such elementary observations yield binary decisions between two alternatives, the experimental answers produced by these key experiments resemble messages sent over digital communication channels in which complex and meaningful messages are made up from individual, but otherwise meaningless, bits [12–14].

While the traditional interpretations of the above key experiments tacitly assumed that particles, waves, and fields are primary entities of physical reality, and that the events of observation are secondary effects produced by the interactions of those primary entities with the experimental equipment, this historic mindset was more recently challenged by the idea that all physical entities at their core are information-theoretic in origin. This latter idea, which was raised by John Archibald Wheeler [15] and aphoristically termed "it from bit", has raised a vivid controversy between the traditional "bit from it" and the more recent "it from bit" approaches [16,17].

In view of this controversy, it appeared to be relevant to re-consider the three key experiments with an informational perspective in mind. In the present paper, we concentrate on those elementary observations that, in the course of time, build up the experimental answers produced by the three key experiments. After a brief review of these experiments in Section 2, we discuss in Sections 3 and 4 the informational and physical characteristics of those elementary observations that show up as macroscopically observable events. On the whole, this discussion reveals that the elements of physical observation have a double nature in that these are abstract pieces of information on the one hand, and concrete physical entities on the other hand. As physical entities, elementary observations reveal as pieces of physical action, produced at the expense of generating entropy. With this conclusion in mind, elementary observations appear as another manifestation of Landauer's original conclusion [18–21], namely that "information is physical" at its origin. The processes of generating and erasing elementary observations and of assigning meaning to discrete patterns of observable events will be discussed in forthcoming papers [22,23].

2. The Three Key Experiments

After the above preliminary considerations, we turn to a more in-depth discussion of those experiments which have been accepted as ground-breaking in the evolution of physical sciences. For the sake of discussion, these historic experiments are sketched in Figures 1–3 below.

Moving from top to bottom, these examples show the Rutherford scattering experiments that convincingly demonstrated the nuclear nature of atoms [1–3] and rejected the earlier "plum pudding model" of atoms proposed by J. J. Thompson [24]. In this way, the road towards the Bohr theory of the hydrogen atom [25] and the modern quantum theories of Heisenberg [26] and Schrödinger [27] were paved.

The double-slit experiments [4–7], on the other hand, confirmed the assumption of a wave–particle duality underlying the Heisenberg [26] and Schrödinger [27] pictures of the atom.

The cloud- [8], bubble- [9] and spark-chamber [10] experiments performed in the realm of high-energy physics finally contributed to the discovery of a vast variety of elementary particles, which led to the standard model of elementary particles [11].

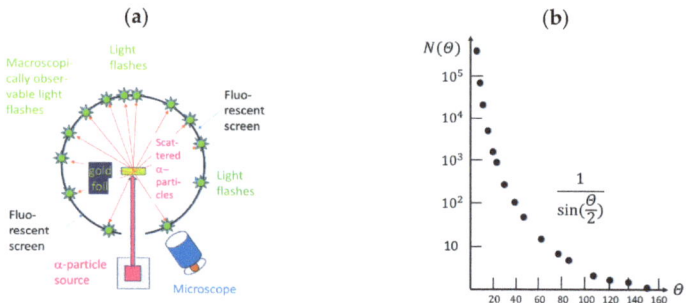

Figure 1. (**a**) Sketch of a Rutherford scattering experiment [1] which proved the nuclear constitution of atomic matter [3]. Alpha-particle scattering from a gold foil produces flashes of light on the fluorescent screen (green stars), whose angular distribution can be interpreted as evidence that most of the mass of Au atoms is concentrated in small volumes with linear dimensions on the order of 10^{-12} cm [3]. (**b**) Angular distribution of light flashes as observed in the original work of Geiger and Marsden in 1913 [1].

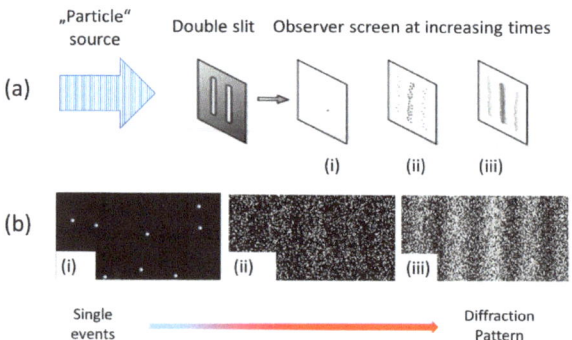

Figure 2. (**a**) Matter in the form of photons, electrons, atoms, and molecules is passed through the double-slit arrangements in (**a**) in one-by-one manner [4–7].; (**b**) After having passed through the double-slit arrangement in (**a**), the transmitted "particles" interact with a photographic screen on the right, producing macroscopically observable events which accumulate in the form of diffraction patterns after more and more "particles" have been processed through the experimental arrangement in (**a**). Screen shots at increasingly larger times are shown in subfigures (i); (ii); (iii) [28].

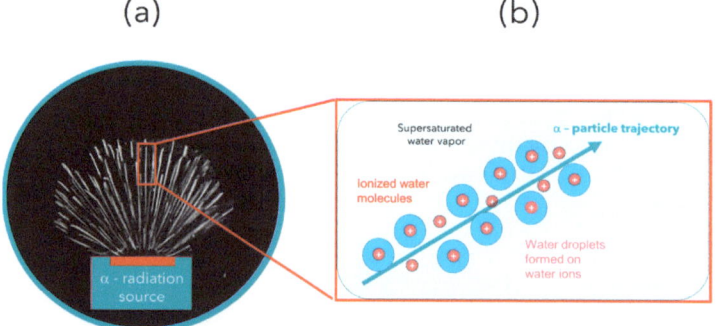

Figure 3. (**a**) α-particle trajectories emerging from an α-particle source immersed inside a cloud chamber [8,29]; (**b**) schematic view of a cloud chamber track of water droplets condensed on water ions formed along the α-particle trajectories [29].

3. Differences and Commonalities between the Three Key Experiments

Considering the above experiments, these share in common that all of them address processes that occur at length and time scales much too small to be directly observable. The key motivation of all these experiments, consequently, was producing macroscopically observable images of those unobservable micro-phenomena.

Depending on the kind of physical questions asked, the experimental arrangements take very different forms. Whereas the Rutherford experiment was intended to measure the momentum transfers to α-particles that occur deep inside the electrostatic fields that surround atomic nuclei, the double-slit experiments addressed interference phenomena and the issue of wave–particle duality while the streaming chamber experiments were designed to reveal particle trajectories with the aim of deriving kinetic energies and momenta of nuclear reaction products.

Concurrent with the architectural differences between the key experiments, the spatio-temporal patterns of events take very different forms. These differences, however, disappear when matter is made to interact with the respective experimental arrangements in a one-by-one manner and when the emerging experimental outputs are monitored as they emerge in the course of time. Looked at as functions of time, all experiments produce phenomena that are localized in space and time, and which are macroscopically observable, i.e., either directly visible by unaided eyes—or at least through some kind of optical instrument such as a microscope, as was used in the Geiger–Marsden experiments [1].

As none of these individual observations form neither an angular distribution of scattering events, nor a diffraction pattern, nor a particle trajectory, the observation of each of these individual events does not yield any other information other than that that an event has happened at a certain space–time location or not. As observation or lack of observation of a single event within an observational time interval decides a simple yes/no alternative, each of these single events has a cognitive value of exactly one bit. This idea of making an elementary observation and of choosing between binary alternatives is pictorially represented in Figure 4. There, a photon is sketched that is moving from the source towards a fluorescent screen through a narrow gap. As, on its way from the source to the fluorescent screen, no observation can be made that would allow us to decide whether the photon is moving along a straight-line particle trajectory or in an undulatory manner as a wave, the observation of a single light flash on a fluorescent screen does not allow any other conclusion to be drawn other than that that an event has happened.

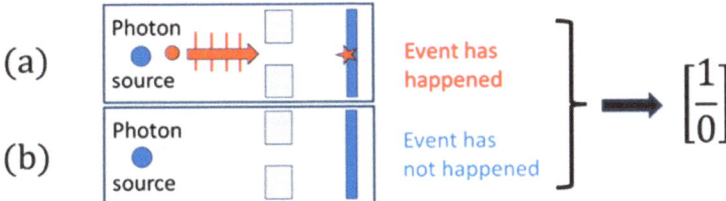

Figure 4. (**a**) A single photon moving from source to fluorescent screen through a narrow slit, either in the form of a particle or in an undulatory manner as a wave; (**b**) no passage of a photon during the observational time period. Elementary observations of this kind produce an information gain equivalent to one binary digit or bit.

Collecting many of such elementary observations, complex multi-bit messages are produced. In a Rutherford scattering experiment, for instance, angular distributions of sufficiently large numbers of scattered particles can be acquired that allow a decision to be made between scattering in nuclear electric force fields with $1/r$, $1/r^2$, or hard sphere potentials [2,3,23]. Similarly, distinctions can be made between wave phenomena occurring at different wavelengths and with different arrangements of slits and screens [4], or between particles moving with different momenta through a given magnetic field [8–10].

4. Emergence and Erasure of Elementary Observations

In the section above, we identified elementary observations as macroscopically observable, binary pieces of information. What has not yet been discussed is how these elementary pieces of information come into existence, and why these occur as temporal transients. In order to move forward into this direction, we re-consider in more detail the processes of Rutherford scattering and of visualizing nuclear particle trajectories in cloud chambers. The time-resolved sketches of these processes in Figures 5 and 6 show that both processes move through a sequence of four steps, namely: initiation, growth, observation, and erasure and reset. All observable effects (light flashes, particle trajectories) that transiently appear on the macro-scale ultimately disappear, as all energy that had produced these effects has finally been dissipated. Such dissipation clearly explains the transient nature of events.

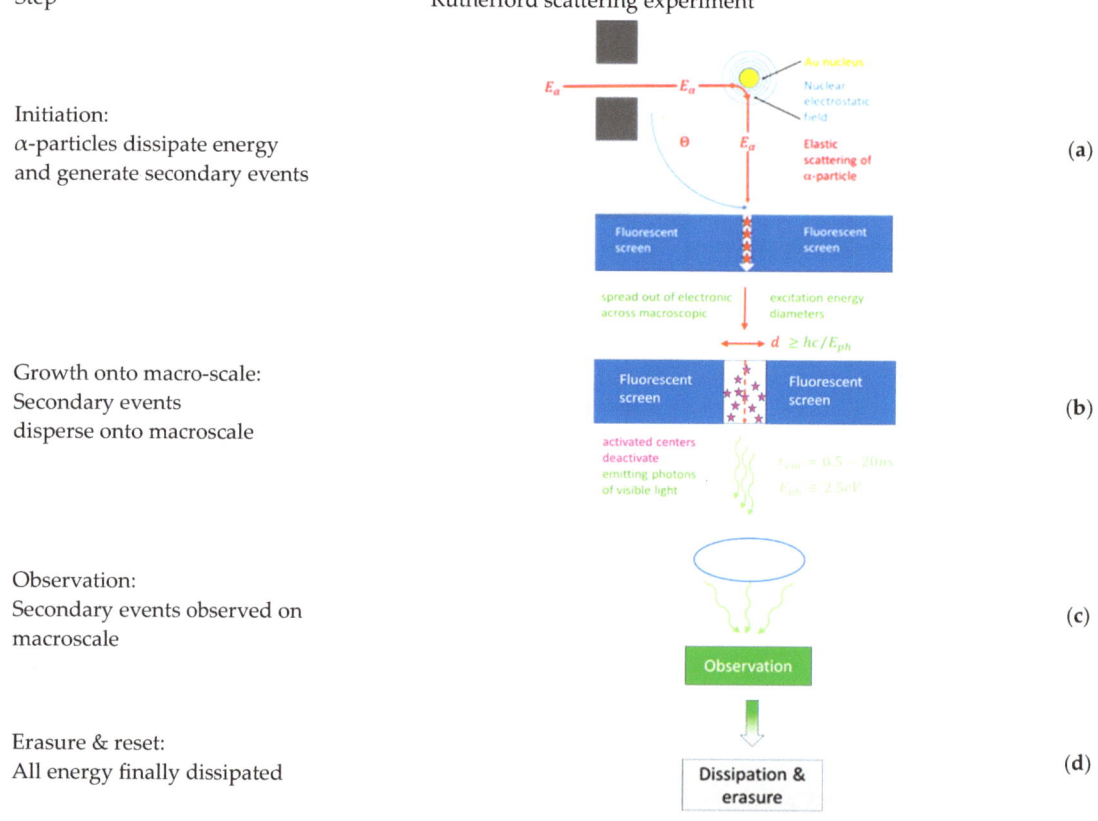

Figure 5. Time-resolved sketch of Rutherford scattering process; sequential steps of information gathering and reset.

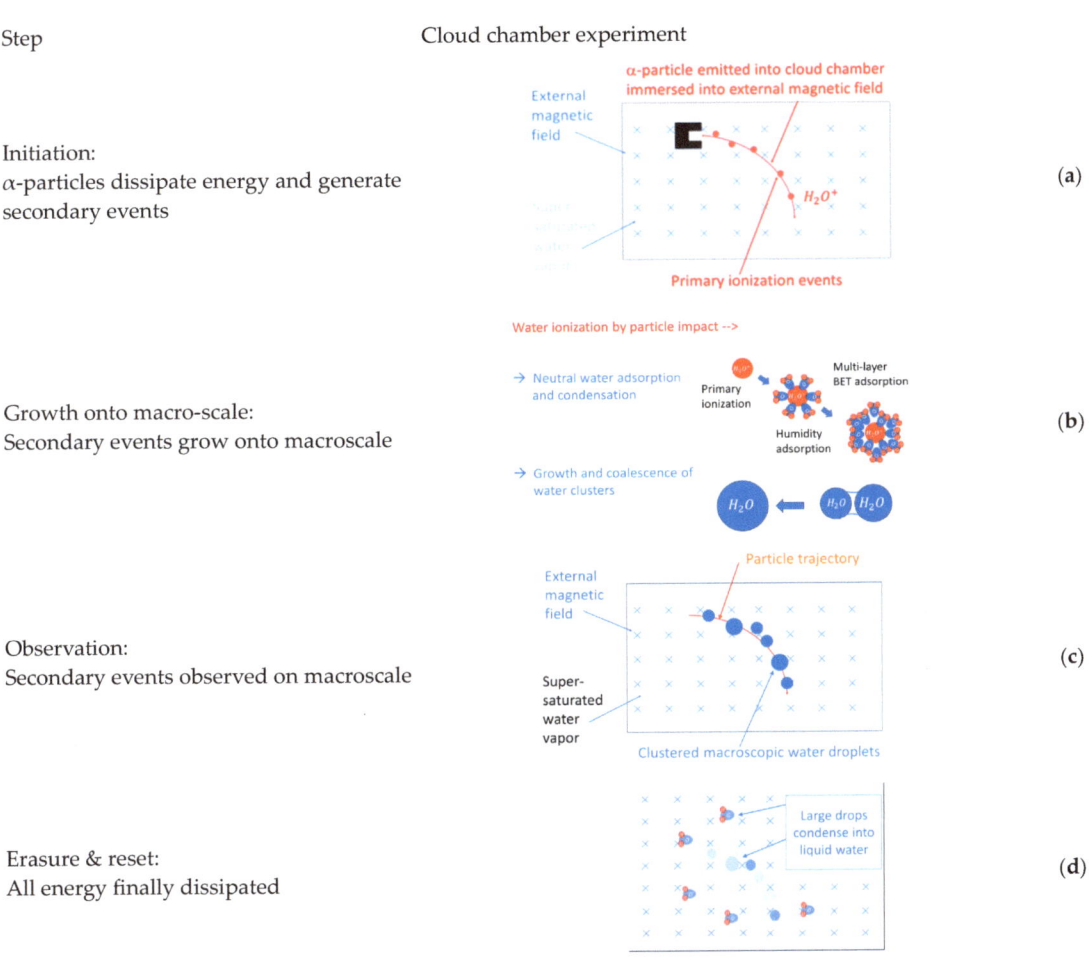

Figure 6. Time-resolved sketch of elementary particle detection in cloud chamber; sequential steps of information gathering and reset.

For the sake of clarity, we now move through these four steps, considering Rutherford scattering and the visualization of particle tracks in a cloud chamber sequentially.

4.1. Rutherford Scattering

The initial step in Rutherford scattering is the approach of an α-particle close to the Au nucleus (Figure 5a). With an α-particle energy of $E_a \cong 5$ MeV, α-particles can approach Au nuclei up to a minimum distance of $r_{min} \cong 5 \times 10^{-12}$ cm, which is still larger than the nuclear radius of $R_{Au} \cong 6 \times 10^{-13}$ cm. The scattering process, therefore, clearly takes place within the strong electrostatic field that surrounds each Au nucleus. During the residence time of $\tau_{int} \approx 2\, r_{min}/v_\alpha$, where v_α is an α-particle velocity of around 5% the speed of light, the physical action associated with the scattering process can be estimated to be $\Delta W \cong E_a \tau_{min} \cong 7$ h. Changes in physical action on the order of a few Planck units are typical of quantum-mechanical interactions.

The second part of the initiation process is the absorption of the scattered α-particle inside the ZnS fluorescent layer, as also shown in Figure 5a, and the generation of secondary ionization events. Estimates based on the Bethe–Boch formula [30] show that roughly

80 – 90 eV of the α-particle's kinetic energy are transferred into ionization and electronic excitation energy within each mean-free path inside the ZnS layer. With the initial α-particle energy of $E_a \cong 5$ MeV and its initial speed of $v_a \cong 0.05c$, each scattered α-particle is found to slow down over a length of approximately 20 μm inside the ZnS layer and within a time span of a few picoseconds. During this short time, the scattered α-particles generate roughly $N_{int} = 6 \times 10^4$ secondary ionization events, which form a narrow, straight line of highly electronically excited ZnS material. Due to the large lateral gradients in electronic excitation energy, intense lateral flows of electrons are initiated away from this line. Assuming that, in the ensuing diffusion- and equilibration processes, one single activated center is formed per primary ionization event, N_{int} green-light luminescence photons will ultimately be emitted from the small cylindrical volume in which the α-particle energy had been dissipated (Figure 5b). With the bulk electron mobility in ZnS on the order of $\mu_n \cong 100$ cm^2/Vs [31], lateral diffusion lengths on the order of several micrometers can be estimated. Although the surface diameters of light-emitting ZnS materials of this size are small, these nevertheless amount to multiples of the wavelength of the green luminescence light of $\lambda_{ph} \cong 0.5$ μm, which allows these light spots to be observed with the help of a microscope (Figure 5c) as actually used in the Geiger–Marsden experiments [1].

With this situation in mind, the amount of physical action W_{obs}, associated with such green-light-emitting cylindrical volumes (Figure 5c), can be estimated. Assuming that each ionization event ultimately leads to the emission of a green-light photon with an energy of $E_{ph} \cong 2.5$ eV [1] and a luminescence lifetime of $\tau_{lum} \cong 10^{-8}$ s [32], a piece of physical action of $W_{obs} \cong N_{int} E_{ph} \tau_{lum}$ is generated which amounts to a quantity of 3.5×10^{11} units of the Planck constant. With a physical action of only 7 units of Planck constant h generated in the initiating scattering process, a huge amount of amplification on the order of $G_{obs} \cong 5 \times 10^{10}$ is inferred to have occurred in the Geiger–Marsden experiment [1]. With this number in place, the macroscopic observability of the initiating microscopic scattering events can be explained. As, finally, after observation, all luminescence light is converted into low-temperature heat (Figure 5d), all of the α-particles' initial kinetic energy has ultimately been dissipated in the detection process.

Taking an overall look at the Rutherford scattering experiment, it becomes apparent that each individual scattering event had ultimately become observable by dissipating the kinetic energy of the incoming α-particles. Dissipation in this context means that the huge initial energy of each α-particle was broken down into increasingly smaller packages of energy which were simultaneously spread out over increasingly larger spatial domains. Whereas, in the final stages of dissipation, the temperature of the entire ZnS fluorescence screen was raised by an immeasurably small amount, macroscopic observability of scattering events relies on the fact that, in the process of dissipation, a large number of visible-light photons are intermittently generated as energy dispersion proceeds. As the emitted photons still carry energies much larger than the mean thermal energy of the ZnS lattice atoms, their informational value stands out from the random thermal noise inside the ZnS layer, which ensures their observability [33]. Again, as the energy of these visible light photons is further dissipated in the detection process [34], all kinetic energy of the initiating α-particles is finally dissipated into low-temperature heat, which completely erases all informational value that had originally been carried by the incoming α-particles in the form of kinetic energy [32].

4.2. Visualization of Nuclear Particle Tracks

In the cloud chamber experiment shown in Figure 6a, the initiating micro-event is the emission of an α-particle from the source and the ensuing travel of the particle through an atmosphere of supersaturated water vapor inside the cloud chamber. Again, with the high kinetic energy of each emitted α-particle of around 5 MeV, a large number of secondary ionization events is triggered along each particle's trajectory. Due to the much lower stopping power of α-particles in super-saturated water vapor [30], however, long tracks of ionization events with lengths on the order of several centimeters are formed [8,29].

After this has happened, the initial ionization is distributed over a large number of H_2O molecules, which, because of the auto-protolysis of water [35], results in a large number of H_3O^+ and OH^- ions. The high electrical fields around each ionized water molecule subsequently encourage neighboring H_2O dipoles to adsorb on the generated water ions, thereby partially shielding the electrostatic field around each molecular ion. After several layers of such dipoles had been adsorbed, the electrical shielding of the H_3O^+ and OH^- ions has been completed, and, apparently, neutral water droplets had been formed (Figure 6b). With diameters in the range of nanometers, these droplets are still far too small to be visually observable. Once this size range had been reached, a second growth process takes over that grows tiny water droplets into visually observable sizes, and which thus enables the α-particle trajectories to become visually observable. This second stage of droplet growth, also shown in Figure 6b, involves the phenomenon of Ostwald ripening [36]. Ostwald ripening involves the fusion of tiny water droplets into aggregates and the growth of the larger fusion partners at the expense of the smaller ones. In this second phase of growth, the driving force towards larger volumes is the minimization of surface area, and, thus, the reduction in weakly bound surface water molecules at the expense of more tightly bound water molecules inside the bulk. In this way, water droplets with higher condensation energy $Q_{H2O}(r)$ are formed with increasing r:

$$Q_{H2O}(r) = \left(\frac{4\pi}{3}r^3\right)\varepsilon_b\left[1 - 3\frac{\gamma_s}{\varepsilon_b}\frac{1}{r}\right] \quad (1)$$

In this equation, $\varepsilon_b = 2.26 \times 10^9$ J/m^3 is the cohesion energy of water [37] and $\gamma_s = 0.073$ J/m^2 is the surface energy of water [38]. The existence of weakly bound water molecules in the near-surface regions and the desire to reduce their numbers exerts a mechanical pressure on the bulk which leads to enhanced vapor pressure in very small droplets. Very small droplets, therefore, easily and rapidly evaporate, thus re-generating individual H_2O molecules which are free to adsorb on larger droplets with lower internal pressures. Quantitatively, this excess pressure inside small drops is given by the Kelvin equation [39,40]:

$$p(r,T) = p_{sat}(T)exp\left[\frac{2\gamma_S V_m}{RT\ r}\right] \quad (2)$$

in which $p_{sat}(T)$ is the vapor pressure over a flat surface at the overall temperature T, R is the universal gas constant, and V_m is the molar volume of water.

In Figure 7a, the condensation energy of water droplets $Q_{H2O}(r)$ is drawn as a function of the drop radius r together with the internal pressure $p(r,T)$ inside these drops. In Figure 7b, the internal pressure data is redrawn, this time, however, with the vapor pressures $p(r,T)$ being converted into time scales $\tau(r,T)$ for the evaporation of drops:

$$\tau_{obs}(r,T) = \tau_{evap}(T,\ r = \infty)exp\left[-\frac{2\gamma_S V_m}{RT\ r}\right] \quad (3)$$

In this mathematical conversion, the assumption has been made that droplets with visually observable sizes evaporate at a time scale of seconds. This latter effect is directly observable in cloud chamber experiments, in which visually observable particle tracks fade away within seconds [8,29].

With the condensation energy $Q_{H2O}(r)$ of the droplets and their evaporative lifetimes $\tau(r,T)$ in place, the physical action W_{obs} of visible droplets can once again be calculated:

$$W_{obs}(r,T) = Q_{obs}(r)\ \tau_{obs}(r,T) \gg h. \quad (4)$$

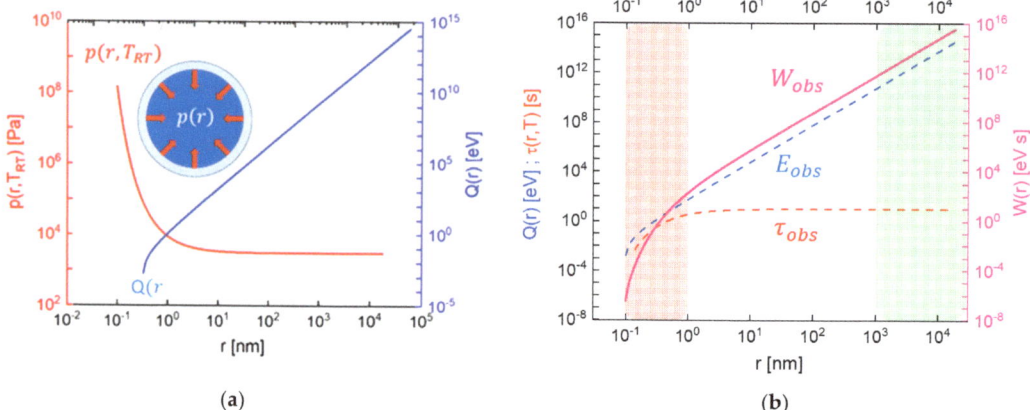

Figure 7. (a) Cohesion energy (blue) and internal pressure of water droplets (red) as a function of drop radius. The development of an inside-oriented pressure resulting from the desire to minimize the numbers of weakly bound H$_2$O molecules on surfaces is shown in the inset. (b) Cohesion energy (blue), evaporative lifetime (red), and observational value (magenta) as a function of drop radius. The colored areas denote the phases of initial growth (red) and of long-lived and macroscopically observable drops that delineate α-particle trajectories.

In Figure 7b, $W_{obs}(r, T_{RT} = 300\ \text{K})$ is plotted as a function of the drop radius. As, in the formation of macroscopically visible and relatively long-lived droplets [8,29], a huge number of water molecules is collected, the magnitudes of $W_{obs}(r, T_{RT})$ are much larger than in the Rutherford scattering case. Once measured in units of the Planck constant of $h = 4.183 \times 10^{-15}$ eVs, the excessively large values of $W_{obs}(r, T_{RT})$ in the cloud chamber case reflect the fact that these tiny water droplets are observable with un-aided eyes as compared to the tiny light flashes in the Rutherford scattering events, which required additional amplification with the help of an optical microscope [1].

Summarizing the considerations about cloud chamber images, some similarity to the case of α-particle scattering can be detected. This similarity is reflected in the formation of primary ionization events in the supersaturated water vapor as highly energetic α-particles are being slowed down, thereby producing drop-initiating H_3O^+ and OH^- ions. Up to the point of drop-initiating water ions, only the kinetic energies of the incoming α-particles had been dissipated. With the onset of adsorption processes on the initiating ions, energetic resources in the experimental equipment become increasingly involved. Once relatively visible droplets start to cluster into rain drops, supersaturated water vapor is finally converted into the more stable phase of condensed water layers, thus completing the overall dissipation of energy. Again, as in the case of Rutherford scattering of α-particles, the phase of macroscopic visibility occurs in a state of partial equilibration and incomplete but ongoing entropy production.

4.3. Producing Permanent Images of Photon Impacts

So far, we have avoided the discussion of photographic images of photon impacts on the photographic screens used in the double-slit experiments. Not considering the complexity of the underlying photo-chemical processes, it is immediately clear that much smaller energies in the range of single electron volts are involved in the photo-chemical processes as compared to the huge α-particle energies in the foregoing examples. Instead of the short lifetimes of the intermittently produced visible-light photons in the Geiger–Marsden experiment or the short evaporative lifetimes in the cloud chamber experiments, the photographic detection of photons in the double-slit experiments produces permanent images of the photon impacts. On the level of observational pieces of physical action,

$W_{obs} = E_{obs}\tau_{obs}$, the lower energies E_{obs} in photography are largely over-compensated by the huge lifetimes τ_{obs} of the photographic images.

5. Summary, Conclusions, and Outlook

In this paper, we have considered historical experiments which were groundbreaking in the development of our modern ideas on processes taking place on the length- and timescales of atoms, nuclei, and elementary particles. Regarding these key experiments as questions posed to nature, it has been revealed that these questions are answered in the form of streams of elementary observations which take the form of temporal transients, which are sharply localized in space but still extended enough to be visually observable. Such observable events were identified as binary pieces of information but also endowed with a firm physical existence as pieces of physical action. Considering in some depth the processes of α-particle scattering on atomic nuclei and the visualization of particle trajectories in cloud chambers, the idea has evolved that these elementary observations are pieces of physical action, produced at the expense of energetic resources either carried with the material objects to be detected or contained in the detection equipment itself. With the elementary observations featuring both as abstract pieces of information and as firm pieces of physical reality, the elementary observations produced by the three key experiments appear as another manifestation of Landauer's initial ideas on memory and switching devices and his conclusive statement of "information is physical" [19].

Introducing the quantity $W_{obs} = E_{obs}\tau_{obs}$, where E_{obs} is the energy expended in turning a quantum-mechanical interaction into a macroscopically observable event and τ_{obs} the lifetime in which an event remains macroscopically observable, a preliminary measure of macroscopic observability has been obtained. Considering the experimental evidence from which this concept was derived, it is revealed that experimentalists have found multiple ways of turning quantum-mechanical interactions on the micro-scale into visually observable events on the macro-scale. Although this is a fascinating proof of experimental creativity, the complexity of the instrumentation and their functional principles are obstacles with regard to accepting elementary observations as theoretically valid concepts. Conceptual devices with simple architectures and easily overseeable physics, such as, for instance, the cylinder–piston-type devices of Szilard engines [41], would allow progress into this direction [22].

Another open question concerning large patterns of observable events is the process of assigning meaning to such patterns, i.e., the process of distinguishing between conceivable alternatives of physical explanation. With each elementary observation contributing one single bit, a multi-element patterns would simply constitute a piece of information consisting of N such bits without revealing anything other than a quantitative aspect of the acquired information. Using the acquired information for deciding between alternatives of physical explanation represents an important qualitative aspect of information. Acquiring quality of information requires matching discrete patterns of events onto mental constructs which mathematically feature in the form of continuous functions. In the past, this task has been performed by experimentalists through least-square fitting of experimental data. A formal connection between statistical data matching and quality of information, however, is unknown to the present author and likely outside the realm of the presently accepted measures of Shannon [13] and thermodynamic measures of information [42].

Funding: This research received no external funding.

Institutional Review Board Statement: Not applicable.

Data Availability Statement: Data is contained within the article.

Conflicts of Interest: The authors declare no conflict of interest.

References

1. Geiger, H.; Marsden, E. The Laws of Deflexion of a-Particles through Large Angles. *Phil. Mag.* **1913**, *25*, 604–623. [CrossRef]
2. Rutherford, E. The Scattering of α and β Particles by Matter and the Structure of the Atom. *Phil. Mag.* **1911**, *21*, 669–688. [CrossRef]
3. Rutherford, E. The Structure of the Atom. *Phil. Mag.* **1914**, *27*, 488–498. [CrossRef]
4. Meschede, D. Youngs Interferenzexperiment mit Licht. In *Die Top Ten der Schönsten Physikalischen Experimente*; Fäßler, A., Jönsson, C., Eds.; Rowohlt Verlag: Hamburg, Germany, 2005; pp. 94–105, ISBN 3-499-61628-9.
5. Jönsson, C. Electron Diffraction at Multiple Slits. *Am. J. Phys.* **1974**, *42*, 4–11. [CrossRef]
6. Carnal, O.; Mlynek, J. Young's double-slit experiment with atoms: A simple atom interferometer. *Phys. Rev. Lett.* **1991**, *66*, 2689–2692. [CrossRef]
7. Nairz, O.; Arndt, M.; Zeilinger, A. Quantum interference experiments with large molecules. *Am. J. Phys.* **2003**, *71*, 319–325. [CrossRef]
8. Wilson, C.T.R. On a Method of Making Visible the Paths of Ionising Particles through a Gas. *Proc. R. Soc. Lond. A Math. Phys. Eng. Sci.* **1911**, *85*, 578.
9. Glaser, D.A. Some Effects of Ionizing Radiation on the Formation of Bubbles in Liquids. *Phys. Rev.* **1952**, *87*, 665. [CrossRef]
10. Griffiths, L.; Symoms, C.R.; Zacharov, B. *Determination of Particle Momenta in Spark Chamber and Counter Experiments*; CERN Yellow Reports: Monographs CERN-66-17; CERN: Geneva, Switzerland, 1966.
11. Dosch, H.G. *Jenseits der Nanowelt—Leptonen, Quarks und Eichbosonen*; Springer: Berlin/Heidelberg, Germany, 2005; ISBN 978-3-540-22889-9.
12. LeSurf, J.C.G. *Information and Measurement*; I.O.P. Publsihing Ltd.: Bristol, UK; Philadelphia, PA, USA, 1995; ISBN 0-7503-0308-5.
13. Shannon, C.E. A Mathematical Theory of Communication. *Bell Syst. Tech. J.* **1948**, *27*, 379–423. [CrossRef]
14. Ben-Naim, A. *Information Theory*; World Scientific: Singapore, 2017.
15. Wheeler, J.A. Information, physics, quantum: The search for links. In Proceedings of the 3rd International Symposium on Foundations of Quantum Mechanics in the Light of New Technology, Tokyo, Japan, 28–31 August 1989; pp. 354–368.
16. Knuth, K.H. Information-Based Physics and the Influence Network. In *It from Bit or Bit from It?* Aguirre, A., Foster, B., Merali, Z., Eds.; Springer: Berlin/Heidelberg, Germany, 2015.
17. Landauer, R. Irreversibility and heat generation in the computing process. *IBM J. Res.* **1961**, *5*, 183–191. [CrossRef]
18. Landauer, R. Information is physical. *Phys. Today* **1991**, *44*, 23–29. [CrossRef]
19. Landauer, R. Minimal energy requirements in communication. *Science* **1996**, *272*, 1914–1918. [CrossRef] [PubMed]
20. Knuth, K.H.; Walsh, J.L. An introduction to influence theory: Kinematics and dynamics. *Ann. Phys.* **2019**, *531*, 1800091. [CrossRef]
21. Bormashenko, E. The Landauer Principle: Re-Formulation of the Second Thermodynamics Law or a Step to Great Unification? *Entropy* **2019**, *21*, 918. [CrossRef]
22. Müller, J.G. *A conceptual Device Turning Quantum-Mechanical Interactions into Macrocopically Observable Events*; Munich University of Applied Sciences: Munich, Germany, 2024; manuscript in preparation.
23. Müller, J.G. *Assigning Meaning to Physical Observations*; Munich University of Applied Sciences: Munich, Germany, 2024; manuscript in preparation.
24. Thompson, J.J. On the structure of the atom. *Phil. Mag.* **1904**, *7*, 237–265.
25. Bohr, N. On the constitution of atoms and molecules. *Phil. Mag. J. Sci.* **1913**, *26*, 1–25. [CrossRef]
26. Heisenberg, W. Über quantentheoretische Umdeutung kinematischer und mechanischer Beziehungen—On the reformulation of kinematic and mechanical relationships. *Z. Phys.* **1925**, *33*, 879–893. [CrossRef]
27. Schrödinger, E. An Undulatory Theory of the Mechanics of Atoms and Molecules. *Phys. Rev.* **1926**, *28*, 1049–1070. [CrossRef]
28. Double-Slit Experiment—Wikipedia. Available online: https://en.wikipedia.org/wiki/Double-slit_experiment (accessed on 1 February 2024).
29. Particle Tracks in AWAN Expansion Cloud Chamber—Cloud Chamber—Wikipedia. Available online: https://en.wikipedia.org/wiki/Cloud_chamber (accessed on 1 February 2024).
30. Jackson, J.D. *Classical Electrodynamics*; John Wiley & Sons: New York, NY, USA, 1975; p. 629.
31. Matossi, F.; Leutwein, K.; Schmid, G. Elektronenbeweglichkeit in Zinksufid-Einkristallen. *Z. Naturforschg.* **1966**, *21*, 461–464. [CrossRef]
32. Fluorescence—Wikipedia. Available online: https://en.wikipedia.org/wiki/Fluorescence (accessed on 1 February 2024).
33. Müller, J.G. Information contained in molecular motion. *Entropy* **2019**, *21*, 1052. [CrossRef]
34. Müller, J.G. Photon detection as a process of information gain. *Entropy* **2020**, *22*, 392. [CrossRef] [PubMed]
35. Christen, H.R. *Grundlagen der Allgemeinen und Anorganischen Chemie*; Otto Salle Verlag: Frankfurt, Germany, 1982; ISBN 3-7935-5394-9.
36. Ostwald, W. Studien über die Bildung und Umwandlung fester Körper—Studies on the formation and transformation of solid bodies. *Z. Phys. Chem.* **1897**, *22*, 289–330. [CrossRef]
37. Enthalpy of Vaporization—Wikipedia. Available online: https://en.wikipedia.org/wiki/Enthalpy_of_vaporization (accessed on 1 February 2024).
38. Surface Tension—Wikipedia. Available online: https://en.wikipedia.org/wiki/Surface_Tension (accessed on 1 February 2024).
39. Thomson, W. On the equilibrium of vapor at a curved surface of liquid. *Phil. Mag.* **1871**, *42*, 448–452. [CrossRef]

40. Von Helmholtz, R. Untersuchungen über Dämple und Nebel, besonders über solche von Lösungen (Investigations of vapors and mists, and especially of such things from solutions). *Ann. Phys.* **1886**, *263*, 508–543. [CrossRef]
41. Szilárd, L. Über die Entropieverminderung in einem thermodynamischen System bei Eingriffen intelligenter Wesen. *Z. Phys.* **1929**, *53*, 840–856. (In German) [CrossRef]
42. Ben-Naim, A. *A Farewell to Entropy: Statistical Thermodynamics Based on Information*; World Scientific Publishing Co. Pte. Ltd.: Singpore, 2008. [CrossRef]

Disclaimer/Publisher's Note: The statements, opinions and data contained in all publications are solely those of the individual author(s) and contributor(s) and not of MDPI and/or the editor(s). MDPI and/or the editor(s) disclaim responsibility for any injury to people or property resulting from any ideas, methods, instructions or products referred to in the content.

Article

Landauer Bound in the Context of Minimal Physical Principles: Meaning, Experimental Verification, Controversies and Perspectives

Edward Bormashenko

Department of Chemical Engineering, Biotechnology and Materials, Engineering Sciences Faculty, Ariel University, Ariel 407000, Israel; edward@ariel.ac.il; Tel.: +972-074-729-68-63

Abstract: The physical roots, interpretation, controversies, and precise meaning of the Landauer principle are surveyed. The Landauer principle is a physical principle defining the lower theoretical limit of energy consumption necessary for computation. It states that an irreversible change in information stored in a computer, such as merging two computational paths, dissipates a minimum amount of heat $k_B T ln 2$ per a bit of information to its surroundings. The Landauer principle is discussed in the context of fundamental physical limiting principles, such as the Abbe diffraction limit, the Margolus–Levitin limit, and the Bekenstein limit. Synthesis of the Landauer bound with the Abbe, Margolus–Levitin, and Bekenstein limits yields the minimal time of computation, which scales as $\tau_{min} \sim \frac{h}{k_B T}$. Decreasing the temperature of a thermal bath will decrease the energy consumption of a single computation, but in parallel, it will slow the computation. The Landauer principle bridges John Archibald Wheeler's "it from bit" paradigm and thermodynamics. Experimental verifications of the Landauer principle are surveyed. The interrelation between thermodynamic and logical irreversibility is addressed. Generalization of the Landauer principle to quantum and non-equilibrium systems is addressed. The Landauer principle represents the powerful heuristic principle bridging physics, information theory, and computer engineering.

Keywords: Landauer principle; entropy; Abbe limit; Margolus–Levitin limit; Bekenstein limit; Planck–Boltzmann time; Szilárd engine

1. Introduction

The Landauer principle is one of the limiting physical principles that constrains the behavior of physical systems. There exist fundamental laws and principles setting the limits of physical systems. These laws do not predict or describe the behavior of physical/engineering systems but limit or restrict their functioning. A realistic natural/engineering system can only provide limited functionalities because its performance is physically constrained by some basic principles [1]. Some of these limits are engineering ones. For example, a key engineering bottleneck for the development of new generations of computers today is integrated circuit manufacturing, which confines billions of semiconducting units in several cm^2 of silicon with extremely low defect rates [2]. Another engineering constraint is imposed by limits on individual interconnects [2]. Despite the doubling of the transistor density according to the Moore law, semiconductor integrated circuits would not operate without fast/dense interconnects. Metallic wires can be either fast or dense but not both at the same time—a smaller cross-section increases electrical resistance, while a greater height or width increases parasitic capacitance with neighboring wires (wire delay grows with RC) [2]. Other constraints limiting the operation of physical (natural or engineering) systems are fundamental ones, and they emerge from the deepest foundations of physics. Limiting physical principles appeared in physics relatively late. It seems that the first limiting principle historically was the Abbe diffraction limit, discovered in 1873, which states that in light with wavelength λ λ, traveling in a medium with refractive index n and converging to a spot with half-angle θ θ, θ will have a minimum resolvable distance of d, as supplied by Equation (1):

$$d = \frac{\lambda}{2n\sin\theta}, \quad (1)$$

where the minimum resolvable distance d is defined as the minimum separation between two objects that results in a certain level of contrast between them [3,4]. The Abbe diffraction limit is the maximum resolution possible for a theoretically perfect, or ideal, optical system [3,4]. Thus, it is not the engineering but the fundamental physical principle. The Abbe diffraction limit arises from the idea that the image arises from a double diffraction process [3,4]. Other diffraction limit formulae, known as the Rayleigh and Sparrow limits, were suggested [3,4]. These formulae coincide with the Abbe limit within a numerical coefficient; thus, the value of the numerical multiplier appearing in Equation (14) is not exact [3–5].

In spite of the fact that the Abbe diffraction limit is rooted in classical physics, the role of the limiting principles in the realm of classical physics is more than modest. The situation has changed dramatically within modern physics. In relativity, the speed of light in a vacuum, labeled c, is a universal physical constant of ca. 300,000 km per second, and according to the special theory of relativity, c is the upper limit for the speed at which conventional matter or energy (and, consequently, any signal carrying information) can travel through space [6,7]. It is impossible for signals or energy to travel faster than c. The speed at which light waves propagate in a vacuum is independent of both the motion of the wave source and the inertial frame of reference of the observer, thus enabling the Einstein synchronization procedure for clocks [6,7]. The limiting status of the speed of light in a vacuum was intensively disputed in the last few decades, and theories assuming a varying speed of light have been proposed as an alternative way of solving several standard cosmological problems [8,9]. Recent observational hints that the fine structure constant may have varied over cosmological scales have given impetus to these theories [8,9]. Theories in which the speed of light traveling in a vacuum appeared as an emerging physical value were suggested [9]. We adopt unequivocally the limiting status of the speed of light in a vacuum c and demonstrate that this status generates other limiting physical principles, and just this status gives rise to consequences emerging from the Landauer principle.

The main limiting principle of quantum mechanics is the Heisenberg uncertainty principle. It states that there is a limit to the precision with which certain pairs of physical properties, such as position x and momentum p (or time t and energy E), can be simultaneously measured. In other words, and more accurately speaking, when one property is measured, the less accurately the other property can be established (see Equations (2) and (3)):

$$\sigma_x \sigma_p \geq \frac{\hbar}{2}, \quad (2)$$

$$\sigma_t \sigma_E \geq \frac{\hbar}{2}, \quad (3)$$

where $\sigma_x, \sigma_p, \sigma_t,$ and σ_E are standard deviations of the position, momentum, time, and energy, respectively, and $\hbar = \frac{h}{2\pi}$ is the reduced Planck constant [10,11]. The time–energy uncertainty principle, supplied by Equation (3), needs more detailed discussion to be supplied in the context of the Mandelstam–Tamm and Margolus–Levitin bounding principles.

The limiting value of the light propagating in a vacuum c combined with the Heisenberg uncertainty principle together yield the Bremermann limit, which supplies a limit on the maximum rate of computation that can be achieved in a self-contained system [12]. The Bremermann limit is derived from Einstein's mass–energy equivalency and the Heisenberg uncertainty principle, and is $\frac{c^2}{\hbar} \cong 1.35 \times 10^{50}$ bits per second per kilogram of the computational system [12]. Consider that the Bremermann limit is built of the fundamental physical constants only.

Quantum mechanics also gives rise to the Mandelstam–Tamm and Margolus–Levitin limiting principles [13,14]. The Mandelstam–Tamm quantum speed limit states the time it takes for an isolated quantum system to evolve between two fully distinguishable states, as given by Equation (4):

$$\tau > \tau_{MT} = \frac{h}{4\Delta E}, \quad (4)$$

where ΔE is the energy uncertainty. The Margolus–Levitin limiting principle supplies a surprising result, predicting the maximum speed of dynamic evolution of the system [15]. The Margolus–Levitin limiting principle supplies the minimum time it takes for the physical system to evolve into an orthogonal state (labeled $\tau_\perp$). It should be emphasized that this minimum time $\tau_\perp$ depends only on the system average energy minus its ground state (denoted $E - E_0$, and not on the energy uncertainty ΔE, as follows from Equation (4) [15]. To simplify the formulae, we chose the zero-level energy in such a way that $E_0 = 0$ so that the Margolus–Levitin limiting principle yields for the minimal time bound, denoted as τ_{ML} in Equation (5):

$$\tau_\perp > \tau_{ML} = \frac{h}{4E} \quad (5)$$

Another important fundamental limiting principle is supplied by the Bekenstein bound [16]. Bekenstein demonstrated that there exists a universal upper bound of the entropy-to-energy ratio $\frac{S}{E}$ for an arbitrary system confined by radius R, and this limit is expressed by $\frac{S}{E} = \frac{2\pi R}{\hbar c}$ [16]. In other words, the Bekenstein bound defines an upper limit on the entropy S, which can be confined within a given finite region of space that has a finite amount of energy E, or conversely, the maximum amount of information required to perfectly describe a given physical system with a given, fixed energy E down to the quantum level [16]. The bound value of entropy S is given by Equation (6):

$$S \leq \frac{2\pi k_B R E}{\hbar c}, \quad (6)$$

where R is the radius of a sphere that can enclose the given system, and E is the total mass–energy including any rest masses [16]. We will discuss below the Margolus–Levitin and the Bekenstein bounds in their relation to the Landauer principle.

2. Results

2.1. What Is Information? The Meaning of the Landauer Principle

What is information? The ambiguity of the notion of information hinders the physical interpretation of this notion. Numerous definitions of information were suggested [17,18]. I am quoting from Ref. [17]: "Information can be data, in the sense of a bank statement, a computer file, or a telephone number. Data in the narrowest sense can be just a string of binary symbols. Information can also be meaning" [17]. Informational theory is usually supplied in a pure abstract form that is independent of any physical embodiment. Intellectual breakthrough in the mathematization of information is related to the pioneering works by Claude Shannon, who introduced the information entropy of a random variable understood as the average level of "information" or "uncertainty" inherent to the variable's possible outcomes [19,20]. Given a discrete random variable X Ψ, which takes values in the alphabet Ψ, X and is distributed according to $p : \Psi \to [0,1]$ $p : X \to [0,1]$, the Shannon measure of information/Shannon entropy, denoted as $H(\Psi)$, is given by Equation (7):

$$H(\Psi) = -\sum_{x \in \Psi} p(x) \log p(x) \quad (7)$$

The Shannon measure of information is a very general mathematical concept, and regrettably, it is often mixed in the literature with thermodynamic entropy [21–25]. A distinction for the Shannon measure of information is made in Refs. [21–25]. Again, the Shannon measure of information is a very useful mathematical concept completely disconnected from the process of recording information, information carrier material, reading, and erasing information.

In contrast, Rolf Landauer, in his pioneering and fundamental papers published in 1961–1996, argued that information is physical and has an energy equivalent [25–29]. It may be stored in physical systems such as books and memory chips and is transmitted by physical devices exploiting electrical or optical signals [26–29]. Indeed (I am quoting from Ref. [29]), "computation, whether it is performed by electronic machinery, on an abacus or in a biological system such as the brain, is a physical process. It is subject to the same questions that apply to other physical processes: How much energy must be expended to perform a particular computation? How long must it take? How large must the computing device be? In other words, what are the physical limits of the process of computation?" If we adopt the idea that computation is a physical process, it must obey the laws of physics, and first and foremost the laws of thermodynamics [26–29]. This thinking leads to the new limiting physical principle, which establishes the minimum energy cost for the erasure of a single memory bit for the system operating at the equilibrium temperature T. This is exactly the Landauer principle. The Landauer principle may be derived in different ways; we start from the one-bit system depicted schematically in Figure 1. The picture depicts the Brownian particle M confined within a double-well potential, shown in Figure 1 and addressed in detail in Refs. [27–30]. When the barrier is much higher than the thermal energy, the Brownian particle will remain in either well (left or right) for a long time. Thus, the particle located in the left or right well can serve as the stable informational states "0" and "1" of a single information bit (the informational states are denoted $m = 0$ and $m = 1$ in Figure 1, where m is the parameter, characterizing the statistical state of the double-well system). The average work W necessary to switch the statistical state of a memory under the isothermal process from the state Ψ with distribution p_m to Ψ' with distribution p'_m is given by Equation (8):

$$W \geq F(\Psi') - F(\Psi), \tag{8}$$

where $F(\Psi)$ is the Helmholtz free energy of the system supplied by Equation (9):

$$F(\Psi) = \sum_m p_m F_m - k_B T H(\Psi) = \sum_m p_m F_m + k_B T \sum_m p_m \ln P_m, \tag{9}$$

where $F_m = E_m - TS_m$ is the Helmholtz free energy of the conditional states, and $H(\Psi) = -\sum_m p_m \ln p_m$ is the Shannon entropy of the informational states, in the Shannon entropy of the informational states, which equals to their entropies S_m [21–25,30]. For a symmetrical well and a random bit $p_0 = p_1 = \frac{1}{2}$, we immediately obtain the Landauer bound, supplied by Equation (10):

$$W = k_B T \ln 2 \tag{10}$$

The exact meaning of Equation (10) supplies the energy necessary for resetting/erasing one random bit stored in a symmetric memory unit [30]. For asymmetric memory units, ΔF_{reset} is not necessarily equal to $-k_B T H(\Psi)$ and the limiting Landauer principle is given by the following inequality:

$$W_{reset} \geq \Delta F_{reset} \tag{11}$$

The exact equality is attained if the reset is thermodynamically reversible [30]. This does not contradict the logical irreversibility of the reset, which implies that the entropy $H(\Psi)$ of the informational states decreases [30,31]. It is noteworthy, that the Landauer bound, given by Equation (10), is related only to a single information-bearing degree of freedom of the entire computing system.

The relation between logic and thermodynamic reversibility will be discussed below. Again, the energetic cost on one random bit is supplied by the limiting physical principle, expressed by Equation (11). A detailed discussion of Equations (10) and (11) is supplied in Ref. [30]. An accurate and rigorous derivation of Equations (10) and (11) emerging from microscopic reasoning is supplied in Ref. [32]. We again consider the particle in the twin-well potential $U(x)$, shown in Figure 1. We assume that before the erasure we want half of the bits to be in the "one" state and the other half to be in the "zero" state. We also adopt the idea that the ensemble of bits is in contact with a thermal reservoir where the temperature of the reservoir T is low enough not to change the state of the bits; in other words, $k_B T < \Delta U$ takes place [32]. The system will instead reach a "local" thermal equilibrium in one of the half-wells. We therefore assume that the initial statistical state is described by the following for the bits before erasure (see Figure 1):

$$\rho_{in}(x,p) = \frac{1}{Z}exp\left\{-\beta\left[U(x) + \frac{p^2}{2M}\right]\right\} \qquad (12)$$

whereas after the erasure, the distribution function is given by Equation (13):

$$\rho_{fin}(x,p) = \left\{\begin{array}{l}\frac{2}{Z}exp\left\{-\beta\left[U(x) + \frac{p^2}{2M}\right]\right\}, \text{ for } x > 0 \\ 0, \text{ for } x < 0\end{array}\right\}, \qquad (13)$$

where x is the position, p is the momentum of the particle M, $\beta = \frac{1}{k_B T}$, and $Z = \int exp - \left\{\left[U(x) + \frac{p^2}{2m}\right]\beta\right\} dpdx$ is the partition function [33,34]. After the routine transformations, it is demonstrated that to erase one bit of information, on average, the work performed on the system has to be equal to or greater than $ln2 k_B T$, or, equivalently, that the heat dissipation by the system into the heat reservoir has to be greater than or equal to the Landauer bound $ln2 k_B T$ [32]. Generalization of the Landauer principle for computing devices based on many-valued logic (N-based logic), exploiting N identical potential wells, was reported [30,35]. The energy necessary for the erasure of one bit of information (the Landauer limiting bound) $W = k_B T ln2$ remains untouched for computing devices exploiting many-valued logic [30,35].

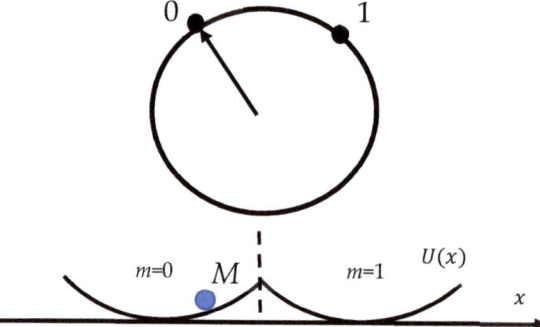

Figure 1. Particle M placed in the twin-well potential is depicted. The position of the particle in the double-well potential will determine the state of the single bit. If the particle is found on the left-hand side of the potential, then we say that the bit is in the "zero" state. If it is found on the right-hand side of the well, then we define that the bit is in the "one" state. The picture is taken from the Bormashenko Ed. "Generalization of the Landauer Principle for Computing Devices Based on Many-Valued Logic" [35].

2.2. The Landauer Limit and the Margolus–Levitin Limiting Principle

Now we are ready to combine the Landauer bound with the Margolus–Levitin limiting principle, given by Equation (5). Consider the computing unit, based on the physical device for which the Landauer limiting principle is true (the device exploiting identical potential wells confining the particle may be taken as an example) [30,32,35]. This device operates in a thermal equilibrium with its surroundings (thermal bath), which is kept at a constant temperature T. Let us pose the following question: What is the minimal time it will take for this device to make a single computing operation? Assuming in Equation (5) that $E \cong k_B T \ln 2$, we obtain the following very rough estimation for the minimum "Margolus–Levitin–Landauer" time necessary for a single computation, denoted as τ_{MLL}:

$$\tau_{MLL} \geq \frac{h}{4 \ln 2 k_B T} = \frac{\tau_{PB}}{4 ln 2} \qquad (14)$$

where $\tau_{PB} = \frac{h}{k_B T}$ is the Planck–Boltzmann thermalization time, which is conjectured to be the fastest relaxation timescale for thermalization of the given system [36]. We assume in Equation (14) that that the energy cost of a single computation equals the energy necessary for the transfer of the system into the orthogonal quantum state. Again, we choose the zero-level energy in such a way that $E_0 = 0$ [15]. The numerical multiplier appearing in Equation (14) should not be taken too seriously. The values of these multipliers are not exact when the limiting physical principles are considered, as already mentioned when the Abbe diffraction limit (see Equation (1)) was discussed. It is noteworthy that the Margolus–Levitin–Landauer time given by Equation (14) is independent of the geometrical dimensions of the computing unit. Formula (14) may be called the Margolus–Levitin–Landauer bound. The Planck–Boltzmann thermalization time should not be mixed up with the Planck time, which is the time span at which no smaller meaningful length can be validly measured due to the indeterminacy expressed in Werner Heisenberg's uncertainty principle.

Let us estimate now the Landauer time for the ambient conditions. Assuming $h \cong 6.626 \times 10^{-34}$ Js, $k_B \cong 1.38 \times 10^{-23} \frac{J}{K}$, $T \cong 300$ K, we calculate $\tau_{MLL} \cong 0.9 \times 10^{-11} \sim 10^{-11}$ s. Thus, a single computing unit may perform not more than 10^{11} erasures per second in ambient conditions.

Other approaches for the bounds of the finite time computation were suggested [37–41]. For a slowly driven (quantum) two-level system weakly coupled to a thermal bath, the finite-time Landauer bound takes the simple form supplied by Equation (15):

$$W \geq k_B T \left(ln 2 + \frac{\pi^2}{4 \Gamma \tau} \right) + O \left(\frac{1}{\Gamma^2 \tau} \right), \qquad (15)$$

where τ is the total time of the computation process and Γ is the thermalization rate. It should be emphasized that all of the approaches suggest the emergence of the Planckian thermalization time scale $\tau_{PB} = \frac{h}{k_B T}$ (we denote it as the Planck–Boltzmann time) as the shortest timescale for information erasure, as also immediately follows from the Margolus–Levitin–Landauer bound supplied by Equation (14) (see Ref. [41]). Finite-size corrections to the Landauer bound are reported in Ref. [42]. Equations (14) and (15) supply the trade-off important for development of the computing devices. Engineers want computing devices to be as energy efficient as possible; thus, they try to diminish the energy necessary for a single computation [43]. It should be emphasized that the Landauer limit establishing the minimal energy cost $W = k_B T ln 2$ for a single erasure operation emerges from the equilibrium thermodynamic considerations, and it is independent of the engineering realization of the computing unit [43]. However, this decrease in the energy cost of computation due to a decrease in the temperature T inevitably results in an increase in a single computation time, as follows from the Margolus–Levitin–Landauer bound supplied by Equation (14).

2.3. The Landauer Limit and the Bekenstein Bound

Now we find ourselves in the realm of relativity. We will demonstrate that the Bekenstein bound [16] also restricts the computation time. Consider a computational unit with a characteristic dimension of R. Cum grano salis we assume that the minimal time of the single computation (we call it the Bekenstein time and denote it as τ_B) is given by $\tau_B \cong \frac{R}{c}$, which is the minimal time possible for the transfer of the particle from one half of the double-well potential to another one. Now we address Equation (6). The entropy change necessary for erasing 1 bit of information is estimated as $S = k_B ln 2$. According to the Landauer principle $E \cong k_B T ln2$, substituting $\tau_B \cong \frac{R}{c}$, $S = k_B ln2$, and $E \cong k_B T ln2$ yields Equation (16):

$$\tau_B \geq \frac{h}{(2\pi)^2 k_B T} = \frac{\tau_{PB}}{(2\pi)^2},\qquad(16)$$

It is immediately recognized that the Planck–Boltzmann thermalization time appears as a single time scale in the eventual bound, supplied by Equation (16). This time scale is independent of the dimensions of the computing unit. Comparing Equation (16) to Equation (14) yields $\tau_B < \tau_{MLL}$; however, the values of these time scales are close one to another. It is seen that the Landauer limiting principle allows for fundamental ideas emerging from relativity and quantum mechanics to be unified. The minimal times of computation arising from the Margolus–Levitin and Bekenstein bounds are close to one to another. Thus, the Landauer principle in a certain sense bridges relativity and quantum mechanics. This idea will be discussed below. It should be emphasized the Landauer principle holds for a variety of quantum systems [39,44–49].

2.4. The Abbe Diffraction Limit and the Landauer Principle

Now we address the Abbe diffraction limit (see Equation (1)) discussed in Section 1 and addressed in detail in the classic textbooks devoted to optics [3,4]. Consider the twin-well computational system depicted in Figure 2 and representing particle M confined within the twin-well potential. We use the monochromatic light ν, λ (ν is a frequency, λ is a wavelength) for identification of the particle location. According to Equation (1), the identification of the particle location is still possible when $\lambda \cong 2dnsin\theta \cong 4Rnsin\theta$ takes place, where n is the refractive index and angle θ is shown in Figure 2. If the same monochromatic light beam ν, λ is used for the erasure of information, i.e., for the transfer of the particle from one half-well to another, and the Landauer principle is adopted, we estimate $h\nu = h\frac{c}{\lambda} \cong k_B T ln2$, where c is the light speed. Thus, we obtain $\lambda \cong \frac{hc}{ln2 k_B T}$. The minimum time necessary for a single computation is roughly estimated as $\tau_{min} \cong \frac{2R}{c}$. Combining these estimations yields the minimum time of a computation:

$$\tau_{min} \cong \frac{1}{2nsin\theta ln2}\frac{h}{k_B T}\qquad(17)$$

The minimum computation time corresponding to $n \cong 1$, $\theta = \frac{\pi}{2}$ is estimated as follows:

$$\tau_{min} \cong \frac{1}{2ln2}\frac{h}{k_B T} \cong \tau_{PB}\qquad(18)$$

Again, the minimum time span of computation scales as the Planck–Boltzmann thermalization time, independent of the geometrical parameters of the system, given by $\tau_{PB} = \frac{h}{k_B T}$.

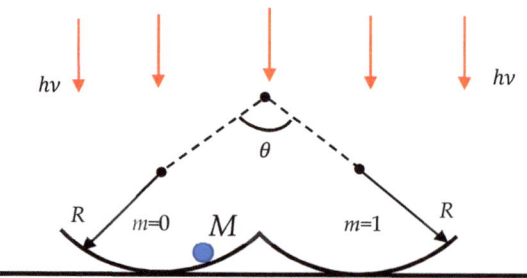

Figure 2. A twin-well system containing particle M illuminated with monochromatic light ν is depicted. The system is in thermal equilibrium with the surrounding T.

2.5. Breaking the Landauer Limit

It should be emphasized that derivation of the Landauer bound emerging from the analysis of the behavior of the particle placed in the twin-well potential, shown in Figures 1 and 2, implies the symmetrical configuration of the potential [30,32]. In the asymmetrical twin-well potential the Landauer bound may be broken [31,50,51]. The Landauer principle for information erasure is valid for a symmetric double-well potential but not for an asymmetric one. Physically, the reduced work arises when the starting state is not in equilibrium, and other degrees of freedom do work that compensates for the work required to erase. More simply, erasing from a small well to a large well transfers a particle from a small box to a larger one but never the reverse [51].

2.6. The Landauer Principle and Thermodynamics of Small Systems

The Landauer principle may be understood in the context of the minimal thermal engine suggested by Leo Szilárd in 1929 [52]. Leo Szilárd is famous for his letter with Albert Einstein's signature that resulted in the Manhattan Project. In Leo Szilárd's original formulation, the engine exploits single-molecule gas confined in a box of volume V_1 contacting a thermal bath at temperature T, as depicted in Figure 3. As in any other thermal engine, the molecule/particle pushes the piston and the engine performs work (say, lifting a load, as shown in Figure 3b,c). Thus, the Szilárd energy transforms heat collected from the bath in the task, being the minimum thermal engine [52]. We are interested in the informational interpretation of the Szilárd engine, which is closely related to the Landauer principle.

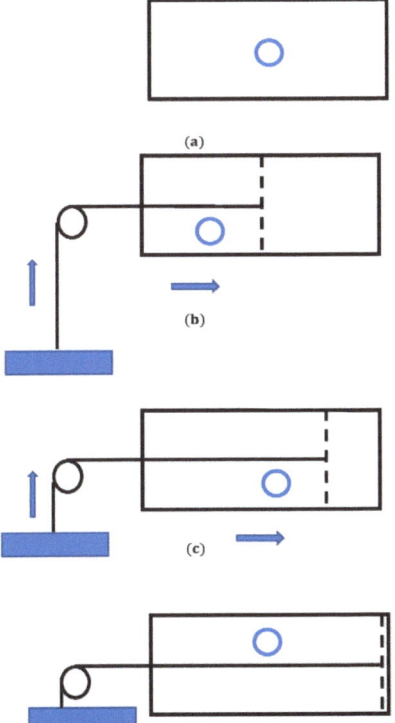

Figure 3. A scheme of the Leo Szilárd minimal engine is depicted. (**a**) A particle in a box is shown; (**b**) the partition defines the location of the particle; (**c**) the particle pushes the piston and the engine performs work; (**d**) one bit of information is erased.

Consider the location of the particle within a box. Divide the box into two equal parts. Actually, the information concerning which side the molecule is in after dividing the box can be utilized to extract work, e.g., via an isothermal expansion, under $T = const$. Let us explain this idea: Isothermal expansion of the single-molecule gas from volume V_1 to volume V_2 followed by the motion of the piston yields the work, given by $= k_B T ln \frac{V_2}{V_1}$. In this particular case, the box is divided into two equal halves: $V_2 = 2V_1$ and $W = k_B T ln 2$. However, this result may be interpreted in terms of the information theory. Indeed, after the expansion we lost the information about the precise location of the particle. Thus, we performed erasure of one bit of information. In other words, we converted one bit of information into the work $W = k_B T ln 2$. This is exactly the Landauer bound [26–29]. Instead of displacement of the piston, we may imagine the Maxwell demon, which introduces or pulls out the impermeable partition that fixes/erases the location of the particle. Thus, it turns out that the Landauer principle is closely related to the famous Maxwell demon paradox [53].

It seems that the action of the Szilárd engine contradicts the second law of thermodynamics. Indeed, let us make the Szilárd engine cyclic. To return the initial state, the partition/piston can be removed without any work consumption, and the whole process can be repeated in a cyclic manner. All thermodynamic processes are defined as isothermal and reversible [53]. This engine apparently violates the Kelvin–Planck statement of the second law (and it is well known that it is actually equivalent to the Clausius and Carnot formulations) by converting heat directly into an equivalent amount of work through a cyclic process [53]. Now it is generally accepted that the measurement process including erasure or reset of the Maxwell demon memory requires a minimum energy cost of at least $W = k_B T ln 2$, associated with the entropy decrease of the engine, and that it saves the second law. A quantum Szilárd engine was addressed [53,54]. A demonless quantum Szilárd engine was studied [53]. It was demonstrated that the localization holds the key along with the Landauer principle to save the second law and presents a complementary resolution of the quantum version of Szilárd's paradox [53]. Quantum mechanics-rooted arguments are necessary for the justification of the third law of thermodynamics. Quantum mechanics also saves the second law, suggesting that quantum mechanics has strong ties in the foundations of thermodynamics and information theory [53].

Numerous questions related to the information interpretation of the Szilárd engine remain open. However, it is clear that the Szilárd engine links the Landauer principle to the thermodynamics of small systems, which was rapidly developed in the past decade [54–57]. For example, it will be instructive to address the minimal (single-particle) Carnot engine, exploited for the erasure of information in heat baths [58]. It is noteworthy that the efficiency of the minimum Carnot is given by the traditional Carnot expression when the motion of gas particles is temporally averaged (instead of the usual spatial averaging) [58]. Only a few experimental realizations of the Szilárd engine have been reported [59–62]. A single-electron box operated as a Szilárd engine enabled the extraction of $k_B T ln 2$ heat from the reservoir at temperature T per one bit of created information [59]. The information was encoded in the position of an extra electron in the box [59].

2.7. The Landauer Principle and the "It from Bit" Archibald Wheeler Paradigm

In 1989, John Archibald Wheeler suggested the global concept aphoristically called "it from bit." "It from bit" symbolizes the idea that every item in the physical world has at the bottom—at a very deep bottom, in most instances—an immaterial source and explanation, that what we call reality arises in the last analysis from the posing of yes–no questions and the registering of equipment-evoked responses—in short, that all things physical are information-theoretic in origin and that this is a participatory universe. Three examples may illustrate the theme of "it from bit." First is the photon. With a polarizer over the distant source and an analyzer of polarization over the photodetector under watch, we ask the yes or no question, "Did the counter register a click during the specified second?" If yes, we often say, "A photon did it." We know perfectly well that the photon existed neither before the emission nor after the detection. However, we also have to recognize that any talk of the photon "existing" during the intermediate period is only a blown-up version of the raw fact, a count. The yes or no that is recorded constitutes an unsplittable bit of information. A photon, Wootters and Zurek demonstrate, cannot be cloned [63]. Actually, the Landauer principle fills the "it from bit" idea with physical content when supplying the link between "information" and physically measurable properties of real systems. This bridge was built in a series of recent papers [64–77]. The principle of mass–energy–information equivalence, which proposes that a bit of information is not just physical, as already demonstrated, but also has a finite and quantifiable mass while it stores information, was suggested [64–71,77]. According to Herrera, a change to one bit of information (provided the temperature is fixed) leads to a decrease in the mass of the system by an amount whose minimal value is [64]:

$$\Delta M = \frac{k_B T}{c^2} ln2 \qquad (19)$$

It is noteworthy that the Landauer principle in Ref. [64] is called "Brillouin's principle". Indeed, the idea that the dissipation of energy associated with a change to one bit of information is a fundamental process independent of the technicalities associated with information processing (regarded today as the Landauer principle) first appears in the work by Leon Brillouin [65].

The idea that mass may be ascribed to information was developed in Refs. [66–75]. According to Vopson, an equivalent mass of excess energy is created in the process of lowering the information entropy when a bit of information is erased, and vice versa. Once a bit of information is created, it acquires a finite mass, denoted as m_{bit} [66]. Using the mass–energy equivalence principle, the mass of a bit of information is given by Equation (20) (compare it to Equation (19)) [66]:

$$m_{bit} = \frac{ln2 k_B T}{c^2} \qquad (20)$$

The idea that a mass may be ascribed to a bit of information was criticized recently, as will be mentioned below. The mass of a bit of information at room temperature calculated with Equation (20) (T = 300 K) is 3.19×10^{-38} kg, as estimated in Ref. [66]. Now consider the particle with energy E in contact (not necessarily in thermal equilibrium) with a thermal bath T. The energy of the particle may be used for erasing information within the thermal bath. The maximum information (as measured in bits), denoted as I_{max}, which may be erased by the particle in contact with the bath, according to the Landauer principle, equals: [75]:

$$I_{max} = \frac{E}{k_B T ln2} = \frac{mc^2}{k_B T ln2}, \qquad (21)$$

where m is the relativistic mass of the particle. The value I_{max} may be seen within the Landauer context as the maximum informational content of a relativistic particle. If the potential energy of the particle is negligible and $\frac{v}{c} \ll 1$ is adopted (v is the velocity of the particle), Equation (21) is re-written as follows [75]:

$$I_{max} = \frac{m_0 c^2}{k_B T ln2} \qquad (22)$$

The value I_{max} supplied by Equation (22) may be understood as the maximum informational content of a particle *at rest* [75]. The particle may exchange information with the medium, if *at least one bit* of information is erased in medium by the particle; thus, inequality $I_{max} \geq 1$ should hold. This inequality yields:

$$m_0 \geq \frac{k_B T ln2}{c^2} \qquad (23)$$

A particle with a rest mass smaller than $\widetilde{m}_0 = \frac{k_B T ln2}{c^2}$ will not erase information in the medium at the temperature T. Assuming $T = 2.73$ K (which is the temperature of the cosmic microwave background [78]), we obtain the estimation $\widetilde{m}_0 \cong \frac{1.6 \times 10^{-4} \text{ eV}}{c^2} \cong 2.0 \times 10^{-40}$ kg. It should be emphasized that all of the elementary particles known today (including neutrino $m_{neutrino} < 0.120 \frac{eV}{c^2}$) are heavier than $\widetilde{m}_0 = 2.0 \times 10^{-40}$ kg. Particles lighter than $\widetilde{m}_0 = 2.0 \times 10^{-40}$ kg will not transform the information to the universe and are expected to be undetectable.

The Landauer principle enables the estimation of the computational capacity of the entire universe, which is large but finite [66,76,79,80]. We denote the total informational capacity of the universe as I_{tot}, which may be estimated as follows:

$$I_{tot} = \frac{m_{tot} c^2}{k_B T}, \qquad (24)$$

where $m_{tot} = 1.5 \times 10^{53}$ kg is the mass of the observable universe [81]. Substituting and $T = 2.73$ K, we obtain $I_{tot} \cong 3.0 \times 10^{92}$ bits, which is in a satisfactory vicinity to the estimation reported in Ref. [80], which was based on quite different considerations.

The Landauer minimum principle enables a fresh glance at the famous "dark matter" problem [82–84]. Dark matter is the mysterious substance that dominates the mass budget of the universe from sub-galactic to cosmological scales, which is arguably one of the greatest challenges of modern physics and cosmology [82–84]. We still do not know how to explain how stars orbit in galaxies or how galaxies orbit in clusters. A wide array of candidates for particle dark matter was suggested, including thermal relics (WIMPs), neutralinos, and sterile neutrinos [83–86]. However, numerous experiments have failed to find evidence for the suggested dark matter particles, and it was hypothesized that gravity theory should be modified [87]. Equation (23), emerging from the Landauer minimum principle, enables revisiting the "dark matter" problem [66,75]. Indeed, if dark matter is built from the particles for which $m < \widetilde{m}_0 \cong \frac{k_B T ln2}{c^2} \cong 2.0 \times 10^{-40}$ kg takes place, they could not be registered due the fact that they do not transform information to the surrounding media and experimental devices [66,75].

Let us continue thinking within the Wheeler "it from bit" paradigm. The Landauer minimum principle supplies a new glance at the problem of the great unification of physics. Equation (21) may be easily extended to fields. Consider a field (for example, an electromagnetic field) in a thermal contact (not necessarily in thermal equilibrium, as it takes place in a black body radiation problem) with a surrounding/thermal bath T. The energy of the field may be used for isothermal erasing of information in the surroundings. The maximum information to be erased by the field (seen as the informational content of the field) according to the Landauer principle is given by:

$$I_{max} = \frac{E_f}{k_B T ln2} \qquad (25)$$

where E_f is the energy of the field. It is noteworthy that the physical nature of the field does not matter. If the information and the temperature are taken as basic physical quantities, Equation (25) will be universal for all kinds of physical fields. The field is capable of isothermally erasing the information if the bounding inequality $E_f > k_B T ln2$ is true. The Landauer principle changes the status of the temperature, usually seen as the derivative of basic physical quantities such as energy and entropy [33,34]. Contrastingly, the Landauer principle tells us that it is just the temperature that determines the possibility of erasing/recording the information, seen as a basic physical value [88].

2.8. Experimental Verification of the Landauer Principle

Landauer bound was tested in a series of experimental investigations [46,59,87–89]. Koski et al. tested the Landauer principle with the minimum Szilárd engine (see Section 2.6 and Figure 3) [52,59]. The main element the Szilárd engine was the single-electron box (abbreviated SEB) [59], which consisted of two small metallic islands connected by a tunnel junction [59]. The SEB was maintained at a dilution-refrigerator temperature in the 0.1 K range. The authors provided an experimental demonstration of extracting nearly $k_B T ln2$ of work for one bit of information, in accordance with the Landauer principle [59]. Use of the trapped ultra-cold ion enabled the demonstration of a quantum version of the Landauer principle in the experimental study by Yan et al. [46]. Ref. [89] reported experimental testing of the Landauer bound at low values of $k_B T$. The authors demonstrated that for the logically reversible operations, energy dissipations much less than $k_B T ln2$ were registered, while irreversible operations dissipated much more than $k_B T ln2$. Measurements of a logically reversible operation on a bit with energy 30 $k_B T$ yielded an energy dissipation of 0.01 $k_B T$ [89]. Experiments performed with a single colloidal particle trapped in a modulated double-well potential demonstrated that the mean dissipated heat saturated at the Landauer bound in the limit of long erasure cycles [90]. An experiment performed with a colloidal particle in a time-dependent, virtual potential created by a feedback trap also confirmed the Landauer limit [91].

2.9. Landauer Limit in the Context of Logical and Thermodynamic Irreversibility

Discussion around the Landauer principle leads to the extremely important distinction between the logic and thermodynamic irreversibility. In order to understand this distinction, we have to start from the separation of the degrees of freedom of the computing device. Some of a computer's degrees of freedom are used to encode the logical state of the computation process, and these information-bearing degrees of freedom (abbreviated IBDF) are by design sufficiently robust that, within limits, the computer's logical state evolves deterministically as a function of its initial value, regardless of fluctuations occurring in the environment (i.e., temperature fluctuations) or in the computer's other non-information-bearing degrees of freedom (NIBDF) [92]. While a computer as an entire physical device (including its power supply and other parts of its environment) may be considered a closed system obeying reversible laws of motion, Landauer noticed that the logical state may evolve irreversibly, with two or more distinct logical states following a single logical successor. Therefore, because Hamiltonian dynamics conserve the fine-grained entropy, the entropy decrease in the IBDF during a logically irreversible operation should necessarily be compensated by an equal or greater entropy increase in the NIBDF and environment. This is the Landauer principle seen in the context of the informational/non-informational degrees of freedom of the computing device [90].

Thus, a clear distinction between thermodynamic and logic reversibility becomes necessary. Following Sagawa, we adopt the following definitions of thermodynamic and logical reversibility: A physical process is thermodynamically reversible if and only if the time evolution of the probability distribution in the process can be time-reversed, where the change in the external parameters is also time-reversed and the signs of the amounts of work and heat are changed [31]. In turn, a computational process $\hat{C}$ is logically reversible if and only if it is an injection. In other words, $\hat{C}$ is logically reversible if and only if, for any output logical state, there is a unique input logical state. Otherwise, $\hat{C}$ is logically irreversible [31]. The logically irreversible erasure can be performed in a thermodynamically reversible manner in the quasi-static limit. This does not contradict the conventional Landauer principle. The logical reversibility is defined only by the reversibility of the logical states, which is related only to the logical entropy. In contrast, the thermodynamic reversibility is related to the reversibility of the relevant total system (i.e., the whole universe), including the heat bath, and to the total entropy production, as discussed in Section 2. Therefore, these logical and thermodynamic reversibilities are not equivalent in general [31,93]. If the erasure is not quasi-static but is performed with a finite velocity (the Margolus–Levitin limit determines only the minimal time of computation; however, in principle it may be infinite; see Section 2.2), the erasure becomes thermodynamically irreversible. In this specific case, we recover the Landauer bound, as a work, which is necessary for the erasure of one bit of information. For the limit of $ln2 k_B T$

heat generation per bit to be reached, the thermodynamic process must be reversible. In practice, logical operations are implemented by sub-optimal physical processes and thus are thermodynamically irreversible [93]. However, this irreversibility is not caused by the nature of the logical operation; it is by way of the operation being implemented by a thermodynamically sub-optimal physical process [93]. This is as true for logically irreversible operations as it is for logically reversible operations [93].

2.10. Generalization of the Landauer Principle

Generalization of the Landauer principle for logically non-deterministic operations was reported by Maroney [94]. The non-equilibrium quantum Landauer principle was reported [45,95]. The Landauer principle at absolute-zero temperatures was introduced recently; a bound tighter than Landauer that remains nontrivial even in the $T \to 0$ was reported [96]. Herrera discussed the Landauer principle in its relation to general relativity [97]. The Landauer principle was applied to the problem of gravitational radiation [97]. The fact that gravitational radiation is an irreversible process entailing dissipation is a straightforward consequence of the Landauer principle and the fact that gravitational radiation conveys information were demonstrated [97]. It should be emphasized that understanding the relativistic extension of the Landauer bound remains an open problem due to the fact that the construction of a relativistic thermodynamics theory is still controversial after more than 110 years of its development. In particular, the problem of the relativistic transformation for temperature remains unsolved [98–102].

2.11. Criticism and Objections to the Landauer Principle

The Landauer principle was intensively criticized by J. D. Norton, who argued that since it is not independent of the second law of thermodynamics, it is either unnecessary or insufficient as an exorcism of Maxwell's demon [103–108]. Lairez suggested a counterexample of physical implementation (that uses a two-to-one relation between logic and thermodynamic states) that allows one bit to be erased in a thermodynamic quasi-static manner (i.e., one that may tend to be reversible if slowed down enough) [109]. The Landauer principle was defended in a series of recent papers [110–114]. Witkowski et al. demonstrated an original proof of the Landauer principle that is completely independent of the second law of thermodynamics [112]. Buffoni et al. demonstrated that the Landauer principle, in contrast to widespread opinion, is not the second law of thermodynamics nor is it equivalent to it; in fact, it is a stricter bound [115]. However, the discussion is far from exhausted.

The mass–energy–information equivalence principle, summarized by Equations (19) and (20), was criticized recently [116]. In particular, Lairez argued that (i) isothermal variation in the entropy-rooted part of the free energy of a body (namely, $T\Delta S$) is not accompanied by any variation in its mass, (ii) the Landauer–Bennet idea is not a general principle and is only true in a particular case, and (iii) the link between information and energy is valid only for fresh information about a dynamic system. Old information, or information detached from its subject matter, is no longer information and has no value [116]. Thus, the physical groundings of the link between the mass, energy, and information remain debatable and should be clarified.

2.12. The Landauer Principle: Open Questions, Perspectives, and Challenges

In spite of the enormous theoretical and experimental effort spent on the understanding and experimental validation of the Landauer principle, a number of challenging problems remain open.

(i) The exact place of the Landauer principle in the structure of thermodynamics should be clarified. Thermodynamics, in contrast to other fields of physics, enables a completely axiomatic approach, as suggested by Carathéodory [117–119]. The second law of thermodynamics was formulated by Carathéodory as follows: "In the neighborhood of any equilibrium state of a system (of any number of thermodynamic coordinates), there exist states that are inaccessible by reversible adiabatic processes." It seems to be instructive to re-shape the axiomatic thermodynamics with the use of the Landauer principle.

(ii) A relativistic extension of the Landauer principle remains one of the unsolved problems (the problem of the accurate derivation of the relativistic transformation of the temperature also remains open [97–102]). This problem is closely related to general cosmology. Calculation of the cosmological constant Λ emerging from the Landauer principle was reported [120].

(iii) It is important to implement the Landauer principle in the development of optimal computational protocols, providing minimal dissipation [37,43,121]. Limitations imposed by the Margolus–Levitin limiting principle should be considered (see Section 2.2). The construction of optimal computers remains an open task and is deeply discussed in Ref. [122], in which restrictions imposed on computation by fundamental physical laws are deeply discussed. Ref. [122] is strongly recommended for readers interested in the physics of computation. It was also mentioned that the transfer of entropy and not entropy itself restricts optimal computational protocols [123].

(iv) The philosophical meaning of the Landauer principle should be clarified [124].

3. Conclusions

The physical roots, justification, interpretation, controversies, and precise meaning of the Landauer principle remain obscure, in spite of the fact that they have been exposed to turbulent and spirited discussion in the last few decades. The Landauer principle (or the Landauer bound), suggested by Rolf Landauer in 1961, is a physical principle predicting the lower theoretical limit of energy consumption of computation [26–29]. It states that an irreversible change in information stored on a computer, such as merging two computational paths, dissipates a minimum amount of heat $k_B T ln 2$ per bit of information to its surroundings. The Landauer principle is discussed in the context of other fundamental physical limiting principles, such as the Abbe diffraction limit, the Margolus–Levitin limit, and the Bekenstein limit [15,16,125]. We demonstrate that the synthesis of the Landauer bound with the Abbe, Margolus–Levitin, and Bekenstein limits quite surprisingly yields the minimum time of computation, which scales as $\tau_{min} \sim \frac{h}{k_B T} = \tau_{PB}$ (where h and k_B are the Planck and Boltzmann constants, respectively), which is exactly the Planck–Boltzmann thermalization time [36,41]. This result leads to a very important conclusion: Decreasing the temperature of a thermal bath will decrease the energy consumption of a single computation, but in parallel, it will slow the computation. The relation between the Landauer bound and the Szilárd minimal engine is discussed.

The Landauer principle bridges John Archibald Wheeler's "it from bit" paradigm and thermodynamics [63,75,76]. This bridge yields the mass–energy–information principle, enables calculation of the informational capacity of the universe, and provides a fresh glance at the dark matter problem [66–71]. The Landauer principle may serve as a basis for the unification of physical theories, enabling a united, unified approach to the informational content of fields and particles. Generalization of the Landauer principle to quantum and non-equilibrium systems is addressed [44,45,125]. The relativistic aspects of the Landauer principle are discussed. Engineering applications of the Landauer principle in the development of optimal computational protocols are considered [37,43,120]. Experimental verifications of the Landauer principle are surveyed [46,59]. The interrelation between thermodynamic and logical irreversibility is addressed. The non-trivial relationship between the Landauer principle and the second law of thermodynamic is considered [115]. Objections and criticism of the Landauer principle are discussed [103,104,109]. The mass–energy–information equivalence principle was criticized recently [116]. Therefore, a lot of questions related to the Landauer principle and its extensions remain debatable. We conclude that the Landauer principle represents a powerful heuristic principle bridging fundamental physics, information theory, and computer engineering. It is suggested that the Landauer principle may serve as a cornerstone of axiomatic thermodynamics.

Funding: This research received no external funding.

Data Availability Statement: No new data were created or analyzed in this study. Data sharing is not applicable to this article.

Acknowledgments: The author is thankful to Oleg Gendelman, M. Frenkel, and A. Gilevich for the extremely fruitful discussions. The author is thankful to the anonymous reviewers for the extremely useful and instructive reviewing of the manuscript.

Conflicts of Interest: The author declares no conflicts of interest.

References

1. Liu, Y.C.; Huang, K.; Xiao, Y.-F.; Yang, L.; Qiu, C.W. What limits limits? *Nat. Sci. Rev.* **2021**, *8*, nwaa210. [CrossRef] [PubMed]
2. Markov, I. Limits on fundamental limits to computation. *Nature* **2014**, *512*, 147–154. [CrossRef]
3. Hecht, E. Chapter 13 Modern Optics. In *Optics*, 4th ed.; Addison-Wesley: Boston, MA, USA, 2002; pp. 609–611.
4. Born, M.; Wolf, E. Chapter 8 Elements of the theory of diffraction. In *Principles of Optics*, 6th ed.; Pergamon Press: Oxford, UK, 1986; pp. 419–424.
5. Zuo, R.; Liu, W.; Cheng, H.; Chen, S.; Tian, J. Breaking the Diffraction Limit with Radially Polarized Light Based on Dielectric Metalenses. *Adv. Opt. Mater.* **2018**, *6*, 1800795. [CrossRef]
6. Einstein, A. Chapter XXII. In *Relativity: The Special and General Theory*; Methuen & Co.: London, UK, 1920; pp. 86–97.
7. Fayngold, M. Chapter 2. In *Special Relativity and How It Works*; John Wiley & Sons—VCH Verlag: Weinheim, Germany, 2008; pp. 17–41.
8. Ellis, G.F.R.; Uzan, J.-P. c is the speed of light, isn't it? *Am. J. Phys.* **2005**, *73*, 240–247. [CrossRef]
9. Anber, M.M.; Donoghue, J.F. Emergence of a universal limiting speed. *Phys. Rev. D* **2011**, *83*, 105027. [CrossRef]
10. Landau, L.D.; Lifshitz, E.M. Chapter 2. In *Quantum Mechanics: Non-Relativistic Theory*, 3rd ed.; Pergamon Press: Oxford, UK, 1977; Volume 3, pp. 46–49.
11. Cohen-Tannoudji, C.; Diu, B.; Laloë, F. *Quantum Mechanics*; Wiley-Interscience: Hoboken, NJ, USA, 1996; pp. 231–233.
12. Bremermann, H.J. Optimization through evolution and recombination. In *Self-Organizing Systems 1962*; Yovits, M.C., Jacobi, G.T., Goldstein, G.D., Eds.; Spartan Books: Washington, DC, USA, 1962; pp. 93–106.
13. Mandelstam, L.; Tamm, I. The uncertainty relation between energy and time in non-relativistic quantum mechanics. In *Selected Papers*; Bolotovskii, B.M., Frenkel, V.Y., Peierls, R., Eds.; Springer: Berlin/Heidelberg, Germany, 1991.
14. Hörnedal, N.; Sönnerborn, O. Margolus-Levitin quantum speed limit for an arbitrary fidelity. *Phys. Rev. Res.* **2023**, *5*, 043234. [CrossRef]
15. Margolus, M.; Levitin, L.B. The maximum speed of dynamical evolution. *Physica D* **1998**, *120*, 188–195. [CrossRef]
16. Bekenstein, J.D. Universal upper bound on the entropy-to-energy ratio for bounded systems. *Phys. Rev. D* **1981**, *23*, 287–298. [CrossRef]
17. Anderson, J.B.; Johnnesson, R. Chapter 1. In *Understanding Information Transmission*; IEEE Press: Piscataway, NJ, USA; John Wiley & Sons, Inc.: Hoboken, NJ, USA, 2005; pp. 2–29.
18. Ash, R.B. Chapter 1. In *Information Theory*; Dover Publications: Mineola, NY, USA, 1990; pp. 2–24.
19. Shannon, C.E. A Mathematical Theory of Communication. *Bell Syst. Tech. J.* **1948**, *27*, 379–423. [CrossRef]
20. Shannon, C.E. A Mathematical Theory of Communication. *Bell Syst. Tech. J.* **1948**, *27*, 623–656. [CrossRef]
21. Ben Naim, A. Shannon's Measure of information and Boltzmann's H-Theorem. *Entropy* **2017**, *19*, 48. [CrossRef]
22. Ben-Naim, A. *Information Theory*; World Scientific: Singapore, 2017.
23. Ben-Naim, A. *A Farewell to Entropy: Statistical Thermodynamics Based on Information*; World Scientific: Singapore, 2008.
24. Ben-Naim, A. An Informational Theoretical Approach to the Entropy of Liquids and Solutions. *Entropy* **2018**, *20*, 514. [CrossRef] [PubMed]
25. Ben-Naim, A. *Entropy, the Truth the Whole Truth and Nothing but the Truth*; World Scientific: Singapore, 2016.
26. Landauer, R. Dissipation and heat generation in the computing process. *IBM J. Res. Dev.* **1961**, *5*, 183. [CrossRef]
27. Landauer, R. Information is physical. *Phys. Today* **1991**, *44*, 23–29. [CrossRef]
28. Landauer, R. Minimal energy requirements in communication. *Science* **1996**, *272*, 1914–1918. [CrossRef] [PubMed]
29. Bennett, C.H.; Landauer, R. The fundamental physical limits of computation. *Sci. Am.* **1985**, *253*, 48–57. [CrossRef]
30. Parrondo, J.M.R.; Horowitz, J.M.; Sagawa, T. Thermodynamics of information. *Nat. Phys.* **2015**, *11*, 131–139. [CrossRef]
31. Sagawa, T. Thermodynamic and logical reversibilities revisited. *J. Stat. Mech.* **2014**, *2014*, P03025. [CrossRef]
32. Piechocinska, B. Information erasure. *Phys. Rev. A* **2000**, *61*, 062314. [CrossRef]
33. Landau, L.D.; Lifshitz, E.M. *Statistical Physics*, 3rd ed.; Course of Theoretical Physics; Elsevier: Oxford, UK, 2011; Volume 5, p. 87.
34. Kittel, C.; Kroemer, H. Chapter 3. In *Thermal Physics*, 2nd ed.; W. H. Freeman and Company: New York, NY, USA, 1980; pp. 61–62.
35. Bormashenko, E. Generalization of the Landauer Principle for Computing Devices Based on Many-Valued Logic. *Entropy* **2019**, *21*, 1150. [CrossRef]
36. Hartnoll, S.A.; Mackenzie, A.P. Colloquium: Planckian dissipation in metals. *Rev. Mod. Phys.* **2022**, *94*, 041002. [CrossRef]

37. Proesmans, K.; Ehrich, J.; Bechhoefer, J. Optimal finite-time bit erasure under full control. *Phys. Rev. E* **2020**, *102*, 032105. [CrossRef] [PubMed]
38. Lee, J.S.; Lee, S.; Kwon, H.; Park, H. Speed Limit for a Highly Irreversible Process and Tight Finite-Time Landauer's Bound. *Phys. Rev. Lett.* **2022**, *129*, 120603. [CrossRef] [PubMed]
39. Van Vu, T.; Saito, K. Finite-Time Quantum Landauer Principle and Quantum Coherence. *Phys. Rev. Lett.* **2022**, *128*, 010602. [CrossRef] [PubMed]
40. Ma, Y.-H.; Chen, J.F.; Sun, C.P.; Dong, H. Minimal energy cost to initialize a bit with tolerable error. *Phys. Rev. E* **2022**, *106*, 034112. [CrossRef] [PubMed]
41. Rolandi, A.; Llobet, M.P. Finite time Landauer Principle beyond weak coupling. *Quantum* **2023**, *7*, 1161. [CrossRef]
42. Reeb, D.; Wolf, M.N. An improved Landauer principle with finite-size corrections. *New J. Phys.* **2014**, *16*, 103011. [CrossRef]
43. Deshpande, A.; Gopalkrishnanm, M.; Ouldridge, T.E.; Jones, N.S. Designing the optimal bit: Balancing energetic cost, speed and reliability. *Proc. R. Soc. A* **2017**, *473*, 0117. [CrossRef] [PubMed]
44. Lorenzo, S.; McCloskey, R.; Ciccarello, F.; Paternostro, M.; Palma, G.M. Landauer's Principle in Multipartite Open Quantum System Dynamics. *Phys. Rev. Lett.* **2015**, *115*, 120403. [CrossRef]
45. Goold, J.; Paternostro, M.; Modi, K. Nonequilibrium Quantum Landauer Principle. *Phys. Rev. Lett.* **2015**, *114*, 060602. [CrossRef]
46. Yan, L.L.; Xiong, T.P.; Rehan, K.; Zhou, F.; Liang, D.F.; Chen, L.; Zhang, J.Q.; Yang, W.L.; Ma, Z.H.; Feng, M. Single-Atom Demonstration of the Quantum Landauer Principle. *Phys. Rev. Lett.* **2018**, *120*, 210601. [CrossRef] [PubMed]
47. Peterson, J.P.S.; Sarthour, R.S.; Souza, A.M.; Oliveira, I.S.; Goold, J.; Modi, K.; Soares-Pinto, D.O.; Céleri, L.C. Experimental demonstration of information to energy conversion in a quantum system at the Landauer limit. *Proc. R. Soc. A* **2016**, *472*, 20150813. [CrossRef] [PubMed]
48. Strasberg, P.; Schaller, G.; Brandes, T.; Esposito, M. Quantum and Information Thermodynamics: A Unifying Framework Based on Repeated Interactions. *Phys. Rev. X* **2017**, *7*, 021003. [CrossRef]
49. Diana, G.; Bagci, G.B.; Esposito, M. Finite-time erasing of information stored in fermionic bits. *Phys. Rev. E* **2013**, *87*, 012111. [CrossRef] [PubMed]
50. Sagawa, T.; Ueda, M. Minimal Energy Cost for Thermodynamic Information Processing: Measurement and Information Erasure. *Phys. Rev. Lett.* **2009**, *102*, 250602. [CrossRef]
51. Gavrilov, M. Erasure Without Work in an Asymmetric, Double-Well Potential. In *Experiments on the Thermodynamics of Information Processing*; Springer Theses; Springer: Cham, Switzerland, 2017.
52. Szilard, L. Über die Entropieverminderung in einem thermodynamischen System bei Eingriffen intelligenter Wesen. *Z. Phys.* **1929**, *53*, 840–856. [CrossRef]
53. Aydin, A.; Sisman, A.; Kosloff, R. Landauer's Principle in a Quantum Szilard Engine without Maxwell's Demon. *Entropy* **2020**, *22*, 294. [CrossRef]
54. Kim, S.W.; Sagawa, T.; De Liberato, S.; Ueda, M. Quantum Szilard Engine. *Phys. Rev. Lett.* **2011**, *106*, 070401. [CrossRef] [PubMed]
55. Chamberlin, R.V. Small and Simple Systems That Favor the Arrow of Time. *Entropy* **2024**, *26*, 190. [CrossRef]
56. Chamberlin, R.V. The Big World of Nanothermodynamics. *Entropy* **2015**, *17*, 52–73. [CrossRef]
57. Hill, T.L. *Thermodynamics of Small Systems, Parts I & II*; Dover Publications: Mineola, NY, USA, 2013.
58. Bormashenko, E.; Shkorbatov, A.; Gendelman, O. The Carnot engine based on the small thermodynamic system: Its efficiency and the ergodic hypothesis. *Am. J. Phys.* **2007**, *75*, 911–915. [CrossRef]
59. Koski, E.V.; Maisi, V.F.; Pekola, J.P.; Averin, D. Experimental realization of a Szilard engine with a single electron. *Proc. Natl. Acad. Sci. USA* **2014**, *111*, 13786–13789. [CrossRef] [PubMed]
60. Koski, J.V.; Kutvonen, A.; Khaymovich, I.M.; Ala-Nissila, T.; Pekola, J.P. On-Chip Maxwell's Demon as an Information-Powered Refrigerator. *Phys. Rev. Lett.* **2015**, *115*, 260602. [CrossRef] [PubMed]
61. Bannerman, T.; Price, G.N.; Viering, K.; Raizen, M. Single-photon cooling at the limit of trap dynamics: Maxwell's demon near maximum efficiency. *New J. Phys.* **2009**, *11*, 063044. [CrossRef]
62. Maruyama, K.; Morikoshi, F.; Vedral, V. Thermodynamical detection of entanglement by Maxwell's demons. *Phys. Rev. A* **2005**, *71*, 012108. [CrossRef]
63. Wheeler, J.A. Information, physics, quantum: The search for links. In Proceedings of the 3rd International Symposium on Foundations of Quantum Mechanics in the Light of New Technology, Tokyo, Japan, 28–31 August 1989; pp. 354–368.
64. Herrera, L. The mass of a bit of information and the Brillouin's principle. *Fluct. Noise Lett.* **2014**, *13*, 1450002. [CrossRef]
65. Brillouin, L. The negentropic principle of information. *J. Appl. Phys.* **1953**, *24*, 1152–1163. [CrossRef]
66. Vopson, M. The mass-energy-information equivalence principle. *AIP Adv.* **2019**, *9*, 095206. [CrossRef]
67. Vopson, M. The information catastrophe. *AIP Adv.* **2020**, *10*, 085014. [CrossRef]
68. Vopson, M. Estimation of the information contained in the visible matter of the universe. *AIP Adv.* **2021**, *11*, 105317. [CrossRef]
69. Vopson, M. Experimental protocol for testing the mass–energy–information equivalence principle. *AIP Adv.* **2022**, *12*, 035311. [CrossRef]
70. Vopson, M.; Lepadatu, S. Second law of information dynamics. *AIP Adv.* **2022**, *12*, 075310. [CrossRef]
71. Vopson, M. The second law of infodynamics and its implications for the simulated universe hypothesis. *AIP Adv.* **2023**, *13*, 105308. [CrossRef]
72. Müller, J.G. Events as Elements of Physical Observation: Experimental Evidence. *Entropy* **2024**, *26*, 255. [CrossRef]

73. Müller, J.G. Photon detection as a process of information gain. *Entropy* **2020**, *22*, 392. [CrossRef] [PubMed]
74. Müller, J.G. Information contained in molecular motion. *Entropy* **2019**, *21*, 1052. [CrossRef]
75. Bormashenko, E. The Landauer Principle: Re-Formulation of the Second Thermodynamics Law or a Step to Great Unification? *Entropy* **2019**, *21*, 918. [CrossRef]
76. Bormashenko, E. Informational Reinterpretation of the Mechanics Notions and Laws. *Entropy* **2020**, *22*, 631. [CrossRef] [PubMed]
77. Bormashenko, E. Rotating Minimal Thermodynamic Systems. *Entropy* **2022**, *24*, 168. [CrossRef] [PubMed]
78. Fixsen, D.J. The Temperature of the cosmic microwave background. *Astrophys. J.* **2009**, *707*, 916–920. [CrossRef]
79. Mikhailovsky, G.T.; Levich, A.P. Entropy, information and complexity or which aims the arrow of time? *Entropy* **2015**, *17*, 4863–4890. [CrossRef]
80. Lloyd, S. Computational capacity of the Universe. *Phys. Rev. Lett.* **2002**, *88*, 237901. [CrossRef] [PubMed]
81. Tatum, E.T.; Seshavatharam, U.V.S.; Lakshminarayan, S. Flat space cosmology as a mathematical model of quantum gravity or quantum cosmology. *Int. J. Astron. Astrophys.* **2015**, *5*, 133–140. [CrossRef]
82. Rubin, V.C.; Burstein, D.; Ford, W.K., Jr.; Thonnard, N. Rotation velocities of 16 Sa galaxies and a comparison of Sa Sb and Sc rotation properties. *Astrophys. J.* **1985**, *289*, 81–104. [CrossRef]
83. Arkani-Hamed, N.; Finkbeiner, D.P.; Slatyer, T.R.; Weiner, N. A theory of dark matter. *Phys. Rev. D* **2009**, *79*, 015014. [CrossRef]
84. de Swart, J.; Bertone, G.; van Dongen, J. How dark matter came to matter. *Nat. Astron.* **2017**, *1*, 0059. [CrossRef]
85. Bertone, G.; Hooper, D.; Silk, J. Particle dark matter: Evidence, candidates and constraints. *Phys. Rep.* **2005**, *405*, 279–390. [CrossRef]
86. Dodelson, S.; Widrow, L.M. Sterile neutrinos as dark matter. *Phys. Rev. Lett.* **1994**, *72*, 17. [CrossRef]
87. Milgrom, M.; Sanders, R.H. Modified Newtonian dynamics and the dearth of dark matter in ordinary elliptical galaxies. *Astrophys. J.* **2003**, *599*, L25–L28. [CrossRef]
88. Bormashenko, E. What Is Temperature? Modern Outlook on the Concept of Temperature. *Entropy* **2020**, *22*, 1366. [CrossRef]
89. Orlov, A.O.; Lent, C.S.; Thorpe, C.C.; Boechler, G.P.; Snider, G.L. Experimental Test of Landauer's Principle at the Sub-k_BY Level. *Jpn. J. Appl. Phys.* **2012**, *51*, 06FE10. [CrossRef]
90. Bérut, A.; Arakelyan, A.; Petrosyan, A.; Ciliberto, S.; Dillenschneider, R.; Lutz, E. Experimental verification of Landauer's principle linking information and thermodynamics. *Nature* **2012**, *483*, 187–189. [CrossRef] [PubMed]
91. Jun, Y.; Gavrilov, M.; Bechhoefer, J. High-precision test of Landauer's principle in a feedback trap. *Phys. Rev. Lett.* **2014**, *113*, 190601. [CrossRef] [PubMed]
92. Bennet, C.H. Notes on Landauer's principle, reversible computation, and Maxwell's Demon. *Stud. Hist. Philos. Mod. Phys.* **2003**, *34*, 501–510. [CrossRef]
93. Maroney, O.J.E. The (absence of a) relationship between thermodynamic and logical reversibility. *Stud. Hist. Philos. Sci. B* **2005**, *36*, 355–374. [CrossRef]
94. Maroney, O.J.E. Generalizing Landauer's principle. *Phys. Rev. E* **2009**, *79*, 031105. [CrossRef]
95. Esposito, M.; Van den Broeck, C. Second law and Landauer principle far from equilibrium. *Europhys. Lett.* **2011**, *95*, 40004. [CrossRef]
96. Timpanaro, A.M.; Santos, J.P.; Landi, G.T. Landauer's Principle at Zero Temperature. *Phys. Rev. Lett.* **2020**, *124*, 240601. [CrossRef]
97. Herrera, L. Landauer Principle and General Relativity. *Entropy* **2020**, *22*, 340. [CrossRef]
98. Farías, C.; Pinto, V.A.; Moya, P.S. What is the temperature of a moving body? *Sci. Rep.* **2017**, *7*, 17657. [CrossRef]
99. Landsberg, P.; Matsas, G.E.A. The impossibility of a universal relativistic temperature transformation. *Phys. A Stat. Mech. Appl.* **2004**, *340*, 92–94. [CrossRef]
100. Papadatos, N.; Anastopoulos, C. Relativistic quantum thermodynamics of moving systems. *Phys. Rev. D* **2020**, *102*, 085005. [CrossRef]
101. Papadatos, N. The Quantum Otto Heat Engine with a Relativistically Moving Thermal Bath. *Int. J. Theor. Phys.* **2021**, *60*, 4210–4223. [CrossRef]
102. Güémez, J.; Mier, J.A. Relativistic thermodynamics on conveyor belt. *Phys. Scr.* **2023**, *98*, 025001. [CrossRef]
103. Norton, J.D. Eaters of the lotus: Landauer's principle and the return of Maxwell's demon. *Stud. Hist. Philos. Sci. B* **2005**, *36*, 375–411. [CrossRef]
104. Norton, J.D. Waiting for Landauer. *Stud. Hist. Philos. Sci. B* **2011**, *42*, 184–198. [CrossRef]
105. Lu, Z.; Jarzynski, C. A Programmable Mechanical Maxwell's Demon. *Entropy* **2019**, *21*, 65. [CrossRef] [PubMed]
106. Leff, H.; Rex, A.F. (Eds.) *Maxwell's Demon 2 Entropy, Classical and Quantum Information, Computing*; CRC Press: Boca Raton, FL, USA, 2002.
107. Rex, A. Maxwell's Demon—A Historical Review. *Entropy* **2017**, *19*, 240. [CrossRef]
108. Bub, J. Maxwell's Demon and the thermodynamics of computation. *Stud. Hist. Philos. Sci. B* **2000**, *32*, 569–579. [CrossRef]
109. Lairez, D. Thermodynamical versus Logical Irreversibility: A Concrete Objection to Landauer's Principle. *Entropy* **2023**, *25*, 1155. [CrossRef] [PubMed]
110. Ladyman, J.; Presnell, S.; Short, A.J.; Groisman, B. The connection between logical and thermodynamic irreversibility. *Stud. Hist. Philos. Sci. B* **2007**, *38*, 58–79. [CrossRef]
111. Ladyman, J.; Robertson, K. Landauer defended: Reply to Norton. *Stud. Hist. Philos. Sci. B* **2013**, *44*, 263–271. [CrossRef]

112. Witkowski, C.; Brown, S.; Truong, K. On the Precise Link between Energy and Information. *Entropy* **2024**, *26*, 203. [CrossRef] [PubMed]
113. Barnett, S.M.; Vaccaro, J.A. Beyond Landauer erasure. *Entropy* **2013**, *15*, 4956–4968. [CrossRef]
114. Lostaglio, M.; Jennings, D.; Rudolph, T. Thermodynamic resource theories, non-commutativity and maximum entropy principles. *New J. Phys.* **2017**, *19*, 043008. [CrossRef]
115. Buffoni, L.; Campisi, M. Spontaneous Fluctuation-Symmetry Breaking and the Landauer Principle. *J. Stat. Phys.* **2022**, *186*, 31. [CrossRef]
116. Lairez, D. On the Supposed Mass of Entropy and That of Information. *Entropy* **2024**, *26*, 337. [CrossRef] [PubMed]
117. Carathéodory, C. Untersuchungen über die Grundlagen der Thermodynamik. *Math. Ann.* **1909**, *67*, 355–386. [CrossRef]
118. Pogliani, L.; Berberan-Santos, M.N. Constantin Carathéodory and the axiomatic Thermodynamics. *J. Math. Chem.* **2000**, *28*, 313–324. [CrossRef]
119. Bubuianu, I.; Vacaru, S.I. Constantin Carathéodory axiomatic approach and Grigory Perelman thermodynamics for geometric flows and cosmological solitonic solutions. *Eur. Phys. J. Plus* **2021**, *136*, 588. [CrossRef]
120. Gkigkitzis, I.; Haranas, I.; Kirk, S. Number of information and its relation to the cosmological constant resulting from Landauer's principle. *Astrophys. Space Sci.* **2013**, *348*, 553–557. [CrossRef]
121. Gingrich, T.R.; Rotskoff, G.M.; Crooks, G.E.; Geissler, P.L. Near-optimal protocols in complex nonequilibrium transformations. *Proc. Natl. Acad. Sci. USA* **2016**, *113*, 10263–10268. [CrossRef] [PubMed]
122. Lloyd, S. Ultimate physical limits to computation. *Nature* **2000**, *406*, 1047–1054. [CrossRef] [PubMed]
123. Prokopenko, M.; Lizier, J. Transfer Entropy and Transient Limits of Computation. *Sci. Rep.* **2015**, *4*, 5394. [CrossRef] [PubMed]
124. Hemmo, M.; Shenker, O. The physics of implementing logic: Landauer's principle and the multiple-computations theorem. *Stud. Hist. Philos. Sci. B* **2019**, *68*, 90–105. [CrossRef]
125. Deffner, S. Quantum speed limits and the maximal rate of information production. *Phys. Rev. R* **2020**, *2*, 013161. [CrossRef]

Disclaimer/Publisher's Note: The statements, opinions and data contained in all publications are solely those of the individual author(s) and contributor(s) and not of MDPI and/or the editor(s). MDPI and/or the editor(s) disclaim responsibility for any injury to people or property resulting from any ideas, methods, instructions or products referred to in the content.

Article

Landauer Principle and the Second Law in a Relativistic Communication Scenario

Yuri J. Alvim and Lucas C. Céleri *

QPequi Group, Institute of Physics, Federal University of Goiás, Goiânia 74690-900, Goiás, Brazil
* Correspondence: lucas@qpequi.com

Abstract: The problem of formulating thermodynamics in a relativistic scenario remains unresolved, although many proposals exist in the literature. The challenge arises due to the intrinsic dynamic structure of spacetime as established by the general theory of relativity. With the discovery of the physical nature of information, which underpins Landauer's principle, we believe that information theory should play a role in understanding this problem. In this work, we contribute to this endeavour by considering a relativistic communication task between two partners, Alice and Bob, in a general Lorentzian spacetime. We then assume that the receiver, Bob, reversibly operates a local heat engine powered by information, and seek to determine the maximum amount of work he can extract from this device. As Bob cannot extract work for free, by applying both Landauer's principle and the second law of thermodynamics, we establish a bound on the energy Bob must spend to acquire the information in the first place. This bound is a function of the spacetime metric and the properties of the communication channel.

Keywords: Landauer principle; second law; general relativity; relativistic communication

1. Introduction

The search for a relativistic theory of thermodynamics has a long history dating back to Einstein [1] and Planck [2], shortly after the discovery of special relativity. Despite ongoing debates and controversies [3,4], the last century has seen numerous advancements exploring the connections between thermodynamics and both special and general relativity (see, e.g., Refs. [5–16]). However, achieving consensus remains elusive, particularly when considering the implications of general relativity.

Quantum information theory, due to its profound connection with thermodynamics [17], offers promising insights into this long-standing problem. Since Landauer's recognition that information is physical and subject to the laws of physics, information theory has become inherently linked to all branches of physics [18]. The foundational Landauer principle asserts that erasing information necessitates dissipating energy as heat, a principle fundamental to both classical and quantum mechanics, and is crucial to resolving Maxwell's demon paradox [19,20]. Subsequent theoretical [21–33] and experimental [34–37] developments have followed these seminal works.

In this study, we explore the intersection of these ideas within the context of relativistic communication. By applying Landauer's principle alongside the second law of thermodynamics, we establish bounds on the energy involved in communication tasks. Specifically, we investigate the transmission of classical information between two parties using a massless scalar quantum field in a general curved spacetime, as discussed in Refs. [38,39]. Building upon this framework, we consider scenarios where one party, Bob, operates a heat engine powered by the information received from the communication channel. This setup enables Bob to locally extract work using the acquired information.

We demonstrate that because only information, not energy, is transmitted via the channel [39], both Landauer's principle and the second law imply that Bob can acquire information from the field only by expending a certain amount of energy. Our main result establishes a lower bound on this energy expenditure.

Our analysis utilizes tools from information theory, quantum field theory in curved spacetimes, general relativity, and thermodynamics to provide insights into relativistic quantum thermodynamics.

The paper is structured as follows: In Section 2, we provide a detailed review of the communication system employed in this study, focusing on classical channel capacity and energy costs for information transmission in globally hyperbolic spacetimes [38,39]. Section 3 applies Landauer's principle and the second law of thermodynamics to this context, forming the core of our investigation. Finally, Section 4 presents our concluding remarks. Throughout, we adopt the metric signature $(-,+,+,+)$ and use natural units where $c = \hbar = 1$.

2. Energy Cost for Conveying Information

In this section, our primary goal is to introduce the system of interest and establish notation. We outline the communication process under consideration and analyse the energies involved, which form the foundation for subsequent discussions in the paper. Specifically, we define the communicating partners and describe the communication channel they use, including its classical capacity $\mathcal{C}$. Furthermore, we discuss the energy changes within the global system (comprising the partners and the channel) during the communication process. This section builds upon the developments presented in Refs. [38,39], and interested readers are referred to these works for more detailed explanations. For a deeper understanding of quantum field theories in curved spacetimes, see Ref. [40].

To start, let us consider two communicating partners, Alice and Bob, each possessing a two-level quantum system (a qubit). The communication channel is physically represented by a quantum scalar (massless) field ϕ. The entire system resides in a globally hyperbolic (asymptotically flat) spacetime $(\mathbb{M}, \mathbf{g})$, where $\mathbb{M}$ denotes the four-dimensional spacetime manifold and $\mathbf{g}$ is a Lorentzian metric.

The communication process unfolds as follows [38,39]: Alice wishes to transmit information to Bob, encoded in her qubit state $\rho_\infty^A \in \mathcal{H}_A$, which was prepared locally at the infinite past. To encode this information into the communication channel, the field ϕ, Alice interacts her qubit with the field over a specific time interval Δt_A. This interval is measured relative to a Cauchy hypersurface Σ_t, where t is a parameter. Once the information is encoded into the field state, the dynamics of the field will mediate its transmission to Bob.

Bob, aiming to retrieve the information sent by Alice, initially prepares his qubit in the quantum state $\rho_{-\infty}^B \in \mathcal{H}_B$ and switches on its interaction with the field for a duration Δt_B, also measured with respect to a parameter t on some Cauchy hypersurface Σ_t. It's important to note that Bob's qubit interaction cannot be excessively strong due to potential decoherence effects.

The dynamics of the field ϕ is determined by the action

$$S = -\frac{1}{2} \int_{\mathbb{M}} d^4x \sqrt{-g} (\nabla_\mu \phi \nabla^\mu \phi), \qquad (1)$$

where $g \equiv \det(g_{\mu\nu})$ stands for the determinant of the metric. From this, we obtain the Klein–Gordon equation

$$\nabla_\mu \nabla^\mu \phi = 0. \qquad (2)$$

The dynamical evolution of ϕ can then be determined by the specification of smooth functions $\phi(t, \mathbf{x})$ and $\pi(t, \mathbf{x})$ on Σ_t, where $\mathbf{x} \equiv (x^1, x^2, x^3)$. As we are working in a globally hyperbolic spacetime, this is always possible.

The canonical momentum π is then defined as

$$\pi = \frac{\partial S}{\partial \dot{\phi}}, \qquad (3)$$

and the pair $(\phi(t,\mathbf{x}), \pi(t,\mathbf{x}))$ represents the state of the field at time t, which can be described as a point in the phase space $\mathcal{M}$

$$\mathcal{M} \equiv \{\phi : \Sigma_t \to \mathbb{C}, \pi : \Sigma_t \to \mathbb{C} \,|\, \phi, \pi \in C_0^\infty(\Sigma_t)\}, \tag{4}$$

with $C_0^\infty(\Sigma_t)$ representing the set of infinitely differentiable compact support functions on Σ_t.

By following the usual quantization procedure, we promote ϕ and π to operators satisfying the equal time canonical commutation relations

$$[\phi(t,\mathbf{x}), \phi(t,\mathbf{x}')]_{\Sigma_t} = [\pi(t,\mathbf{x}), \pi(t,\mathbf{x}')]_{\Sigma_t} = 0 \tag{5}$$

and

$$[\phi(t,\mathbf{x}), \pi(t,\mathbf{x}')]_{\Sigma_t} = i\delta^3(\mathbf{x}, \mathbf{x}'). \tag{6}$$

Using these operators, we define a symplectic structure $\Omega : \mathcal{S}^\mathbb{C} \times \mathcal{S}^\mathbb{C} \to \mathbb{C}$ as

$$\Omega([\phi_1, \pi_1], [\phi_2, \pi_2]) \equiv \int_{\Sigma_t} (\pi_1 \phi_2 - \pi_2 \phi_1) \mathrm{d}^3\mathbf{x}, \tag{7}$$

where each one of the pairs (ϕ_1, π_1) and (ϕ_2, π_2) leads us to a unique element ψ of $\mathcal{S}^\mathbb{C}$ —$\mathcal{S}^\mathbb{C}$ is the space of complex solutions to Equation (2).

The symplectic structure $\Omega(\psi_1, \psi_2)$, with $\psi_1, \psi_2 \in \mathcal{S}^\mathbb{C}$, can then be used to define the Klein–Gordon inner product as

$$\langle \psi_1 | \psi_2 \rangle_{\mathrm{KG}} \equiv -i\Omega(\overline{\psi_1}, \psi_2), \tag{8}$$

which is not positive definite on $\mathcal{S}^\mathbb{C}$. Therefore, the one-particle Hilbert space, $\mathcal{H}$, must be chosen as a subspace of $\mathcal{S}^\mathbb{C}$, where the inner product in Equation (8) is positive definite. Additionally, the space of complex solutions is comprised as $\mathcal{S}^\mathbb{C} \simeq \mathcal{H} \oplus \overline{\mathcal{H}}$, with $\overline{\mathcal{H}}$ being the dual Hilbert space.

Defining now a test function $f \in C_0^\infty(\mathbb{M})$, we can describe the generalised solution to Equation (2) as an operator-valued distribution. Formally, this operator is a mapping that associates each test function with an operator. More precisely, let us define $\mathcal{S} \in \mathcal{S}^\mathbb{C}$ as the space of real solutions, the projection operator $K : \mathcal{S} \to \mathcal{H}$ and the map $E : C_0^\infty(\mathbb{M}) \to \mathcal{S}$, which acts on the test functions f, such that

$$Ef(x) \equiv Af(x) - Rf(x), \tag{9}$$

where Af and Rf are the advanced and retarded solutions, respectively, to the non-homogeneous field equation, and Ef is a solution to Equation (2). Therefore, the quantum field operator is defined as an operator-valued distribution for some test function f as

$$\phi(f) \equiv i\left[a(\overline{KEf}) - a^\dagger(KEf)\right], \tag{10}$$

and satisfies the relation

$$[\phi(f_1), \phi(f_2)] = -i\Delta(f_1, f_2)\mathbb{I}, \tag{11}$$

where $f_1, f_2 \in C_0^\infty(\mathbb{M})$, $\mathbb{I}$ represents the identity operator while $\Delta(f_1, f_2)$ is defined as [40]

$$\Delta(f_1, f_2) \equiv \int_\mathbb{M} \sqrt{-g} f_1(x) Ef_2(x). \tag{12}$$

The problem with this method is that it involves arbitrarily many choices of Hilbert spaces and, thus, also vacuum and particles representations. Fortunately, we can circumvent this problem by using an algebraic approach, which is a formulation of the quantum field theory that provides a powerful tool for understanding the dynamics and properties of quantum fields (see Ref. [40] for more details). In short, while in the usual approach, we define states as vectors in Hilbert spaces and observables as operators acting on these spaces, in the algebraic approach, we build operators as elements of an algebraic space over which the states will act by means of the identification of a number to each operator [40]. Mathematically, let $\mathcal{W}(\mathbb{M})$ be the exponential version of the algebraic algebra of the fundamental observables. The generators of the elements of this Weyl algebra are defined as

$$W(Ef) = e^{i\phi(f)}, \tag{13}$$

and satisfies the relations $W^*(Ef) = W(-Ef)$, $W[E(\nabla^\mu \nabla_\mu - m^2)f] = \mathbb{I}$ and $W(Ef_1)W(Ef_2) = e^{i\Delta(f_1,f_2)/2}W(Ef_1 + Ef_2)$, with $f_1, f_2 \in C_0^\infty(\mathbb{M})$. Additionally, we define the algebraic quasi-free state as a positive and normalised linear functional $\omega : \mathcal{W}(\mathbb{M}) \to \mathbb{C}$, such that

$$\omega_\nu[W(Ef)] = e^{-\nu(Ef,Ef)/2}, \tag{14}$$

with ν being an inner product on $\mathcal{S}$ satisfying the relation

$$\nu(Ef_1, Ef_1)\nu(Ef_2, Ef_2) \geq \frac{1}{4}|\Omega(Ef_1, Ef_2)|^2. \tag{15}$$

In this way, we can describe the states of the communication channel without making any preferred choices of Hilbert spaces [40].

We are interested in the maximum amount of information that Alice can reliably convey to Bob. In other words, we are interested in the capacity of the communication channel. As mentioned before, we need to determine the dynamics of our system. Let us then employ the above formalism in order to determine the time evolution of the state of Bob's qubit, which is the receiver.

If $\rho_{-\infty}^A$ and $\rho_{-\infty}^B$ are the initial states of the Alice and Bob qubits, respectively, we can write the system initial state as $\rho_{-\infty} \equiv \rho_{-\infty}^A \otimes \rho_{-\infty}^B \otimes \rho_\omega$, where ρ_ω is the density operator associated with the field algebraic state ω_ν (see Equation (14)). Also, we define $\omega_\nu[W(Ef)] \equiv \text{Tr}\{\rho_\omega W(Ef)\}$.

Time evolution is governed by the total Hamiltonian of the system, which can be written as

$$H(t) \equiv H_\phi(t) + H_{\text{int}}(t), \tag{16}$$

where $H_\phi(t)$ is the Hamiltonian of the field and $H_{\text{int}}(t)$ is the Hamiltonian associated with the qubits' interaction with the field. It is mathematically more convenient to change to the interaction picture with respect to the free Hamiltonian. In this representation, the time evolution operator takes the form

$$U \equiv \vec{T} \exp\left\{-i \int_{-\infty}^{\infty} dt\, H_I(t)\right\}, \tag{17}$$

where $\vec{T}$ is the time ordering operator while $H_I(t)$ is the interaction picture representation of the Hamiltonian.

Under these definitions, the final state of the system is given by $\rho_{+\infty} \equiv U\rho_{-\infty}U^\dagger$, from which we determine Bob's qubit final state by tracing out the field and Alice's qubit degrees of freedom

$$\rho^B = \text{Tr}_{A,\phi}\left\{U\rho_{-\infty}^A \otimes \rho_{-\infty}^B \otimes \rho_\omega U^\dagger\right\}, \tag{18}$$

whose explicit expression, that is not important for our purposes here, can be found in Ref. [38]. This is the state where the information transmitted by the channel is codified. So, we can think about this state as a quantum memory.

In our investigation, we focus on examining the balance between the energy expended in the communication process and the energy Bob can generate using the acquired information. Therefore, our first task is to quantify the amount of information available to Bob. In the ideal scenario we are considering, this is represented by the channel capacity C.

By choosing the initial state for Bob's qubit in such a way that the signalling amplitude of the communication is maximised, and using the Holevo–Schumacher–Westmoreland [17] theorem, the classical capacity of the quantum channel is given by [38]

$$\mathcal{C} = S\left(\frac{1}{2} + \frac{\nu_B}{2}|\cos[2\Delta(f_A, f_B)]|\right) - S\left(\frac{1}{2} + \frac{\nu_B}{2}\right), \quad (19)$$

where S is the Shannon entropy and ν_B is defined as

$$\nu_B \equiv \omega_\nu[e^{i\phi(2f_B)}], \quad (20)$$

while the indexes A and B labelling the test functions f_A and f_B stand for Alice and Bob, respectively.

The channel capacity is the maximum rate at which one can reliably convey information. Therefore, Equation (19) represents the maximum amount of classical information Bob can obtain from Alice per use of the quantum channel. As we are interested in a lower bound of the energy Bob must spend in order to acquire the information, we assume that this is the case.

Some comments are in order here. First, from Equations (11) and (19), we observe that if Alice and Bob are not causally related, i.e., when the spacetime causality makes it impossible for Alice and Bob to have any influence over each other, $\Delta(f_A, f_B) = 0$ and, consequently, the channel capacity vanishes, as it should. If they are causally related, then $\Delta(f_A, f_B) \neq 0$ and $\mathcal{C} > 0$, such that it will be possible for them to communicate over this channel [38]. In this last case, Bob's final state will contain the amount of information given by $\mathcal{C}$.

Now that we know how much information is available to Bob, we need to understand the energy balance related to this process. We briefly discuss this now and point the reader to Ref. [39] for more details.

We want to study how the energy of the total system (two qubits plus the field) changes in time when the state evolves from $\rho_{-\infty}$ to $\rho_{+\infty}$. In order to do this, we just need to compute the total energy variation of the system, which is simply given by [39]

$$\Delta E \equiv \langle H(+\infty)\rangle_{\rho_{+\infty}} - \langle H(-\infty)\rangle_{\rho_{-\infty}}, \quad (21)$$

with $\langle \cdot \rangle_\rho$ representing the expectation value taken with respect to the state ρ.

Note that as the qubits interact with the field for a finite amount of time, the interaction part of the Hamiltonian does not contribute, and the total energy change can be recast into the form

$$\Delta E = E_\phi + E_A + E_B + E_{AB}, \quad (22)$$

whose formal expressions can be found in Ref. [39]. Physically, E_ϕ is the contribution coming from the effect of particle creation due to the dynamic nature of the metric. $E_A + E_B$ are the energies arising from the work that must be performed in order to turn on and off the interaction between the field and the qubits. This term is a function of the qubit trajectories, the coupling constants, and the metric. The last term, E_{AB}, is the contribution associated to the communication process itself. This depends on the metric, the relative motion between Alice and Bob, and the initial states of the qubits. Such dependence can be tailored to make $E_{AB} = 0$, while maximising the channel capacity, by a convenient choice of the initial state of Bob's qubit [39]. Remember that Alice's qubit state cannot be fixed as it contains the information she wants to convey to Bob. Therefore, the total change in energy takes the form

$$\Delta E = E_\phi + E_A + E_B. \quad (23)$$

This result is particularly interesting because it tells us that we can convey an arbitrary amount of information without any extra energy cost. This is the main fact on which the results presented in the next section are build.

3. Information Driven Heat Engine

Let us consider the simplest scenario of inertial Alice and Bob in Minkowski spacetime, as it is sufficient to illustrate our argument. We assume the initial state of the field is the vacuum, thus avoiding additional noise from finite temperature. In this case, as the metric remains unchanged, E_ϕ vanishes, and the only contribution to the energy change comes from the coupling of the qubits with the field. For efficient communication, Alice needs to strongly interact her qubit with the field. This energy is provided by a battery in Alice's lab and is not transmitted to Bob [39]. Therefore, as our interest lies in what happens at Bob's location, the only relevant energy is E_B. This is our contribution: We apply both the Landauer principle and the second law at Bob's laboratory to show that there must be a bound on Bob's ability to couple his qubit with the field to prevent him from violating the second law.

The argument proceeds as follows. Suppose Bob has a heat engine in his lab with two finite-size reservoirs at the same temperature. The second law states that it is impossible to extract work from this engine. Now, assume Bob has a memory (in equilibrium with the local environments) where he stores the information received from Alice. Bob can erase this information by allowing the memory to reversibly thermalize with one of the environments, using an arbitrarily small amount of energy. It is important to mention here that Bob has to invest energy in order to acquire information, thus changing the state of his qubit (memory). After this, Bob can simply couple his qubit with his environment without any extra energy environment. The information will be erased and there will be a flux of energy (in the form of heat) from the qubit to the environment. So, there must be a cost of acquiring information. This cannot be arbitrarily small, but must respect Landauer's bound.

The heat flux generated in this way will increase the energy in the environment. Although the effect is small, it is present. Now, Bob has a heat engine with a temperature gradient, from which work can be extracted. We argue that, as no energy was transmitted along with the information, there must be a lower bound on the energy Bob spends to couple his memory (qubit in our case) with the field to acquire the information. Otherwise, Bob would be able to extract work without investing energy, violating the second law. The aim of this section is to compute this bound.

Bob's qubit must interact with the field weakly and for a short duration to avoid decoherence. This coupling can be adjusted to maximize information transfer without incurring additional energy costs. Recall that in this scenario, information is transferred without energy flowing through the field. Bob can then recover an arbitrary amount of information by expending only a minimal amount of energy.

In the case of the Minkowski spacetime, it is possible to analytically compute the change in the energy of the qubits [39]

$$E_X = \frac{\lambda_X^2}{\tau_X}, \qquad (24)$$

where λ_X is the coupling constant of qubit X with the field, while τ_X is the time scale associated with the process of switching on and off this interaction. This is a trade-off relation between energy and time. From here on, we assume that $\tau_A = \tau_B = \tau$ is a fixed time scale that only depends on the switching the detectors. Therefore, the only important variable here is the coupling constant between the qubit and the field.

Now, as mentioned before, we assume that Alice has a local battery that provides her the necessary energy to turn on and off the coupling of her qubit with the field. In order to maximise the communication rate, we should choose λ_A to be as big as possible, implying that Alice can transfer the information to the field very efficiently, while spending a reasonable amount of energy.

The key focus is on Bob in this scenario. We are considering that Bob possesses a local battery that he utilizes to connect his qubit to the field (to acquire information). Additionally, Bob has a heat engine with two finite environments at the same temperature, denoted as T_c. It is important to note that this system is contained within Bob's laboratory, where both quantum mechanics and thermodynamics are applicable, thus presenting no ambiguity to define physical quantities like temperature. The second law of thermodynamics states that to effectively operate the heat engine, Bob must establish a temperature gradient. While he could use his own battery to create this gradient and operate the engine to generate work, Bob can also employ the information he obtained from Alice, converting it into useful work using the heat engine. This is where the Landauer principle comes into play.

The Landauer principle states that in order to erasure an amount $\mathcal{I}$ of information, we must dissipate energy in the form of heat Q, such that

$$Q \geq \beta^{-1} \mathcal{I} \ln 2, \tag{25}$$

where β is the inverse temperature of the environment where the heat goes [18].

Now, by assuming that the communication process is performed in the best possible way, Bob receives an amount of information that equals the channel capacity $\mathcal{I} = \mathcal{C}$. So, by reversibly erasing this information, the equality in Landauer's principle is achieved and Bob can increase the temperature of one of his environments as

$$T_c \to T_h = T_c + \frac{Q}{c_T} > T_c, \tag{26}$$

where c_T represents the thermal capacity of the environment. This can be achieved, for instance, by weakly coupling the qubit to the environment and allowing the system to reversibly thermalize, a process that can be achieved with an arbitrarily small energy cost. It is important to note that this occurs in Bob's laboratory, thus eliminating any issues related to coupling with gravity. The specific method through which this process occurs is not crucial. The key point is that some heat will be transferred to the environment during the erasure process, raising its temperature and creating the necessary temperature gradient to operate the heat engine. Given that Bob is assumed to achieve the exact channel capacity, this represents the maximum temperature gradient he can create.

The Carnot efficiency of this engine is simply given by

$$\eta = 1 - \frac{T_c}{T_h} > 0. \tag{27}$$

Using Equation (26), which is a consequence of the Landauer principle, we obtain

$$\eta = 1 - \left[1 + \frac{\mathcal{C} \ln 2}{c_T}\right]^{-1}. \tag{28}$$

This implies that the maximum work extracted from the heat engine is given by $W = \eta Q > 0$, which is a function of the relativistic channel capacity and, thus, of the metric and the trajectories followed by Alice and Bob.

Therefore, by erasing the information he received from Alice, Bob can operate an information-fueled heat engine, from which he can extract work W, while expending an arbitrarily small amount of energy in the process. However, as discussed in the preceding section, Alice can convey an arbitrary amount of information to Bob with no extra energy cost for him than E_B. We thus conclude that, in order for the second law to be obeyed, we must have

$$W \leq E_B, \tag{29}$$

as what happens on Alice's side does not matter to the heat engine. This directly implies a lower bound on the interaction strength between Bob's qubit and the field

$$\lambda_B^2 \geq \tau \mathcal{C} T_c \left[1 - \frac{1}{1 + \mathcal{C} \ln 2 / c_T}\right] \ln 2. \tag{30}$$

Note that such a bound depends on the spacetime metric and on the Alice and Bob trajectories, as these variables determine the channel capacity.

4. Discussion

In this contribution, we consider a relativistic communication scenario in which Alice sends information to Bob via a massless scalar field. The information is encoded and decoded through local interactions between the field and Bob's and Alice's detectors (qubits). An energy analysis revealed that the energy cost of this protocol is concentrated in the coupling of Alice's and Bob's qubits to the field, with no additional energy required for information transmission [39]. In this context, we considered that Bob operates a locally reversible heat engine. By applying Landauer's principle and the second law of thermodynamics, we derive a lower bound on the strength of the coupling between Bob's qubit and the field. This bound depends on the channel properties and the spacetime metric.

Some comments on our assumption of a finite-size environment are necessary here. The work extracted from the engine is indeed slightly less than what we previously considered. However, the general arguments remain valid as we are considering the best-case scenario. In this case, any amount of work that Bob can extract from the engine must set a limit on the energy he must spend to couple his qubit with the field. Furthermore, we are consider the case where the heat engine operates reversibly—zero power output—which implies that the environments are always in equilibrium, even with temperature variations. Note that our reference temperature in Equation (30) is the cold, initial, one.

The predicted effect is expected to be very small. The environments were considered finite as an infinite environment would have infinite thermal capacity, resulting in no temperature change. However, every physical system is finite, and this assumption is crucial for ensuring locality and consistency when defining thermodynamic laws in curved spacetimes. Landauer's bound predicts that $\beta^{-1} \ln 2$ of heat will be generated per bit erasure, so even with finite environments, a strong effect is not expected. Nevertheless, the important message is that the effect must exist for the second law of thermodynamics to hold in Bob's laboratory.

One consequence of this lower bound is that Bob's qubit will experience unavoidable decoherence. For any finite coupling strength, a finite amount of time is required for information transfer from the field to the qubit. During this time, the qubit interacts with the quantum field, leading to decoherence. This reduces the amount of information Bob receives and, consequently, the extracted work.

To illustrate our argument, we considered the simplest case of two qubits in flat spacetime. However, according to the general theory, if Alice and Bob are not causally disconnected, a positive channel capacity is always achievable, implying that our result holds for general spacetimes. The general case includes energy associated with particle creation from the vacuum due to metric changes, which tends to destroy the information flowing through the channel and decrease the heat engine's efficiency. Despite this, the effect is not expected to vanish unless the channel capacity does.

This work raises several questions, including the study of general spacetimes, especially those with event horizons. Another important issue is the propagation of information through the channel and its relation to energy balance during the dynamics. Additionally, what happens when transmitting quantum information instead of classical information, as considered in this work? These questions will be the subject of future research.

Author Contributions: All of the authors contributed equally to this work. All authors have read and agreed to the published version of the manuscript.

Funding: This work was supported by the National Institute for the Science and Technology of Quantum Information (INCT-IQ), Grant No. 465469/2014-0, the National Council for Scientific and Technological Development (CNPq), Grant No. 308065/2022-0, and the Coordination of Superior Level Staff Improvement (CAPES).

Data Availability Statement: There are no data associated to this work.

Conflicts of Interest: The authors declare no conflicts of interest.

References

1. Einstein, A. Über das Relativitätsprinzip und die aus demselben gezogenen Folgerungen. *Jahrb. Radioakt. Elektron.* **1907**, *4*, 411.
2. Planck, M. Zur Dynamik bewegter Systeme. *Ann. Phys.* **1908**, *331*, 1. [CrossRef]
3. Ott, H. Lorentz-Transformation der Wärme und der Temperatur. *Z. Phys.* **1963**, *175*, 70. [CrossRef]
4. Landsberg, P.T. Does a moving body appear cool? *Nature* **1966**, *212*, 571. [CrossRef]
5. Tolman, R.C. On the weight of heat and thermal equilibrium in general relativity. *Phys. Rev.* **1930**, *35*, 904. [CrossRef]
6. Cavalleri, G.; Salgarelli, G. Revision of the relativistic dynamics with variable rest mass and application to relativistic thermodynamics. *Nuovo Ciment. A* **1969**, *62*, 722. [CrossRef]
7. Newburgh, R.G. Relativistic thermodynamics: Temperature transformations, invariance and measurement. *Nuovo Ciment. B* **1979**, *52*, 219. [CrossRef]
8. Landsberg, P.T.; Matsas, G.E.A. The impossibility of a universal relativistic temperature transformation. *Phys. A* **2004**, *340*, 92. [CrossRef]
9. Dunkel, J.; Hänggi, P.; Hilbert, S. Non-local observables and lightcone-averaging in relativistic thermodynamics. *Nat. Phys.* **2009**, *5*, 741. [CrossRef]
10. Jacobson, T. Thermodynamics of spacetime: The Einstein equation of state. *Phys. Rev. Lett.* **1995**, *75*, 1260. [CrossRef]
11. Eling, C.; Guedens, T.; Jacobson, T. Nonequilibrium thermodynamics of spacetime. *Phys. Rev. Lett.* **2006**, *96*, 121301. [CrossRef] [PubMed]
12. Rovelli, C. Statistical mechanics of gravity and the thermodynamical origin of time. *Class. Quantum Grav.* **1993**, *10*, 1549. [CrossRef]
13. Rovelli, C.; Smerlak, M. Thermal time and Tolman-Ehrenfest effect: Temperature as the speed of time. *Class. Quantum Grav.* **2011**, *28*, 075007. [CrossRef]
14. Rovelli, C. General relativistic statistical mechanics. *Phys. Rev. D* **2013**, *87*, 084055. [CrossRef]
15. Padmanabhan, T. Thermodynamical aspects of gravity: New insights. *Rep. Prog. Phys.* **2010**, *73*, 046901. [CrossRef]
16. Basso, M.L.W.; Maziero, J.; Céleri, L.C. The irreversibility of relativistic time-dilation. *Class. Quantum Grav.* **2023**, *40*, 195001. [CrossRef]
17. Wilde, M.M. *Quantum Information Theory*; Cambridge University Press: Cambridge, UK, 2013.
18. Landauer, R. Irreversibility and heat generation in the computing process. *IBM J. Res. Dev.* **1961**, *5*, 183. [CrossRef]
19. Bennett, C.H. The thermodynamics of computation—A review. *Int. J. Theor. Phys.* **1982**, *21*, 905. [CrossRef]
20. Bennett, C.H. Notes on Landauer's principle, reversible computation, and Maxwell's demon. *Stud. Hist. Philos. Mod. Phys.* **2003**, *34*, 501. [CrossRef]
21. Georgescu, I. 60 years of Landauer's principle. *Nat. Rev. Phys.* **2021**, *3*, 770. [CrossRef]
22. Xu, H. Distinguishing pure and thermal states by Landauer's principle in open systems. *Eur. Phys. J.* **2024**, *84*, 357. [CrossRef]
23. Zivieri, R. From Thermodynamics to Information: Landauer's Limit and Negentropy Principle Applied to Magnetic Skyrmions. *Front. Phys.* **2022**, *10*, 769904. [CrossRef]
24. Reeb, D.; Wolf, M.N. An improved Landauer principle with finite-size corrections. *New J. Phys.* **2004**, *16*, 103011. [CrossRef]
25. Norton, J.D. Eaters of the lotus: Landauer's principle and the return of Maxwell's demon. *Stud. Hist. Philos. Sci. B.* **2005**, *36*, 375. [CrossRef]
26. Norton, J.D. Waiting for Landauer. *Stud. Hist. Philos. Sci. B.* **2011**, *42*, 184. [CrossRef]
27. Esposito, M.; van den Broeck, C. Second law and Landauer principle far from equilibrium. *EPL* **2011**, *95*, 40004 [CrossRef]
28. Goold, J.; Paternostro, M.; Modi, K. Nonequilibrium quantum Landauer Principle. *Phys. Rev. Lett.* **2015**, *114*, 060602. [CrossRef]
29. Hilt, S.; Shabbir, S.; Anders, J.; Lutz, E. Landauer's principle in the quantum regime. *Phys. Rev. E.* **2011**, *83*, 030102. [CrossRef] [PubMed]
30. Ladyman, J.; Presnell, S.; Short, A.J.; Groisman, B. The connection between logical and thermodynamic irreversibility. *Stud. Hist. Philos. Sci. B.* **2007**, *38*, 58. [CrossRef]
31. Barnett, S.M.; Vaccaro, J.A. Beyond Landauer erasure. *Entropy* **2013**, *15*, 4956. [CrossRef]
32. Maroney, O.J.E. Generalizing Landauer's principle. *Phys. Rev. E* **2009**, *79*, 031105. [CrossRef] [PubMed]
33. Timpanaro, A.M.; Santos, J.P.; Landi, G.T. Landauer's principle at zero temperature. *Phys. Rev. Lett.* **2020**, *124*, 240601. [CrossRef] [PubMed]
34. Bérut, A.; Arakelyan, A.; Petrosyan, A.; Ciliberto, S.; Dillenschneider, R.; Lutz, E. Experimental verification of landauer's principle linking information and thermodynamics. *Nature* **2012**, *483*, 187. [CrossRef] [PubMed]
35. Jun, Y.; Gavrilov, M.; Bechhoefer, J. High-precision test of Landauer's principle in a feedback trap. *Phys. Rev. Lett.* **2014**, *113*, 190601. [CrossRef] [PubMed]
36. Peterson, J.P.S.; Sarthour, R.S.; Souza, A.M.; Oliveira, I.S.; Goold, J.; Modi, K.; Soares-Pinto, D.O.; Céleri, L.C. Experimental demonstration of information to energy conversion in a quantum system at the Landauer limit. *Proc. R. Soc. A* **2016**, *472*, 20150813. [CrossRef] [PubMed]

37. Hong, J.; Lambson, B.; Dhuey, S.; Bokor, J. Experimental test of Landauer's principle in single-bit operations on nanomagnetic memory bits. *Sci. Adv.* **2016**, *2*, e1501492. [CrossRef] [PubMed]
38. Landulfo, A.G.S. Nonperturbative approach to relativistic quantum communication channels. *Phys. Rev. D* **2016**, *93*, 104019. [CrossRef]
39. Barcellos, I.B.; Landulfo, A.G.S. Relativistic quantum communication: Energy cost and channel capacities. *Phys. Rev. D* **2021**, *104*, 105018. [CrossRef]
40. Wald, R.M. *Quantum Field Theory in Curved Spacetime and Black Hole Thermodynamics*; University of Chicago Press: Chicago, IL, USA, 1994.

Disclaimer/Publisher's Note: The statements, opinions and data contained in all publications are solely those of the individual author(s) and contributor(s) and not of MDPI and/or the editor(s). MDPI and/or the editor(s) disclaim responsibility for any injury to people or property resulting from any ideas, methods, instructions or products referred to in the content.

Article

Elementary Observations: Building Blocks of Physical Information Gain

J. Gerhard Müller

Department of Applied Sciences and Mechatronics, Munich University of Applied Sciences,
D-80335 Munich, Germany; gerhard.mueller@hm.edu or jgmuegra@t-online.de

Abstract: In this paper, we are concerned with the process of experimental information gain. Building on previous work, we show that this is a discontinuous process in which the initiating quantum-mechanical matter–instrument interactions are being turned into macroscopically observable events (EOs). In the course of time, such EOs evolve into spatio-temporal patterns of EOs, which allow conceivable alternatives of physical explanation to be distinguished. Focusing on the specific case of photon detection, we show that during their lifetimes, EOs proceed through the four phases of initiation, detection, erasure and reset. Once generated, the observational value of EOs can be measured in units of the Planck quantum of physical action $h = 4.136 \times 10^{-15}$ eVs. Once terminated, each unit of entropy of size $k_B = 8.617 \times 10^{-5}$ eV/K, which had been created in the instrument during the observational phase, needs to be removed from the instrument to ready it for a new round of photon detection. This withdrawal of entropy takes place at an energetic cost of at least two units of the Landauer minimum energy bound of $E_{La} = \ln(2) k_B T_D$ for each unit of entropy of size k_B.

Keywords: physical measurement; information gain; event generation; physical action; energy dissipation; spacetime extension; Landauer principle

1. Introduction

The idea that matter is composed of indivisible elementary building blocks has been around since ancient times and has become widely known under the headline of "Greek atomism [1]". The mental concept of atomism turned into a seriously considered scientific reality with the rise of modern chemistry and the discovery of the periodic table of elements [2]. At its time of publication, the atoms in the periodic table were still considered indivisible building blocks of matter, a point of view that was shattered in the early years of the 20th century with the discovery of the electron [3], the proton [4], and later with the neutron [5]. In the year of 1932, when the neutron was discovered, the idea emerged that all matter in the universe might ultimately be composed of only three kinds of elementary particles. This idea was later shattered by the research into cosmic rays, and even more by experiments with high-energy accelerators [6]. The bewildering variety of "elementary particles" that emerged from this research was later consolidated into the standard model of elementary particles [6], which contains no less than 18 constituent particles. The increasing number of "elementary particles" raised an increasing discomfort in the scientific community, a situation that has been aggravated as new ideas of unexplained "dark matter" and "dark energy" have come up [7,8].

Returning to the subject matter of this paper, it is suggested that ultimate simplicity may not necessarily exist on the level of matter but rather on the level of observation. Being inspired by the idea of John Archibald Wheeler [9] that all physical entities at their bottom might be information-theoretic in origin, we have re-considered in a recent paper [10] three key experiments that were groundbreaking in the evolution of our modern ideas of matter at the atomic, nuclear and elementary particle scales, with an informational perspective in mind. The experiments re-considered were the Rutherford scattering experiments of Geiger and Marsden [11,12], the double-slit experiments with photons, electrons and other pieces of matter [13–16], and the visualization of nuclear particle trajectories in cloud, bubble and streaming chambers [17–19]. In re-considering these key experiments, we have taken the standpoint that these experiments can be regarded as questions posed to nature, and we asked ourselves how these questions are being answered by nature itself. A key result was that in spite of the different questions posed, all experimental answers are structured in a remarkably similar way, namely, in producing streams of macroscopically observable events (EOs) in the first place, which accumulate in the long run into spatio-temporal patterns of EOs, which represent the expected experimental answers, and which finally allow decisions to be taken regarding the validity of competing alternatives of physical explanation. In this previous work [10], we also arrived at the conclusion that EOs by themselves exhibit a double nature, being both abstract pieces of binary information, on the one hand, and concrete physical entities, endowed with the property of physical action, on the other hand:

$$W_{obs} = E_{obs}\tau_{obs} \gg h. \qquad (1)$$

In this equation, E_{obs} stands for the energy expended in producing a macroscopically observable EO, τ_{obs} for the lifetime during which the EO had remained macroscopically observable and h for Planck's constant of physical action. The inequality $W_{obs} \gg h$, moreover, indicates that EOs can be regarded as macroscopic images of the initiating micro-events and that the observational value of EOs can be measured in multiples of the elementary quantum of h. In this paper, we concentrate on EOs that have been produced by photon–matter interactions, and we aim to arrive at a set of figures of merit (FOMs) that characterize the observational value and the statistical significance of the produced EOs. Finally, we assess the energetic and entropic costs of producing such EOs.

2. Photons as Key Carriers of Physical Information

The choice of concentrating on photons and the process of photon detection is motivated by the fact that photons are the most important carriers of information, and that photon detection is the key process through which our material world becomes visible and accessible to physical investigation. This latter fact is demonstrated in a cartoon-like manner in Figure 1.

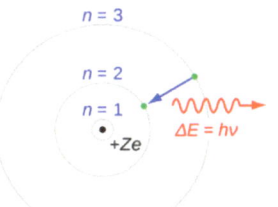  

Figure 1. Situations where matter becomes visible through the interaction with photons.

The above figure demonstrates that the information-carrying potential of photons is not at all limited to normal macroscopic dimensions, but that it extends all throughout the entire range of atomic and nuclear dimensions up to the length scale of truly cosmic dimensions measuring in billions of light years. We show in a mathematical appendix (Appendix A) that this information-carrying capacity of photons derives from the fact that in the course of electromagnetic wave propagation, quanta of physical action of size h are continually generated and erased while being shifted in space in discrete steps of length $\Delta x = \lambda/2$, where λ is the photon wavelength and x the direction of propagation. Such propagation processes continue up to the point at which the quanta of physical action become absorbed either inside a passive piece of matter or in some kind of photon detector. Whereas in both cases the quanta of physical action are absorbed, a macroscopically observable output signal is generated when the absorption takes place inside a suitably designed photon detector. The above figure, moreover, shows that without the possibility of photon detection, we would not be able to observe our own macroscopic environments, nor would the sciences of physics and astronomy exist at all, as without electromagnetic interaction and the possibility of photon detection, all kinds of matter would disappear into eternal darkness and unobservability.

In Figure 2, we also sketch in a cartoon-like manner an experiment in which single photons were processed in a one-by-one manner through a double-slit arrangement, fitted with a fluorescent detection screen behind the double slits [13]. This picture vividly demonstrates that each single photon becomes detected in the form of a "particle impact" and that the individual "particle impacts" converge in the long run towards a "diffraction pattern", which is taken as evidence that photons, on their travel from source to detection screen, propagate in the form of waves that had become diffracted upon passage through the double-slit arrangement.

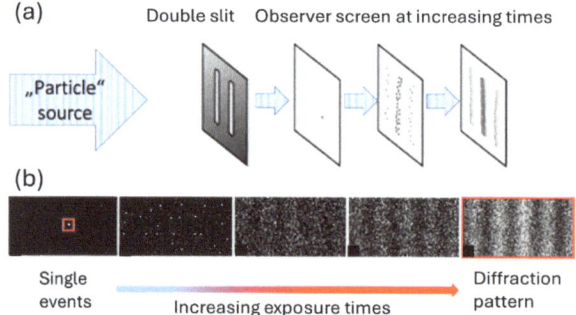

Figure 2. (**a**) Sketch of a double-slit experiment with photons, conducted for increasingly longer periods of time. Photon impacts on the detector screen feature as black dots; (**b**) developed photographic plates exposed to photons for increasingly longer times. After development of the photographic plates, individual "photon impacts" appear as small, permanently whitened spots, approximating diffraction patterns in the long run.

Looking at this same experiment from an informational point of view, it is suggested that the individual "particle impacts" are binary pieces of information that decide between two simple alternatives (event has happened at the particular "impact site"/event has not happened at this "site"). As the decision of a binary alternative provides the minimum possible information gain of one single binary digit, the seeming "particle impacts" can rightly be considered as "elementary observations (EOs)" and the "diffraction patterns" that emerge in the long run as complex pieces of information, built up from individual EOs. This latter interpretation puts well-designed physical experiments in parallel with technical information channels in which meaningful messages, such as texts and images, are transported from information source to information sink in the form of meaningless binary bits [20–23].

As similar conclusions concerning EOs were also reached in our previous work [10] with regard to the individual light flashes produced in a Rutherford scattering experiment, or the individual liquid droplets that had formed around ionized particle tracks in a cloud chamber, we extrapolated that experimental answers, in general, are being built up in a discontinuous manner from elementary pieces of information, i.e., EOs. Once looked at as wholes, such experimental answers raise informational questions on two different levels:

(a) What is the physical and informational nature of the individual EOs?
(b) What are the mental processes that allow physical meaning to be assigned to the patterns of EOs that emerge from the accumulation of huge numbers of EOs?

In the present paper, we concentrate on the first question and leave the discussion of the second question to a forthcoming paper [24].

3. Photon Detection with the Help of a Conceptual Device

In the following, we present the idea of a conceptual device that turns quantum-mechanical photon–matter interactions into macroscopically observable EOs. The principal architecture of such a device is sketched in Figure 3. There, a photo-ionization detector (PID) is shown, which consists of a pair of metal or semiconductor electrodes that are positioned facing each other in the form of a parallel-plate capacitor that is housed in a fully evacuated box with side lengths L and an entrance window through which photons can penetrate this box. In case an externally generated photon gets trapped inside this box, and in case the energy E_{ph} of this photon exceeds the electron work function $q\phi_m$ of the metal or semiconductor electrodes, a mobile electron is generated that in principle can flow from one electrode to the other. Provided a bias potential, V_b, is applied across the electrode pair, a directional electron current is initiated, which takes the form of a triangular current pulse, and which can be observed in the external circuit. Inside this circuit, a macroscopically observable image of the initiating micro-event of photon excitation is formed. While the generation of the mobile electron is an intrinsically quantum-mechanical measurement process that likely proceeds through the process of wavefunction collapse, the transport of the liberated electron is a process that can be described in a purely classical manner, and which thus allows those processes to be elucidated in which an intrinsically unobservable micro-event is transformed into a macroscopically observable event, i.e., into an EO.

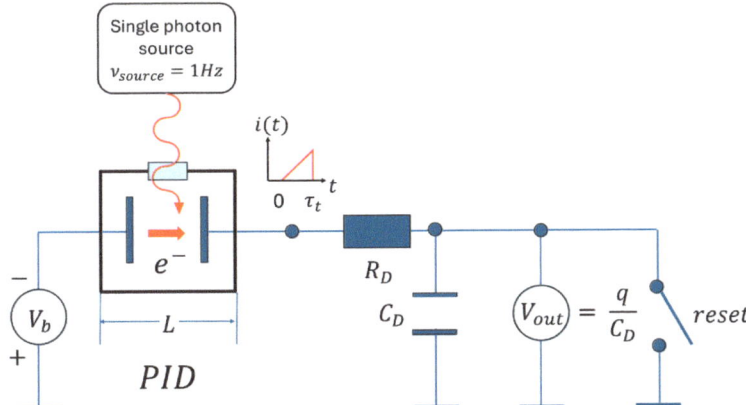

Figure 3. Schematic view onto a photo-ionization detector (PID). While the thick red arrow inside the box indicates the internal photoelectron current flow, the thin blue lines on the exterior are electrical wires that allow for current continuity throughout the whole device; R_D and C_D form an integrator circuit that converts the very short electron pulses into quasi-permanent output voltage readings. The frequency ν_{source} that is much lower than the inverse transit time through the electrode gap was chosen to conform with the conditions of single-photon detection.

In the present paper we build on the results obtained in our first paper on photon detection [25] where we have shown that the technical performance parameters [26] of signal-to-noise ratio (*SN*), noise-equivalent power (*NEP*) and detectivity (*D* and *D**) can be neatly translated into informational language by making the following assignment:

$$i_D(E_{ph}, T_D) = \frac{1}{ln(2)} ln[SN] = \frac{1}{ln(2)} ln\left[\frac{N_s}{N_n}\right] \qquad (2)$$

There, SN is the conventionally defined signal-to-noise ratio, N_s and N_n the numbers of signal and noise electrons that build up the output signal currents $I_s(t)$ and $i_D(E_{ph}, T_D)$ the informational value that can be assigned to the current transients $I_s(t)$. Using Equation (2) and transforming the conventional signal-to-noise ratio SN into informational language, three contributions to $i_D(E_{ph}, T_D)$ can be identified:

$$i_D(E_{ph}, T_D, V_D, V_b) = i_{diss}(E_{ph}, T_D) - i_{loc}(E_{ph}, V_{gap}) - i_{time}(L, V_b) \qquad (3)$$

As discussed in our previous paper [25], the first contribution $i_{diss}(E_{ph}, T_D)$ largely corresponds to the potential information $i_{pot}(E_{ph}, T_D)$ that the travelling photon had carried prior to its detection. This first term simply measures the potential of a photon of energy E_{ph} to generate entropy $S_D = E_{ph}/T_D$ inside a thermal reservoir maintained at a temperature T_D. In case this thermal reservoir is a detector operated at the temperature T_D, the generated information $i_{pot}(E_{ph}, T_D)$ can only partly be retrieved as realized observational information $i_D(E_{ph}, T_D)$:

$$i_D(E_{ph}, T_D) \leq i_{pot}(E_{ph}, T_D) = \frac{1}{\ln(2)} \frac{E_{ph}}{k_B T_D}. \qquad (4)$$

The second and third contributions to i_D, which reduce i_D below its maximum value of i_{pot}, arise when detector volumes are increased beyond their minimum sizes of $V_D = [\lambda/2]^3$, where λ is the photon wavelength and when electron transit times τ_t are increased beyond the photon transit times $\tau_{ph} = L/c$ through the detector gap. Under these latter conditions externally captured photons are increasingly likely to coexist with internally generated black-body photons inside the gap, which can trigger photon detection events as well and which thereby reduce the confidence level of the produced photon-detection EOs.

In the present paper we return to our previous work on PID detectors [25], and we focus on the special problem of single-photon detection and on those processes which turn single quantum-mechanical photon-detector interactions into macroscopically observable events, i.e., photon-detection EOs. Key result of these latter considerations is that the technical performance parameters of signal-to-noise ratio and/or their informational translations of $i_D(E_{ph}, T_D)$ fall short of completely specifying the observational value of photon-detection EOs. The reason for this incomplete match is that signal-to-noise ratios and/or their informational translations do not specify the observational value of photon-detection EOs that had been gained by expanding the space-time volume of the initiating photon-detector interactions into the hugely enhanced spacetime dimensions of the ensuing photon-detection EOs. In order to amend this situation we derive in Sections 4 and 5 two figures of merit (FOM), where the first FOM quantifies the level of macroscopic observability OV_{EO} gained in a photon detection process, and the second the level of confidence SI_{EO} that the observed photon-detection EO had actually been triggered by a photon that had originated from outside the detector itself. In Section 6 we discuss the entropy cost of observation. There, we show that EOs with optimum observability OV_{EO} and optimum statistical significance SI_{EO} can be obtained at minimum entropic cost in case photon and detector share evenly in the energetic cost of generating an EO. In Section 7 we consider the time evolution of EOs, and we show that, during their finite lifetimes, EOs proceed through the four stages of initiation, detection, erasure and reset. In this way a connection between PIDs and the widely discussed Szilard-type engines [27] and the Landauer principle [28–32] is established. In Section 8 we briefly summarize our results and present an outlook towards other types of EOs which are not photon-detection-related.

4. Making Microscopic Interaction Events Macroscopically Observable

Returning to Figure 3, we note that the triangular current pulses that emerge from PIDs in response to the internal absorption of a single photon can be described by [26]

$$I_s(t, L, V_b) = 2q \frac{t}{\tau_t(L, V_b)^2} \; ; (0 \leq t \leq \tau_t), \tag{5}$$

with

$$\tau_t(L, V_b) = \frac{L}{c} \sqrt{\frac{2m_e c^2}{qV_b}} \tag{6}$$

standing for the transit time of the photoelectron through the electrode gap. In the two equations above, q stands for the electron charge, c for the speed of light and $m_e c^2$ for the rest energy of the photoelectron. An integration of $I_s(t, L, V_b)$ over the transit time interval $[0, \tau_t]$ yields the magnitude q of the transported charge, and thus establishes the fact of single-photon detection.

Multiplying Equation (5) by the bias potential V_b that was applied across the electrode gap, the signal power emerges as

$$P_S(t, L, V_b) = 2qV_b \frac{t}{\tau_t(L, V_b)^2}. \tag{7}$$

A double integration of $P_S(t, L, V_b)$ over the transit time interval $[0, \tau_t]$ first yields the kinetic energy $E_{kin}(L, V_b)$ that the photoelectron had gained upon its impact at the anode surface,

$$E_S(L, V_b) = qV_b, \tag{8}$$

and secondly the physical action that can be associated with the photoelectron transit and the concomitant production of an EO:

$$W_S(L, V_b) = \frac{1}{3} q V_b \tau_t(L, V_b). \tag{9}$$

Considering that the function $W_S(L, V_b)$ has the dimension of physical action and that a travelling photon, prior to its detection, carried a single quantum of physical action h towards the detector (Appendix A), a dimensionless measure of macroscopical observability of a detection event can be defined:

$$OV_{EO}(L, V_b) = W_S(L, V_b)/h. \tag{10}$$

In Figure 4a, the variation of $OV_{EO}(L, V_b)$ with increasing bias potential V_b is shown. This first result shows that $W_S(L, V_b)$ can grow to large multiples of the Planck quantum of physical action h when the bias potential is increased. Photon detection EOs, therefore, can be regarded as hugely amplified images of the tiny packages of physical action that had been carried by the photon prior to its detection. Returning to Figure 4a, we additionally see that such gains in observability, $OV_{EO}(L, V_b)$, need to be paid for in terms of entropy as the energetic photoelectrons will impact on the anode with increasingly larger energies as bias potentials are being increased and as this excess energy needs to be dissipated there. We mention here without proof that this entropy—when written in information units—amounts to

$$MI_D(E_{ph}, V_b, T_d) = \frac{1}{\ln(2)} \left[\frac{E_{ph} + qV_b}{k_B T_D} \right]. \tag{11}$$

We will come back to a discussion of Equation (11) in Section 6.

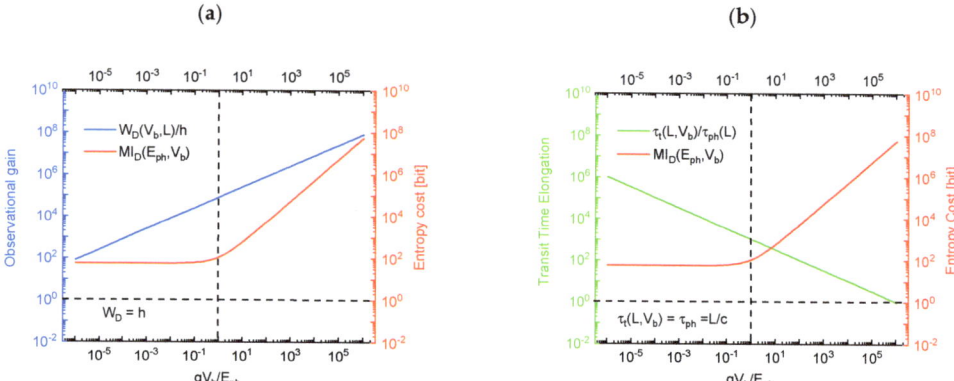

Figure 4. (a) Observational gain $OV_{EO}(L, V_b)$ as measured in multiples of the Planck constant h versus the normalized bias potential qV_b/E_{ph}. For the sake of good macroscopic observability, a device with a length extension of 300 μm $\gg \lambda$ was chosen ; (b) electron transit time through the electrode gap as a function of the normalized bias voltage. As shown in Section 6, the specific choices of $qV_b \approx E_{ph}$ represent conditions under which optimum observabilty is ensured at minimum entropic cost.

We have already shown in our previous paper that the figure of merit (FOM) of $OV_{EO}(L, V_b)$ cannot be increased indefinitely, as the vacuum inside the electrode gap will break down and become permanently electrically conducing when the energy of the photoelectrons impacting on the anode increases beyond the threshold energy of electron–positron pair production of $E_{th} \geq 2m_e c^2$.

Another possible option for arriving at even larger values of OV_{EO} is increasing the electrode gap width L, or the detector volume $V_D = L^3$ as a whole. We will see in the following section that this latter option fails as huge detector volumes tend to contain large amounts of thermally generated radiation, i.e., noise photons, which deteriorate the statistical significance of the detected EOs.

5. Statistical Significance of Detected Events

In addition to the observational value $OV_{EO}(L, V_b)$, which measures the level of spacetime expansion of an observed EO beyond the initiating photon-detector interaction event, the statistical significance $SI_{EO}(E_{ph}, T_D, L, V_b)$ of an observed EO can be defined as

$$SI_{EO}(E_{ph}, T_D, L, V_b) = 1 - \frac{1}{SN(E_{ph}, T_D, L, V_b)} \quad (12)$$

where $SN(E_{ph}, T_D, L, V_b)$ is the conventionally defined signal-to-noise ratio of a PID [26,33]. In this way another dimensionless FOM is obtained, which takes on the value of one when the observed EO has been generated by an outside photon, and the value of zero when the observed EO has been generated with equal probability by an outside or a thermally generated inside photon. In this first case of $SI_{EO} = 1$, the photon detection EO conforms to the nature of an EO, as discussed in our previous paper [10]. There, we argued that EOs feature a double nature, being abstract pieces of binary information, on the one hand, and concrete physical entities endowed with the property of physical action, on the other hand.

With the signal-to-noise ratio SN standing for the ratio of the numbers of signal (N_s) versus noise (N_n) electrons inside the electrode gap, Equation (12) takes on a particularly simple form in the limit of single-photon detection, i.e., ($N_s = 1$) and $N_n \approx 0$. In this latter case, the statistical significance of an EO reduces to the particularly simple form of

$$SI_{EO}(E_{ph}, T_D, L, V_b) = 1 - N_n. \quad (13)$$

Considering that the signal-to-noise ratio of PIDs is given by [25]

$$SN(E_{ph}, T_D, L, V_b) = \frac{1}{\sqrt{\pi}} \sqrt{\frac{\left[\frac{E_{ph}}{k_B T_D}\right] exp\left[\frac{E_{ph}}{k_B T_D}\right]}{\left[\frac{V_{gap}}{V_{min}}\right]\left[\frac{V_{b\_max}}{V_b}\right]}}, \qquad (14)$$

it is revealed that the condition $N_n \approx 0$ is easily obtained by detecting high-energy photons in a detector operated at a temperature T_D fulfilling the condition $E_{ph} \gg k_B T_D$. Or, in case this first condition cannot be fulfilled, another option is reducing the detector volume $V_D = L^3$ towards its minimum size of $V_{D\_min} = (\lambda/2)^3$ with λ standing for the photon wavelength. Alternatively, the bias voltage of the PID can be raised towards its maximum value of $qV_{b\_max} = 2m_e c^2$. Whereas reduced detector volumes are likely to run into conflict with the requirement of large levels of macroscopic observability OV_{EO}, the second measure drastically increases the entropy cost that needs to be paid for obtaining high levels of SI_{EO} (see Figure 4b).

6. The Entropy Cost of Observation

As high levels of macroscopic observability and concomitantly high levels of statistical significance require contradictory demands on optimum detector volumes and biasing conditions, compromises need to be sought. A guiding principle towards optimizing both FOMs is considering the entropy costs that are associated with obtaining the particular values of OV_{EO} and SI_{EO} at the chosen level of bias potential V_b.

In order to assess the level of entropy production, consider Figure 5a,b. While Figure 5a shows, in the form of a semiconductor-like band profile, a PID as operated under zero-bias conditions, Figure 5b shows this same device with the applied bias potential satisfying the condition $qV_b = E_{ph}$.

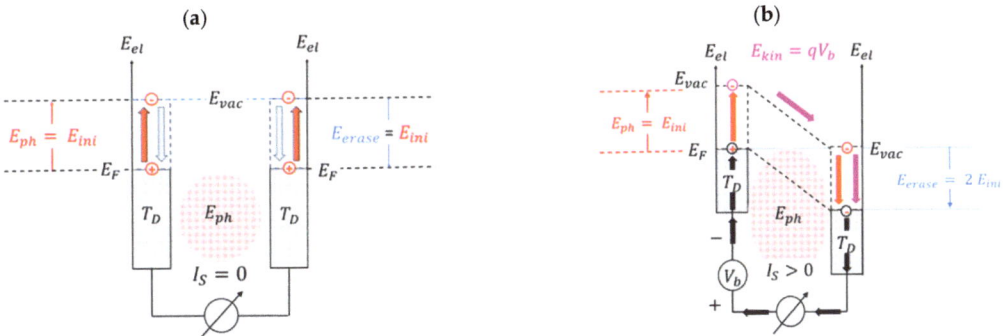

Figure 5. Pathways of photoelectrons in a band profile picture of a PID: (**a**) unbiased condition; (**b**) bias conditions optimally chosen to convert initiating photon energy into the kinetic energy of an emitted photoelectron (see Figure 6).

Turning to Figure 5a first, it can be seen that with the electron work function $q\phi_m$ of the metal electrodes matching the photon energy E_{ph} to be detected, a photon entering the detector can be absorbed at either of the two electrodes. Upon absorption in either of these electrodes, an electron may be raised from the Fermi energy E_F of the affected electrode up to the vacuum level E_{vac} at this same electrode. In such an event, the electron has gained potential energy amounting to $E_{pot} = E_{vac} - E_F = E_{ph}$. After having stayed at E_{vac} for a very short time, the excited electron returns to the Fermi level and deposits its extra energy inside the electrode in the form of a small quantity of heat. With the electrode temperature having been raised above the ambient temperature T_D, the excess heat will subsequently flow away, either by means of heat conduction or by thermal radiation, thus re-establishing T_D again.

Further, as no electrical potential had been applied across the electrode gap, no displacement current had been induced, and no externally observable signal had been generated.

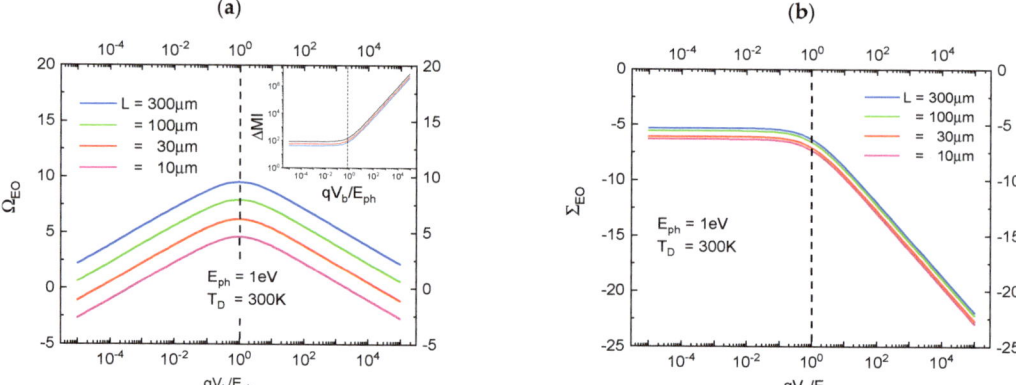

Figure 6. (a) Observability Ω_{EO} as a function of the normalized bias potential qV_b/E_{ph} with the device size L as a parameter. The different curves in the inset show the impact of temperature on entropy production; (b) statistical significance Σ_{EO} as a function of the normalized bias potential qV_b/E_{ph} and as evaluated for different device sizes L. For clarity of presentation, the curves in (b) had been slightly offset from each other.

This situation drastically changes as a potential difference is applied between both electrodes. Once an electron has been excited to the vacuum level of the cathode, the excited electron does no longer return to the cathode Fermi energy but, rather, gets attracted by the electric field that was built up inside the electrode gap. With this field being present, the excited electron gets attracted to the vacuum level of the anode. Once it arrives there, the electron has gained a kinetic energy $E_{kin} = qV_b$ equivalent to the bias potential difference that had been applied across the electrode gap as shown in Figure 5b. With a current now flowing through the electrode gap, current continuity will assure that an electron current will not only be flowing through the electrode gap but also through the entire external circuit. As the current in this external circuit experiences friction, the energy qV_b that is transported with this flow will finally be dissipated inside the external circuit and generate an entropy $S_{D1} = qV_b/T_D$ there. With the photoelectron having arrived at the vacuum level of the anode, the electron still has potential energy equivalent to the photon energy E_{ph}, as by assumption the electron work function $q\phi_m$ of both electrodes had satisfied the condition $q\phi_m = E_{ph}$. As in the case of Figure 5a, the collected electron will continue to fall onto the Fermi energy of the anode, thus producing another bit of entropy equivalent to $S_{D2} = E_{ph}/T_D$ there. Adding both entropic contributions and writing their sum in informational units [33,34], the result already reported in Equation 4 is retained. With MI_D again being a dimensionless number, a logarithmic quantity Ω_{EO} can be defined that represents the gain in observational value relative to the entropy cost that had been invested at the particular level of bias potential:

$$\Omega_{EO}(E_{ph}, T_D, L, V_b) = \frac{1}{ln(2)} ln\left\{\frac{1}{3}\left[\frac{k_B T_D}{h}\right]\left[\frac{\tau_t(L, V_b)}{\left(1 + \frac{E_{ph}}{qV_b}\right)}\right]\right\}. \quad (15)$$

In this latter equation

$$\tau_{t\_red}(L, V_b) = \left[\frac{\tau_t(L, V_b)}{\left(1 + \frac{E_{ph}}{qV_b}\right)}\right] \quad (16)$$

is the reduced transit time of the electron through the electrode gap, and $\tau_{PB}(T_D)$ the Planck–Boltzmann thermalization time [32,35]

$$\tau_{PB}(T_D) = \frac{h}{k_B T_D}. \qquad (17)$$

Similarly, a second logarithmic function can be defined, which measures the statistical significance of the generated EO relative to its entropic cost:

$$\Sigma_{EO}(E_{ph}, T_D, L, V_b) = \frac{1}{\ln(2)} \ln\left\{ \frac{SI_{EO}(E_{ph}, T_D, L, V_b)}{MI_D(E_{ph}, V_b, T_D)} \right\}. \qquad (18)$$

In Figure 6a,b, both FOMs are plotted as functions of the normalized bias potential qV_b/E_{ph}. Both figures show that an optimum compromise between high levels of macroscopic observability, statistical significance and minimum entropy cost can be obtained when the applied bias potential is chosen to match the energy of the travelling photon prior to its detection.

7. Time Evolution of Elementary Observations

Accepting the above result of $qV_b = E_{ph}$, we now turn to the time evolution of an EO, i.e., to the kind of journey an excited photoelectron takes as it is circled through a PID device. This kind of travel is visualized in Figure 7, again in the form of a semiconductor-like band profile and with the electron travel directions being indicated by bold, red arrows.

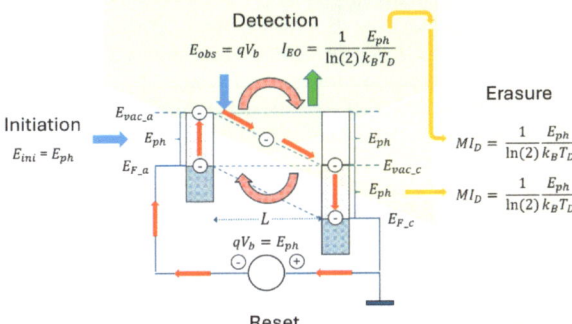

Figure 7. Time evolution of an EO as displayed in a band profile picture. Energy flows into the PID are denoted by blue arrows. Red arrows denote the cyclic progress of a photoelectron through the band profile during the four phases of initiation, detection, erasure, and reset. The green arrow indicates the outward flow of signal information when measured in conventional binary information units. Orange arrows denote outward entropy flows into the wider environments of the PID, causing erasure of the intermittently produced information. Reset to the pre-detection state is affected by the PID power supply, causing the electron to be lifted from the Fermi energy of the anode "upstairs" towards the Fermi energy of the cathode.

In the first two steps of initiation and detection, external energy had to be introduced into the device in the forms of photon energy and externally supplied electrical energy; these inputs are indicated by bold, blue, inward-pointing arrows. With the excited electron moving through the electrode gap and the entire external circuit, a macroscopically observable electrical signal is generated at the sensor output during the detection phase. As this flow carries the energy $E_{EO}(L, V_b) = qV_b$ (Equation (8)) that the electron had gained upon its travel through the electrode gap, a flow of potential information equivalent to

$$i_{pot}(E_{ph}, T_D) = \frac{1}{\ln(2)} \frac{E_{ph}}{k_B T_D} \qquad (19)$$

can be viewed as circling through the external circuit, and that is ready to transfer a maximum amount of information i_{pot} to a potential observer. This flow of thermodynamic information is indicated by a bold, green and outward-pointing arrow on the detection side. Whether used for observational purposes or not, this potential information will ultimately end up as an increased amount of missing microscopic information inside the infinitely large thermal reservoir in which the detector had been embedded, and will thereby be erased:

$$MI_{env}(E_{ph}, T_D) = \frac{1}{ln(2)} \frac{E_{ph}}{k_B T_D} \qquad (20)$$

This latter effect of energy dispersion and entropy generation inside the reservoir is indicated by a thinner, wavy arrow pointing towards the right-hand side, and denoted by "Erasure".

Up to this point, the photoelectron has progressed up to the vacuum level of the anode, where it still carries excess energy amounting to $E_{rest} = E_{ph}$. Upon returning to the anode Fermi energy, this energy will be dissipated inside the anode, thereby raising its temperature beyond the environmental temperature T_D, which will cause an outward energy flow into the reservoir, where a second piece of missing information will be created. In this way, the potential information of the electron, that had been sitting on the anode vacuum level, is finally erased. As in this downward transition no displacement current had been generated, the potential information in this latter case is directly erased, with no intermediate step of information gain.

As an overall result, one piece of potentially useful information, i_{pot}, had been generated during the detection phase, and two equally large pieces of missing information had been generated inside the thermal reservoir during the erasure phase. With the Landauer minimum amount of energy of $E_{La} = \ln(2) k_B T_D$ per bit, the total energy expense for erasing one potentially useful bit of potential information is affected by the transfer of two units of energy of size E_{La} to the thermal reservoir, thereby completely erasing the intermittently produced and potentially useful information that had been generated in the detection phase.

With the photoelectron having arrived at the anode Fermi energy, the photoelectron has lost all its acquired energy. In order to end up at a fully cyclic process of EO generation, information erasure, and reset, the photoelectron still needs to be "pumped up" by the external voltage source to arrive back at the cathode Fermi energy. In case this upward shift is not associated with any additional entropy production, the total energy expense in the initiation, detection, erasure and reset cycle still remains at two units of the Landauer minimum amount of energy, and larger amounts otherwise [31,32]:

$$E_{erasure} \geq 2E_{La} = 2\ln(2) k_B T_D. \qquad (21)$$

8. Summary and Conclusions

The results presented in this paper are a follow-up to our previous paper [10], in which we discussed historic experiments performed at the scale of atoms, nuclei and elementary particles, with an informational perspective in mind. There, it was shown that those experiments produced complex experimental answers that were composed out of streams of elementary observations (EOs) and which provide simple binary answers to the question of whether a matter–instrument interaction had taken place in the micro-domain of quantum phenomena or not.

In the present paper, we have concentrated on the specific case of single-photon detection, and we have made use of the easily overseeable physics of PID photon detectors to develop a more detailed picture of EOs, both as novel physical entities and as pieces of abstract information. In brief, our key results are the following:

- EOs appear in the form of spatio-temporal transients with spatial dimensions larger than the observability limits set by the Abbe diffraction limit [36,37] and the temporal limits imposed by the Planck–Boltzmann equilibration time constant [32,35].

- Within the finite lifetime of EOs, EOs proceed through the four phases of initiation, detection, erasure and reset.
- EOs are pieces of physical action, formed at the expense of generating entropy and endowed with the informational properties of macroscopic observability Ω_{EO} and statistical significance Σ_{EO}.
- Once detected, EOs appear as macroscopic images of the initiating photon–detector interactions that had occurred at the micro-scale of quantum phenomena. The observability gain obtained in the micro–macro conversion of detection events can be measured in units of the Planck constant h. In the limit of $\Sigma_{EO} = 1$, the generated EOs represent the binary answers concerning the initiating matter–instrument interactions that have already been discussed in our previous paper [10].
- The present investigations have further shown that EOs with optimum properties of Ω_{EO} and Σ_{EO} are produced when photon and detector share evenly in the energetic and entropic costs required for turning unobservable micro-events into macroscopically observable EOs. This picture of EO formation is in accordance with the view of a participatory process of information gain [9].
- Once the detection phase of EOs has ended, both the energy of the initiating photon and the energy supplied by detector-internal resources are dissipated and turned into missing information ΔMI_{env} concerning the unobservable microstate of the wider environment of the PID.
- After energy dissipation and spatial dispersion have taken place, the intermittently generated information has been removed from the PID device and has been distributed in the wider environment of the PID and, thus, been erased. In terms of energy consumption, this erasure has been performed at the expense of transferring two units of the Landauer minimum energy bound of $E_{La} = \ln(2)k_B T_D$ per bit from the PID and towards the thermal reservoir in which the PID had been embedded. In the final step of reset, additional energy needs to be supplied from external resources to reset the instrument for a new round of photon detection. In cases where this final step is associated with an additional entropy production, the total energy cost for erasure and reset exceeds the Landauer minimum energy cost of two units of E_{La}.

$$E_{erasure} \geq 2E_{La} = 2\ln(2)k_B T_D. \tag{22}$$

- Looking beyond the field of photon detection, we propose that the above considerations regarding photon detection may be generalized in diagrams, as displayed in Figure 8. In this figure, the cyclic process of EO initiation, detection, erasure and reset is displayed in two diagrams, with the first one emphasizing the energy inputs and outputs in the course of an EO cycle, and the second focusing on the timing issues in response to the energy inputs and outputs.

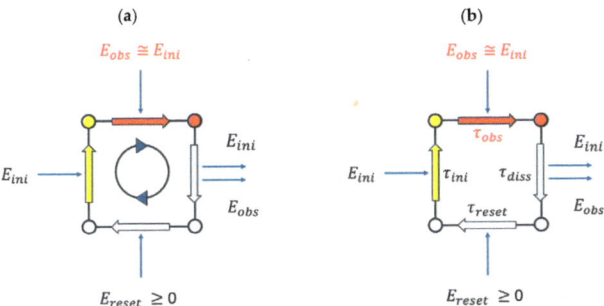

Figure 8. Generalized picture of EOs displayed as cyclic processes of initiation, detection, erasure and reset: (**a**) energy inputs and outputs in the different phases; (**b**) timing sequence of the four steps in response to energy inputs and outputs.

Assuming that $E_{ini} \gg k_B T$, the parameter Ω_{EO} is the dominant figure of merit (FOM), which characterizes the observational value of an EO. Following Equation (15), this can be approximated as

$$\Omega_{EO}(E_{ph}, T_D, L) \cong \frac{1}{ln(2)} ln\left[\frac{\tau_{obs}}{\tau_{PB}(T_D)}\right]. \tag{23}$$

High values of Ω_{EO} obviously rely on the efficiency of extending the observational time span τ_{obs} of EOs beyond the Planck–Boltzmann equilibration time of $\tau_{PB}(T_D) = h/k_B T$, which is a combination of the two natural constants of h and k_B.

Turning to the parameter τ_{obs}, the comparison in Table 1 shows that τ_{obs} is most likely that EO-related parameter that exhibits the largest range of variability. This latter comparison shows that EOs should not be confused with the reversible thermal fluctuations of size $E_{ini} \gg k_B T_D$ that can occur within a heat reservoir of temperature T_D, and whose lifetimes τ_H are dictated by the Heisenberg time–energy uncertainty relationship, and that, in the case of large energies E_{ini}, are much shorter than the Planck–Boltzmann thermalization time of $\tau_{PB}(T)$ [32,35]:

$$\tau_H = \left(\frac{h}{E_{ini}}\right) \cong 10^{-15} s \ll \tau_{PB}(T_D) = \left(\frac{h}{k_B T_D}\right) \cong 10^{-13} s. \tag{24}$$

Extremely long times of τ_{obs}, as for instance in photography, rather point to the fact that the art of creating particularly long-lived EOs relies on the art of using the energy inputs E_{ini} and E_{obs} to drive the detection instrument into a deeply trapped observational state with huge thermal release times. Principally, such a situation of deep trapping can be achieved by large energy barriers of E_{reset} and long associated waiting times τ_{reset}, which both inhibit a detector reset and which trap the detector in a long-lived observational state.

Table 1. Observational lifetimes and EO figures of merit in different experimental circumstances.

EO Origin	Thermal Fluctuation Time $\tau_{PB}(RT)$	Observational Lifetime τ_{obs}	FOM$_{EO}$
Photon detection (PID) This work	1.5×10^{-13} s	$\cong 10^{-9}$ s	$\cong 12$
α-particle detection(fluorescence) [12,13]	1.5×10^{-13} s	$\cong 10^{-8}$ s	$\cong 17$
Wilson cloud chamber [18]	1.5×10^{-13} s	$\cong 3$ s	$\cong 44$
Double-slit experiments (photography) [14]	1.5×10^{-13} s	$\cong 100\, a \cong 3 \times 10^9$ s	$\cong 74$

Overall, what we have achieved in the end is the introduction of a new vehicle of experimental information gain and information erasure that goes beyond the traditional Szilard cylinder and piston-type approaches [27], which had been borrowed from the age of steam engines. The proposed picture of EOs is much closer to actual experiments [10] that had been performed in unravelling processes inside the quantum domain. EOs, in addition, involve interactions of single particles with detection instruments and, thus, more directly conform to the requirements of minimum thermal engines.

Funding: This research received no external funding.

Institutional Review Board Statement: Not applicable.

Data Availability Statement: All relevant data are contained in the main text.

Conflicts of Interest: The author does not declare any conflict of interest.

Appendix A. Photon Propagation

In the main text, we have arrived at the conclusion that EOs are physical entities endowed with the property of physical action $W_{EO}(L, V_b) \gg h$. In order to support our interpretation that EOs can be regarded as hugely amplified images of the tiny packages of physical action h that had been carried with the photons prior to their detection, we show in this appendix that freely propagating electromagnetic waves can be viewed as repeatedly generating and erasing single quanta of physical action h.

With $\varphi(x, t)$ standing for one of the electrical or magnetic field components, plane electromagnetic waves can be described by

$$\varphi(x,t) = \sin\left\{2\pi\left[\frac{x}{\lambda} - \frac{t}{\tau}\right]\right\} \tag{A1}$$

where λ stands for the photon wavelength and τ for the photon vibrational period. Physically, such sine wave functions arise from the fact that within each half-wave period, time-varying electric fields generate time-varying magnetic fields, and vice-versa. As predicted by Maxwell's equations, such electromagnetic field disturbances move forward along the x-axis with a phase velocity of $c = \nu\lambda$ until the wave either becomes absorbed in a solid piece of matter or inside a detector, where the field disturbance can trigger a detection event.

Mathematically, sine waves, as described above, can be constructed by rotating a unit vector around the origin of a circle with a unit radius and with its terminal point moving along its periphery with angular speed $\omega = 2\pi/\tau$ and spanning an arc length ranging from 0 to 2π (Figure A1). The sine wave in Figure A1 can also be viewed in a somewhat different manner by replacing λ and $\tau = 1/\nu$ with their quantum analogs of $\lambda = h/p_{ph}$ and $\tau = h/E_{ph}$, where E_{ph} and p_{ph} stand for the photon energy and the photon momentum and h for Planck's constant. With these substitutions, Equation (A1) takes the form

$$\varphi(x,t) = \sin\left\{2\pi\left[\frac{p_{ph}x - E_{ph}t}{h}\right]\right\}. \tag{A2}$$

This latter form can be interpreted in the way that the repeated interconversion of electric into magnetic fields and vice versa gives rise to a repeated generation and erasure of quanta of physical action of size h, which causes these quanta to be shifted along the x-axis in discrete steps of length $\Delta x = \lambda/2$. In Figure A1, this kind of transport is indicated in the form of colored boxes. Specifically, these boxes indicate that within the first quarter of each full wave, a quantum of physical action is gradually generated, whereas it is gradually erased as it moves through the second quarter-wave period. Upon entering the second half-wave period, the package is re-generated and re-erased again, and then arrives with zero amplitude at the onset of the second full-wave period again. In essence, this view of wave propagation can also be viewed as an alternative form of particle motion in which the quanta of physical action are shifted in discrete steps whenever an interconversion of electrical into magnetic fields and vice versa occurs within the driving electromagnetic wave that propagates into the x-direction.

As such a kind of transport cannot be ascertained by direct observation, we call these discrete shifts of action quanta "propagational events". In the main text, we are concerned with the transformation of "propagational events" into macroscopically observable "photon detection EOs" with the help of a conceptual device. These latter considerations confirm the point of view that photon detection EOs are hugely amplified images of the initiating quanta of physical action of size h.

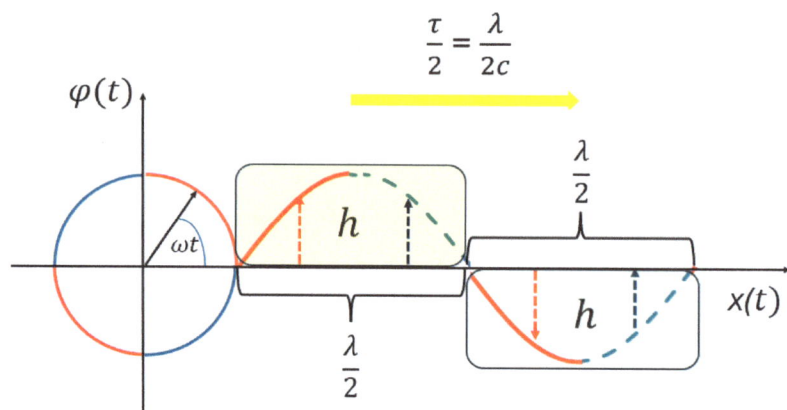

Figure A1. Propagation of an electromagnetic wave $\varphi(x,t)$ as visualized as a shift of packages of physical action of the size of a single Planck unit h.

References

1. Atomism—Wikipedia. Available online: https://en.wikipedia.org/wiki/Atomism_(social) (accessed on 12 May 2024).
2. Periodic Table—Wikipedia. Available online: https://en.wikipedia.org/wiki/Periodic_table (accessed on 12 May 2024).
3. Electron—Wikipedia. Available online: https://en.wikipedia.org/wiki/Electron (accessed on 12 May 2024).
4. Proton—Wikipedia. Available online: https://en.wikipedia.org/wiki/Proton (accessed on 12 May 2024).
5. Neutron—Wikipedia. Available online: https://en.wikipedia.org/wiki/Neutron (accessed on 12 May 2024).
6. Dosch, H.G. *Jenseits der Nanowelt—Leptonen, Quarks und Eichbosonen*; Springer Verlag: Berlin/Heidelberg, Germany, 2005; ISBN 978-3-540-22889-9. [CrossRef]
7. Dark Matter—Wikipedia. Available online: https://en.wikipedia.org/wiki/Dark_matter (accessed on 12 May 2024).
8. Dark Energy—Wikipedia. Available online: https://en.wikipedia.org/wiki/Dark_energy (accessed on 12 May 2024).
9. Wheeler, J.A. Information, physics, quantum: The search for links. In *Feynman and Computation*; CRC Press: Boca Raton, FL, USA.
10. Müller, J.G. Events as elements of physical observation: Experimental evidence. *Entropy* **2024**, *26*, 255. [CrossRef] [PubMed]
11. Geiger, H.; Marsden, E. On a Diffuse Reflection of the α-Particles. *Proc. R. Soc. Ser. A* **1909**, *82*, 495–500.
12. Rutherford, E. The Scattering of α and β Particles by Matter and the Structure of the Atom, Phil. Mag., Series 6. *Lond. Edinb. Dublin Philos. Mag. J. Sci.* **1911**, *21*, 669–688. [CrossRef]
13. Meschede, D. Youngs Interferenzexperiment mit Licht. In *Die Top Ten der Schönsten Physikalischen Experimente Fäßler*; Fäßler, A., Jönsson, C., Eds.; Rowohlt Verlag: Hamburg, Germany, 2005; pp. 94–105. ISBN 3-499-61628-9.
14. Jönsson, C. Electron Diffraction at Multiple Slits. *Am. J. Phys.* **1974**, *42*, 4–11. [CrossRef]
15. Carnal, O.; Mlynek, J. Young's double-slit experiment with atoms: A simple atom interferometer. *Phys. Rev. Lett.* **1991**, *66*, 2689–2692. [CrossRef] [PubMed]
16. Nairz, O.; Arndt, M.; Zeilinger, A. Quantum interference experiments with large molecules. *Am. J. Phys.* **2003**, *71*, 319–325. [CrossRef]
17. Wilson, C.T.R. On a Method of Making Visible the Paths of Ionising Particles through a Gas. *Proc. R. Soc. Lond. A Math. Phys. Eng. Sci.* **1911**, *85*, 578.
18. Glaser, D.A. Some Effects of Ionizing Radiation on the Formation of Bubbles in Liquids. *Phys. Rev.* **1952**, *87*, 665. [CrossRef]
19. Griffiths, L.; Symoms, C.R.; Zacharov, B. *Determination of Particle Momenta in Spark Chamber and Counter Experiments*; CERN-66-17; CERN Yellow Reports: Monographs; Corpus ID: 116490066; CERN: Geneva, Switzerland, 1966.
20. Shannon, C.E. A Mathematical Theory of Communication. *Bell Syst. Tech. J.* **1948**, *27*, 379–423+623–656. [CrossRef]
21. Young, J.F. Einführung in die Informationstheorie. R. Oldenbourg: München, Germany; Wien, Austria, 1975.
22. Kraus, G. Einführung in die Datenübertragung. R. Oldenbourg Verlag: München, Germany; Wien, Austria, 1978.
23. Lesurf, J.C.G. *Information and Measurement*; I.O.P. Publishing Ltd.: Bristol, UK; Philadelphia, PA, USA, 1995; ISBN 0 7503 0308 5.
24. Müller, J.G. Assigning meaning to physical observations. *Entropy* **2024**. to be published.
25. Müller, J.G. Photon detection as a process of information gain. *Entropy* **2020**, *22*, 392. [CrossRef] [PubMed]
26. Kingston, R.H. *Detection of Optical and Infrared Radiation*; Springer: Berlin/Heidelberg, Germany, 1978.
27. Szilard, L. Über die Entropieverminderung in einem thermodynamischen System bei Eingriffen intelligenter Wesen. *Z. Phys.* **1929**, *53*, 840–856. (In German) [CrossRef]
28. Landauer, R. Irreversibility and heat generation in the computing process. *IBM J. Res.* **1961**, *5*, 183–191. [CrossRef]
29. Landauer, R. Information is physical. *Phys. Today* **1991**, *44*, 23–29. [CrossRef]
30. Landauer, R. Minimal energy requirements in communication. *Science* **1996**, *272*, 1914–1918. [CrossRef] [PubMed]

31. Witkowski, C.; Brown, S.; Truong, K. On the Precise Link between Energy and Information. *Entropy* **2024**, *26*, 203. [CrossRef] [PubMed]
32. Bormashenko, E. Landauer Bound in the Context of Minimal Physical Principles: Meaning, Experimental Verification, Controversies and Perspectives. *Entropy* **2024**, *26*, 423. [CrossRef] [PubMed]
33. Ben-Naim, A. *A Farewell to Entropy: Statistical Thermodynamics Based on Information*; World Scientific: Singapore, 2008.
34. Müller, J.G. Information contained in molecular motion. *Entropy* **2019**, *21*, 1052. [CrossRef]
35. Proesmans, K.; Erich, J.; Bechhoefer, J. Optimal finite time bit erasure under full control. *Phys. Rev. E* **2020**, *102*, 032105. [CrossRef] [PubMed]
36. Hecht, E. Chapter 13 Modern Optics. In *Optics*, 4th ed.; Addison-Wesley: Boston, MA, USA, 2002; pp. 609–611.
37. Born, M.; Wolf, E. Chapter 8 Elements of the theory of diffraction. In *Principles of Optics*, 6th ed.; Pergamon Press: Oxford, UK, 1986; pp. 419–424.

Disclaimer/Publisher's Note: The statements, opinions and data contained in all publications are solely those of the individual author(s) and contributor(s) and not of MDPI and/or the editor(s). MDPI and/or the editor(s) disclaim responsibility for any injury to people or property resulting from any ideas, methods, instructions or products referred to in the content.

Article
Modified Landauer Principle According to Tsallis Entropy

Luis Herrera

Instituto Universitario de Física Fundamental y Matematicas, Universidad de Salamanca, 37007 Salamanca, Spain; lherrera@usal.es

Abstract: The Landauer principle establishes a lower bound in the amount of energy that should be dissipated in the erasure of one bit of information. The specific value of this dissipated energy is tightly related to the definition of entropy. In this article, we present a generalization of the Landauer principle based on the Tsallis entropy. Some consequences resulting from such a generalization are discussed. These consequences include the modification to the mass ascribed to one bit of information, the generalization of the Landauer principle to the case when the system is embedded in a gravitational field, and the number of bits radiated in the emission of gravitational waves.

Keywords: Landauer principle; information theory; general relativity; gravitational radiation

1. Introduction

The Landauer principle ref. [1], which is a cornerstone in the theory of information, states that the erasure of one bit of information stored in a system implies the dissipation of energy, whose value cannot be smaller than

$$\triangle E = kT \ln 2, \tag{1}$$

where k is the Boltzmann constant and T denotes the temperature of the environment. The important point to keep in mind here is that even though the value of dissipated energy depends on the erasure procedure, it cannot be lower that Equation (1).

At this point, some remarks are needed, as follows:

- It has been argued in the past (see for example ref. [2]) that the main idea stated in the Landauer principle appears already in some Brillouin works ref. [3]. We shall skip this controversy and shall adopt the notation used by most of researchers, and we shall refer to it as the Landauer principle.
- In spite of some arguments put forward in the past questioning the relevance of the Landauer principle (see ref. [4] and references therein), the important point to retain here is that on the one hand it allows an "informational" reformulation of thermodynamics, as stressed in ref. [4], and on the other hand brings out a link between information theory and different branches of science refs. [5–7]. This allows us to approach some physical problems from the point of view of information theory.
- The expression Equation (1) for the dissipated energy heavily relies on the concept of entropy. More specifically, such an expression was found using the Gibbs entropy. Therefore, we should expect different expressions for alternative definitions of entropy.

2. Landauer Principle and Definition of Entropy

In order to exhibit the link between the Landauer principle and the definition of entropy, let us present a very simple proof of this principle.

Thus, let us consider a physical system which may be in two possible states, e.g., a particle whose spin may point upward or downward. The particle is inside a black box, and for an observer outside the box, the particle may be in either state with the same probability. Then, using the Gibbs definition of entropy given by

$$S = -k \sum_{i=1}^{N} p_i \ln p_i, \qquad (2)$$

where N denotes the total number of accessible states and p_i is the probability of each state (i.e., $\sum_{i=1}^{N} p_i = 1$), we find that the Gibbs entropy of our system is

$$S = k \ln 2. \qquad (3)$$

Let us now apply a magnetic field to our system as a consequence of which the spin is set to point to a determined direction (upward or downward). Obviously after such operation the entropy of the system becomes equal to zero, implying that there has been a decreasing of entropy equal to

$$\Delta S = k \ln 2, \qquad (4)$$

which according to the second law of thermodynamics should be accompanied by an increasing of, at least, the same amount, producing a dissipation of energy equals to

$$\Delta E = kT \ln 2, \qquad (5)$$

where T is the temperature of the environment.

Now, applying a magnetic field to our system, we set the direction of the spin in a predetermined direction, thereby erasing the information about where the spin was pointed to before switching on the magnetic field ref. [8]. Since this information is contained in the answer to the single question, "where is the spin pointing to?", the amount of this information is one bit.

Thus, we have proved that erasing one bit of information implies that an amount of energy not smaller than Equation (5) must be dissipated, which is just the statement of the Landauer principle. The purpose of the above exercise being to bring out the relationship between the minimal amount of dissipated energy with the definition of entropy Equation (2).

Arriving at this point the obvious question arises: what could be the corresponding minimal amount of dissipated energy in the process of erasure of one bit of information if we resort to a definition of entropy different from Equation (2)?

We endeavor in this work to answer to the above question in the case when we use the Tsallis entropy (instead of using Equation (2)).

However, it would be legitimate to ask why, in particular, we have chosen Tsallis entropy, instead of any other definition of entropy? The answer to this question is based on the great deal of attention received by Tsallis proposal and its applications (see for example refs. [9–13] and references therein). Nevertheless, it goes without saying, that resorting to any other alternative definition of entropy would also deserve to be considered.

3. Tsallis Entropy and Modified Landauer Principle

Some years ago Tsallis proposed a generalization of Gibbs definition of entropy, which reads ref. [14]

$$S = k \frac{1 - \sum_{i=1}^{N} p_i^q}{q - 1}, \qquad (6)$$

where q is a real number.

It is a simple matter to check that

$$\lim_{q \to 1} k \frac{1 - \sum_{i=1}^{N} p_i^q}{q - 1} = -k \sum_{i=1}^{N} p_i \ln p_i. \qquad (7)$$

Thus, deviations from the Gibbs entropy correspond to values of q different from 1.

Since its publication the Tsallis proposal has received a great deal of attention, and therefore we find it useful to evaluate its impact in the Landauer principle.

The Lower Bound of the Dissipated Energy Ensuing the Erasure of One Bit of Information According to the Tsallis Entropy

In order to calculate the minimal amount of energy that must be dissipated when erasing on bit of information according to Tsallis entropy, let us retrace the steps of the exercise proposed in the previous section, leading to Equations (4) and (5).

Thus, let us consider a system with two possible accessible states ($N = 2$) the probability of each of which is $1/2$. Then, it follows from Equation (6) that the Tsallis entropy of our system is given by

$$S = \frac{k}{q-1}\left[1 - 2^{(1-q)}\right]. \tag{8}$$

We now proceed to apply a magnetic field to our system, after which the system is in a single state with probability 1, implying the erasure of one bit of information, and the vanishing of the entropy. Thus, the decreasing of entropy is given by

$$\Delta S = \frac{k}{q-1}\left[1 - 2^{(1-q)}\right], \tag{9}$$

producing an amount of dissipated energy equal to

$$\Delta E \equiv T\Delta S = \frac{kT}{q-1}\left[1 - 2^{(1-q)}\right]. \tag{10}$$

As depicted in Figure 1, the above expression decreases monotonically with q for any $q > 0$. It is a simple matter to check that in the limit $q \to 1$, expressions Equations (9) and (10) become Equations (4) and (5), respectively.

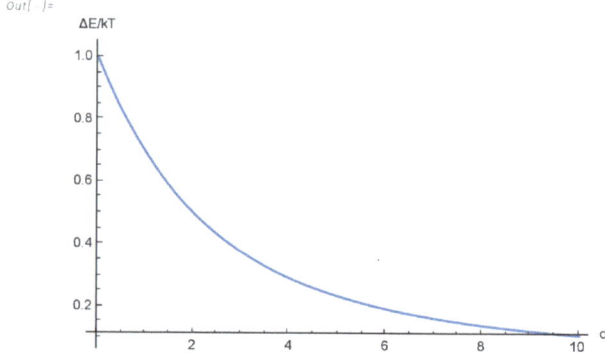

Figure 1. $\Delta E/kT$ as function of q for the Tsallis entropy.

Thus, using the Tsallis entropy we see that the minimal energy dissipated in the erasure of one bit of information depends on the parameter q as expressed by (10).

We shall next see how this change affects some consequences derived from the Landauer principle.

4. The Mass of a Bit of Information

As we have seen above, the Landauer principle based on the Gibbs definition of entropy, asserts that a minimal amount of energy given by Equation (1), should be dissipated when erasing one bit of information. This fact implies the association of such an amount of energy with one bit of information. From the previous comment it follows at once, recalling the well-known fact that a mass E/c^2 has to be ascribed to energy E, and that a mass should be ascribed to a bit of information ref. [15] (see also refs. [4,16]), specifically

$$\triangle M = \frac{kT}{c^2} \ln 2, \tag{11}$$

where c denotes the speed of light.

Following the same reasoning leading to Equation (11), but using Equation (10) instead of Equation (1) we obtain for the mass associated with a bit of in formation

$$\Delta M = \frac{kT}{c^2(q-1)} \left[1 - 2^{(1-q)}\right], \tag{12}$$

which of course becomes Equation (11) in the limit $q \to 1$.

From the above it follows that for one bit of information, at room temperature, the minimal dissipated energy is

$$\triangle E \approx \frac{4.04}{q-1} \left[1 - 2^{(1-q)}\right] \times 10^{-14} erg \tag{13}$$

and the associated mass is:

$$\triangle M \approx \frac{4.33}{(q-1)} \left[1 - 2^{(1-q)}\right] \times 10^{-35} g. \tag{14}$$

In the limit $q \to 1$, the above expressions yield $2.8 \times 10^{-14} erg$ and $3 \times 10^{-35} g$, respectively.

Also it is worth noticing that according to the uncertainty principle, there is a minimal time interval required to measure a given amount of energy. In our case this implies that for the energy Equation (13) the minimal time interval is

$$\triangle t \approx \frac{\hbar}{\triangle E} \approx \frac{2.56(q-1)}{1 - 2^{1-q}} \times 10^{-14} s, \tag{15}$$

where $\hbar$ is the Planck constant divided by 2π, thereby imposing a limit in the speed of information processing which in the case $q \approx 1$ is $\approx 10^5$ GHz.

We shall next consider the case, when the system is placed in a gravitational field.

5. Landauer Principle in a Gravitational Field

If the system is located in a (weak) static gravitational field, then the gravitational potential affects the Landauer principle. This important result was obtained by Daffertshoffer and Plastino ref. [17]. More specifically, these authors show that in this case (assuming for the entropy the Gibbs definition Equation (2)) the minimal amount of energy dissipated in the erasure of one bit of information is given by

$$\triangle E = kT(1 + \frac{\phi}{c^2}) \ln 2. \tag{16}$$

where ϕ denotes the (negative) gravitational potential, and $T(1 + \frac{\phi}{c^2})$ (the Tolman's temperature) is the quantity which is constant in thermodynamic equilibrium ref. [18].

Now, Equation (16) was obtained in the context of Newtonian gravity (weak field approximation). The extension of the above result to the general relativistic case is simple to achieve if we recall that in such a case Tolman's temperature becomes $T\sqrt{g_{tt}}$, where g_{tt} denotes the tt component of the metric tensor (the coefficient of dt^2 in the expression for the line element). Therefore, Equation (16) generalizes to

$$\triangle E = kT\sqrt{g_{tt}} \ln 2, \tag{17}$$

producing for the mass ascribed to a bit of information

$$\triangle M = \frac{kT}{c^2}\sqrt{g_{tt}}\ln 2. \tag{18}$$

So, the question is: how does the Landauer principle change in the presence of a gravitational field if we use the Tsallis entropy Equation (6) instead of Equation (2)?

Retracing the same steps followed in ref. [17], we obtain for the energy dissipated in the erasure of one bit of information and for the corresponding mass

$$\Delta E = \frac{kT}{q-1}\left[1 - 2^{(1-q)}\right]\left(1 + \frac{\phi}{c^2}\right), \tag{19}$$

and

$$\Delta M = \frac{kT}{c^2(q-1)}\left[1 - 2^{(1-q)}\right]\left(1 + \frac{\phi}{c^2}\right). \tag{20}$$

The generalization of the above expressions to the general relativistic case may be easily obtained by replacing $(1 + \frac{\phi}{c^2})$ with $\sqrt{g_{tt}}$.

After the formation of a black hole ($g_{tt} = 0$), it follows from Equation (17) or Equation (19) that the energy dissipated during the erasure of one bit of information vanishes (assuming that the proper temperature is not singular), leading to a vanishing mass for a bit of information.

Now, the change of information without dissipation implies that all bits are already in one state only ref. [8]. This result agrees with the well-known assumption that the quantum radiation emitted by the black hole is nearly thermal (i.e., it conveys no information) refs. [19,20], thereby suggesting the "bleaching" of information at the horizon.

Thus, the well-known fact that after the formation of the horizon ($g_{tt} = 0$), no further information leaves the system, follows in a simple way from information theory.

If the gravitational field does not correspond to a black hole ($g_{tt} \neq 0$), then we see a decreasing of the corresponding mass of a bit of information. Such a decreasing value depending on the parameter q occurs if we assume the Tsallis definition of entropy. At any rate such a decreasing value is very small for a weak gravitational field ($\frac{\phi}{c^2} \approx 10^{-9}$ for the case of the earth).

6. Gravitational Radiation, Radiated Information, and the Landauer Principle

Finally, we would like to consider the relationship between the energy and the information conveyed by gravitational radiation and the definition of entropy.

As we know from field theory (at classical level and for any spin), information about changes in the structure and/or state of motion of the source is propagated by radiation. Once the observers have received this information, the information encrypted in the "old" multipole structure is erased. In other words, the process of radiation implies not only propagation of information but also erasure of information, from which it is obvious that the Landauer principle should be implicated in the whole process.

The above comments imply that according to the Landauer principle, gravitational radiation entails a dissipation of energy. This conclusion was proved to be true in ref. [21] and is a consequence of the fact that gravitational radiation is an irreversible process, and this irreversibility should show up in the equation of state of the source.

This "informational" approach to radiation is particularly manifest in the Bondi formalism refs. [22,23].

In this approach there is a function (called "news function" by Bondi), which entails all the information required to forecast the evolution of the system (besides the initial data) and is identified with gravitational radiation itself. Such an identification is possible because the news function describe all changes in the field produced by changes in the source. Moreover, the vanishing of the news function is the necessary and sufficient condition for the total energy of the system to be constant. This scheme applies to Maxwell systems in Minkowski spacetime ref. [24] as well as to Einstein–Maxwell systems ref. [25].

Once we admit that a bit of radiated information implies a bit of erased information at the radiating system, which in turn leads to a decreasing of its total mass (energy), then it is legitimate to ask: what part of the total radiated energy (mass) corresponds to the radiated information?

We shall answer to this question, adopting the Tsallis definition of entropy.

In ref. [26] an answer was provided to the above question, based in the Landauer principle expressed through the Gibbs entropy Equation (1).

Thus, one obtains for the total dissipated energy (see ref. [26] for details)

$$E_{rad}^{(L)} = \int_{r_\Sigma}^{\infty} \int_0^{\pi} \int_0^{2\pi} \sqrt{|g|} \mu_{rad}^{(L)} dr d\theta d\phi, \qquad (21)$$

where $|g|$ is the absolute value of the determinant of the metric tensor, $r = r_\Sigma$ is the equation of the boundary surface of the source, and $\mu^{(L)}$ is the energy–density of the radiation associated exclusively with the dissipative processes related to the emission of gravitational radiation.

The above expression may be transformed further using a central result by Bondi Ref. [22], relating the rate at which the energy is being radiated, with the news function, which reads:

$$\frac{dm(u)}{du} = -\frac{1}{2} \int_0^{\pi} \frac{(dc(u,\theta))^2}{du} \sin\theta d\theta, \qquad (22)$$

where $\frac{dc(u,\theta)}{du}$ is the news function, u is the timelike coordinate in the Bondi frame, $c(u,\theta)$ is a function entering into the power series expressions of the Bondi metric, and $m(u)$ denotes the energy of the system (the Bondi mass).

Therefore, the total radiated energy in the timelike interval $u_1 \leq u \leq u_2$ is given by

$$E_{rad}^{(L)} = \int_{u_1}^{u_2} \left[\frac{1}{2} \int_0^{\pi} \frac{(dc(u,\theta))^2}{du} \sin\theta d\theta\right] du, \qquad (23)$$

(please notice a misprint in the sign of Equations (31) and (32) in ref. [26]).

On the other hand, according to the Landauer principle Equation (19), we obtain for the total number N of bits erased (radiated) in the process of the emission of gravitational radiation

$$N = \frac{E_{rad}^{(L)}}{kT\sqrt{|g_{tt}|}\ln 2}, \qquad (24)$$

Feeding back Equation (23) into Equation (24) we find an explicit relationship linking the news function with the total number of bits radiated in the assumed time interval,

$$N = \frac{\int_{u_1}^{u_2} \left[\frac{1}{2} \int_0^{\pi} \frac{(dc(u,\theta))^2}{du} \sin\theta d\theta\right] du}{kT\sqrt{|g_{tt}|}\ln 2} = \frac{\left[\int_{r_\Sigma}^{\infty} \int_0^{\pi} \int_0^{2\pi} \sqrt{|g|} \mu_{rad}^{(L)} dr d\theta d\phi\right]}{kT\sqrt{|g_{tt}|}\ln 2}, \qquad (25)$$

which measure the total erased information during the radiation process.

The expressions above have been obtained by resorting to the Landauer principle based on the Gibbs entropy; therefore, in the context of this work it is legitimate to ask how do the expressions above change if we use the Landauer principle based in the Tsallis entropy Equation (6). Using Equation (19) and retracing the same steps leading to Equation (25), we obtain

$$N = \frac{(q-1)\int_{u_1}^{u_2} \left[\frac{1}{2} \int_0^{\pi} \frac{(dc(u,\theta))^2}{du} \sin\theta d\theta\right] du}{kT\sqrt{|g_{tt}|}[1 - 2^{(1-q)}]} = \frac{\left[\int_{r_\Sigma}^{\infty} \int_0^{\pi} \int_0^{2\pi} \sqrt{|g|} \mu_{rad}^{(L)} dr d\theta d\phi\right](q-1)}{kT\sqrt{|g_{tt}|}[1 - 2^{(1-q)}]}, \qquad (26)$$

bringing out the role played by the parameter q in the number of bits radiated in a given burst of gravitational radiation.

It would be most desirable to relate the above expressions with the data obtained from the LISA program (see ref. [27] and references therein). Unfortunately, at this point we do not see how to exactly establish such a link.

7. Discussion

Motivated by the fact that the specific value of the lower bound of energy—which according Landauer principle should be dissipated in the erasure of one bit of information—depends on the definition of entropy, we have addressed the question about the value of this bound for the Tsallis entropy, obtaining the expression Equation (10).

Once this value has been established, we have considered how deviations of this value, with respect to the one obtained from the Gibbs entropy, affects different scenarios where the Landauer principle is involved. In particular we have brought out how different values of q modify the values of different observational variables.

The first important result resides in the expression for the lower bound of energy dissipated after the erasure of one bit of information for the Tsallis entropy, which is now given by Equation (10). Figure 1 shows that for any value of temperature, such dissipated energy is a monotonically decreasing function of q, which is larger than the corresponding value for the Gibbs entropy for any value of q in the interval $[0,1]$ and smaller in the interval $[1,\infty]$.

Next, we have considered the mass associated with a bit of information, which for the Tsallis entropy is given by Equation (14) in contrast with expression Equation (11) obtained from the Gibbs entropy. This result also affects the limitation on the speed of processing, as expressed by Equation (15).

The generalization of the Landauer principle for systems embedded in a gravitational field has been achieved following the work by Daffertshoffer and Plastino ref. [17]. The corresponding expression for the energy dissipated in the erasure of one bit of information is now given by Equation (19), leading to the expression Equation (20). Once again we see how q affects the values of the two above mentioned variables.

Finally, we addressed the question about the number of bits radiated (erased) in the emission of gravitational radiation. By using the Tsallis entropy, we found that such a number is given by Equation (26) instead of the expression Equation (25) corresponding to the Gibbs entropy.

In all these examples the role of the parameter q is clearly displayed. This fact brings us back to the leitmotiv of our work.

Indeed, it is to be expected that for any physical scenario, the experimental data could differentiate between what is the correct definition of entropy that should be adopted. In the case of Tsallis entropy, this implies a specific value of q. Since the scenarios analyzed above imply observed quantities, we harbor the hope that some of the expressions found here could help in a process of verification of the appropriate definition of entropy. Moreover, we believe that the extension of the program followed in this work to other definitions of entropy is an issue that deserves to be considered in the future.

Funding: This work was partially supported by the Spanish Ministerio de Ciencia, Innovación, under Research Project No. PID2021-122938NB-I00.

Data Availability Statement: Data are contained within the article.

Conflicts of Interest: The author declares no conflicts of interest. The funders had no role in the design of the study; in the collection, analyses, or interpretation of data; in the writing of the manuscript; or in the decision to publish the results.

References

1. Landauer, R. Dissipation and heat generation in the computing process. *IBM J. Res. Dev.* **1961**, *5*, 183. [CrossRef]
2. Kish, L.B.; Granqvist, C.G. Electrical Maxwell demon and Szilard engine utilizing Johnson noise, measurement, logic and control. *PLoS ONE* **2012**, *7*, e46800. [CrossRef] [PubMed]
3. Brillouin, L. The negentropic principle of information. *J. Appl. Phys.* **1953**, *24*, 1152–1163. [CrossRef]
4. Bormashenko, E. The Landauer Principle: Re–Formulation of the Second Thermodynamics Law or a Step to Great Unification. *Entropy* **2019**, *21*, 918. [CrossRef]
5. Plenio, M.B.; Vitelli, V. The physics of forgetting: Landauer's erasure principle and information theory. *Contemp. Phys.* **2001**, *42*, 25–60. [CrossRef]
6. Bais, F.A.; Farmer, J.D. The physics of information. *arXiv* **2007**, arXiv:0708.2837v2.
7. Bormashenko, E. Generalization of the Landauer Principle for Computing Devices Based on Many-Valued Logic. *Entropy* **2019**, *21*, 1150. [CrossRef]
8. Piechocinska, B. Information erasure. *Phys. Rev. A* **2000**, *61*, 062314-9. [CrossRef]
9. Teimoori, Z.; Rezazadeh, K.; Rostami, A. Inflation based on the Tsallis entropy. *Eur. Phys. J. C* **2024**, *84*, 80. [CrossRef]
10. EPiceno-Martínez, A.E.; Rosales-Zárate, L.E. A generalized entropic measure of steering using Tsallis entropies and the relationship with existent steering criteria. *J. Opt.* **2024**, *26*, 105702. [CrossRef]
11. Ebrahimi, E.; Sheykhi, A. Ghost dark energy in Tsallis and Barrow cosmology. *Phys. Dark Univ.* **2024**, *45*, 101518. [CrossRef]
12. Anastasiadis, A. Special issue: Tsallis entropy. *Entropy* **2012**, *14*, 174–176. [CrossRef]
13. Furuichi, A review of the mathematical properties of the Tsallis entropies. *AIP Conf. Proc.* **2008**, *1045*, 11–20.
14. Tsallis, C. Possible generalization of Boltzmann-Gibbs entropy. *J. Stat. Phys.* **1988**, *52*, 479–487. [CrossRef]
15. Herreral, L. The mass of a bit of information and the Brillouin's principle. *Fluc. Noise Lett.* **2014**, *13*, 1450002. [CrossRef]
16. Vopson, M.M. The mass–energy–information equivalence principle. *AIP Adv.* **2019**, *9*, 095206. [CrossRef]
17. Daffertshoffer, A.; Plastino, A.R. Forgetting and gravitation: From Landauer's principle to Tolman temperature. *Phys. Lett. A* **2007**, *362*, 243–245. [CrossRef]
18. Tolman, R. On the weight of heat and thermal equilibrium in general relativity, *Phys. Rev.* **1930**, *35*, 904–924..
19. Hawking, S.W. Particle creation by black holes. *Commun. Math. Phys.* **1975**, *43*, 199. [CrossRef]
20. Hawking, S.W. Breakdown of predictability in gravitational collapse. *Phys. Rev. D* **1976**, *14*, 2460. [CrossRef]
21. Herrera, L.; Di Prisco, A.; Ospino, J. Irreversibility and gravitational radiation: A proof of Bondi's conjecture. *Phys. Rev. D* **2024**, *109*, 024005. [CrossRef]
22. Bondi, H.; van der Burg, M.G.J.; Metzner, A.W.K. Gravitational waves in general relativity VII. Waves from axi–symmetric isolated systems. *Proc. Roy.Soc. A* **1962**, *269*, 21–52.
23. Sachs, R. Gravitational waves in general relativity VIII. Waves in asymptotically flat space–time. *Proc. R. Soc. A* **1962**, *270*, 103–126.
24. Janis, A.I.; Newman, E.T. Structure of Gravitational Sources. *J. Math. Phys.* **1965**, *6*, 902. [CrossRef]
25. van der Burg, M.G.J. Gravitational Waves in General Relativity X. Asymptotic Expansions for the Einstein-Maxwell Field. *Proc. R. Soc. A* **1969**, *310*, 221.
26. Herrera, L. Landauer principle and general relativity. *Entropy* **2020**, *22*, 340. [CrossRef]
27. Abac, A.G.; Abbott, R.; Abe, H.; Acernese, F.; Ackley, K.; Adamcewicz, C.; Adhicary, S.; Adhikari, N.; Adhikari, R.X.; Adkins, V.K.; et al. Search for Eccentric Black Hole Coalescences during the Third Observing Run of LIGO and Virgo. *Astrophys. J.* **2024**, *973*, 132.

Disclaimer/Publisher's Note: The statements, opinions and data contained in all publications are solely those of the individual author(s) and contributor(s) and not of MDPI and/or the editor(s). MDPI and/or the editor(s) disclaim responsibility for any injury to people or property resulting from any ideas, methods, instructions or products referred to in the content.

Article

Evidence for Dark Energy Driven by Star Formation: Information Dark Energy?

Michael Paul Gough

School of Engineering and Informatics, University of Sussex, Brighton BN1 9QT, UK; m.p.gough@sussex.ac.uk

Abstract: Evidence is presented for dark energy resulting directly from star formation. A survey of stellar mass density measurements, SMD(a), as a function of universe scale size a, was found to be described by a simple CPL $w_0 - w_a$ parameterisation that was in good agreement with the dark energy results of *Planck* 2018, Pantheon+ 2022, the Dark Energy Survey 2024, and the Dark Energy Spectroscopic Instrument 2024. The best-fit CPL values found were $w_0 = -0.90$ and $w_a = -1.49$ for SMD(a), and $w_0 = -0.94$ and $w_a = -0.76$ for SMD(a)$^{0.5}$, corresponding with, respectively, good and very good agreement with all dark energy results. The preference for SMD(a)$^{0.5}$ suggests that it is the temperature of astrophysical objects that determines the dark energy density. The equivalent energy of the information/entropy of gas and plasma heated by star and structure formations is proportional to temperature, and is then a possible candidate for such a dark energy source. Information dark energy is also capable of resolving many of the problems and tensions of ΛCDM, including the cosmological constant problem, the cosmological coincidence problem, and the H_0 and σ_8 tensions, and may account for some effects previously attributed to dark matter.

Keywords: Landauer's principle; dark energy; dark energy experiments

1. Introduction

The ΛCDM model has been very successful despite our inability to account for either the cosmological constant, Λ, or cold dark matter, CDM. It is well known that the natural value of Λ is a factor of $\sim 10^{120}$ different from the observed value. Also, there has not been a single confirmed detection of a CDM particle of any type, including WIMP, axion, etc. In addition, when using ΛCDM to extrapolate from early universe measurements to the late universe, there appears to be a significant difference, or tension, with the Hubble constant, H_o, and with the σ_8 matter fluctuation parameter measured today. Therefore, despite the success of ΛCDM, we are encouraged to also consider alternative explanations. Here, we consider the role of information energy.

Information must play a significant physical role in the universe. Rolf Landauer [1,2] showed that "*Information is Physical*", as each bit of information in a system at temperature T has an energy equivalence of $k_B T \ln(2)$. Laboratory experiments have proven the Landauer information energy equivalence [3–6]. John Wheeler [7] even considered information to be more fundamental than matter, with all things physical being information-theoretic in origin, a view encapsulated by his famous slogan "*It from Bit*". In the same vein, Anton Zeilinger [8] proposed a "*Foundational Principle*" whereby the attributes of all particles at their most fundamental level correspond with elemental systems, each with just one classical bit or quantum qubit of information.

A strong similarity was found [9] between information energy and a cosmological constant. Consider a Zeilinger elemental bit of a particle attribute in a simple universe, without star formation. The Landauer equivalent energy of such a bit has been shown to be defined exactly the same as, and have the same value as, the characteristic energy of a cosmological constant [9,10].

These ideas of information have encouraged research [11–15] into the possible role information energy may play as a source of dark energy. Such a source would be governed by the product of the source bit number total, N [16,17], with a typical source temperature, T. Previously, the time history of alternative dark energy contributions was compared with the generally assumed cosmological constant Λ. By definition, Λ has a constant energy density, or a total energy proportional to a^3, where a is the scale size of the universe, given by $a = 1/(1+z)$; z is redshift; and $a = 1$ today. A time history of information energy was obtained by combining the stellar mass density history, SMD(a), for T, with the holographic principle [18–20] for N. During late-universe times, $z < 1.35$; the NT product was found to also vary as a^3 with a near-constant information energy density, emulating a cosmological constant. During earlier times, $z > 1.35$; the steeper gradient would provide a means by which the information dark energy could be differentiated from a cosmological constant and effectively falsified [15].

However, the universe information content is well below the holographic bound (~10^{124} bits) and, so far, the holographic principle has only been verified to apply to black holes at that bound. The approach taken in the present work was to show that information energy could account for dark energy history based solely on the measured SMD(a), without invoking the holographic principle. Compared with the most recent work [15], the approach here is simpler and more natural. Moreover, the predicted time history of this information dark energy is provided in the same form as the results from dark energy measurements, enabling a direct comparison between theory and experiments.

2. Information Dark Energy (IDE)

The equation of state parameter, w, of dark energy sets the time variation in the dark energy density as being proportional to $a^{-3(1+w)}$. While baryon and dark matter energy densities vary as a^{-3} and $w = 0$, the energy density of a cosmological constant is, by definition, constant, unchanging as a^0 and $w = -1$. In contrast, a dynamic form of dark energy varies at different rates at different times. In order to take any such time variation into account, most dark energy studies have adopted the CPL [21] parameters w_0 and w_a for a variable equation of state parameter, $w(a) = w_0 + (1-a)\,w_a$. This provides $w(a)$ with a smooth variation from the very early value of $w_0 + w_a$ to the present value of w_0. While there is no reason to expect that any source of dark energy with a time varying $w(a)$ can be fully described by CPL parameters, it does have the advantage of being simple and, for that reason, it is widely applied to studies of dark energy. CPL provides a common testing ground between experiments and theory. Dark energy measurements were originally expected to strengthen the cosmological constant hypothesis by converging on the values of $w_0 = -1$ and $w_a = 0$, but recent dark energy measurements [22–24] clearly tend towards a dynamic dark energy description, with $w_0 > -1$ and $w_a < 0$.

As the main source of information dark energy, IDE(a) is the information energy of hot gases and plasma heated by star and general structure formations [15], we must consider the stellar mass density, SMD(a), as a function of universe scale size, a. Figure 1 provides a survey of SMD(a) measurements in units of solar masses per cubic co-moving megaparsec. A total of 121 SMD(a) measurements from 27 published sources [25–51] (some of which were covered in a review [52]) are plotted in Figure 1 on a logarithmic scale of stellar mass density against the logarithm of universe scale size, a. Note that only values of $a > 0.2$ are used in the analysis below. This is because values of a < 0.2 would correspond to times when the information energy density was so much weaker, <<1%, of the matter energy density (varying as a^{-3}), and thus could not affect universe expansion measurements. Dark energy is only evident from measurements of the expansion rate history.

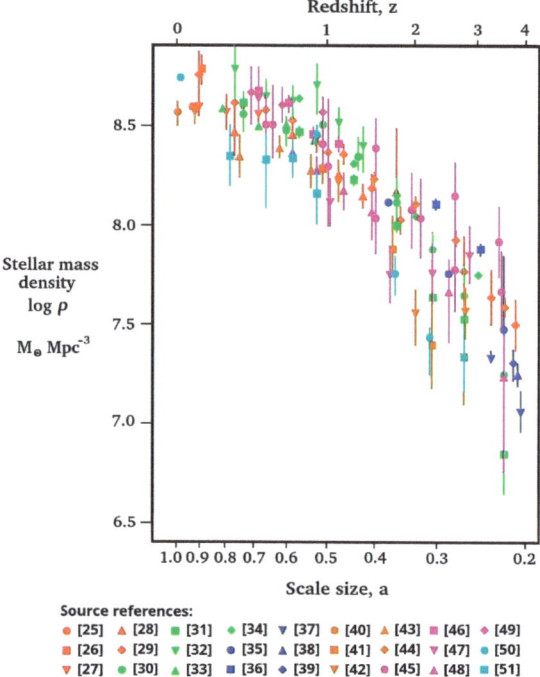

Figure 1. Survey of 121 measurements of stellar mass density measurements. Data sources: [25–51].

As SMD(a) is a universe-wide average mass density and IDE(a) is a universe-wide average information energy density—both effectively energy densities—we expect IDE(a) to vary at some power, p, of proportionality as SMD(a)^p. In this way, we can account for time variations in the NT product (without recourse to employing the holographic principle, as it was previously).

The Friedmann equation [53] describes the Hubble parameter $H(a)$ in terms of the Hubble constant, H_0, and dimensionless density parameters, Ω, expressed as a fraction of today's total energy density. We can assume that the curvature term is zero and that the radiation term has been negligible for some time. The ΛCDM model is then given by Equation (1). The equivalent IDE model is then described by Equation (2), where the present fractional energy density contributions are Ω_{tot} from all matter (baryons + dark matter); Ω_Λ is the cosmological constant and Ω_{IDE} is information dark energy (IDE).

$$\text{ΛCDM:} \quad (H(a)/H_0)^2 = \Omega_{\text{tot}}\, a^{-3} + \Omega_\Lambda \quad (1)$$

$$\text{IDE:} \quad (H(a)/H_0)^2 = \Omega_{\text{tot}}\, a^{-3} + \Omega_{\text{IDE}}\, (\text{SMD}(a)/\text{SMD}(1.0))^p \quad (2)$$

Note that the energy density terms Ω_{tot} and Ω_{IDE} are energy density fractions, assuming the mc^2 energy equivalence of mass, and the Landauer, k$_B$ T ln(2), energy equivalence of information. No matter needs to be destroyed, nor information erased, nor such processes identified in order to use these energy equivalences in these equations.

It seems most natural to assume that the heating of gases and plasmas is directly proportional to the amount of star formation, $p = +1$. However, we see in Section 4 that there are many general cases in the universe where temperatures closely follow the square root of mass, corresponding with $p = +0.5$. As the Landauer information equivalent energy is proportional to temperature, we therefore examined both cases, IDE(a) α SMD(a) and IDE(a) α SMD(a)$^{0.5}$, as shown in Figure 2.

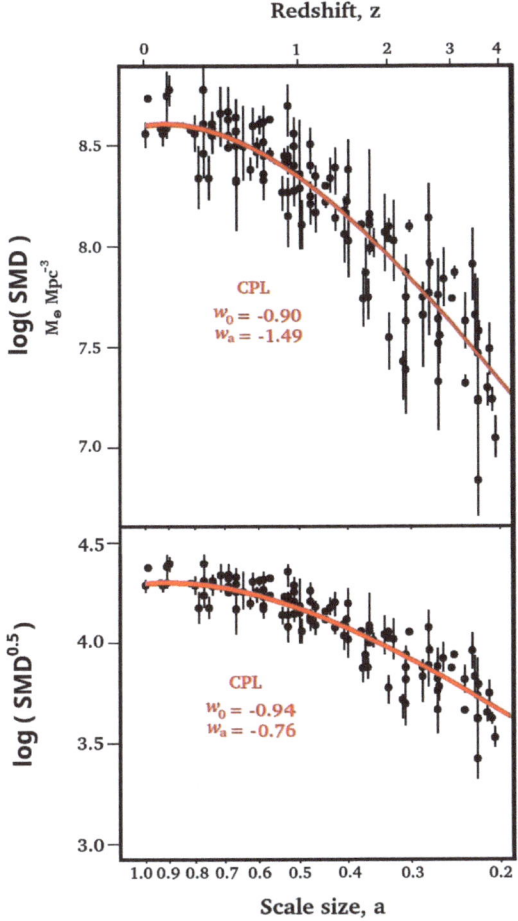

Figure 2. Measured stellar mass densities [25–51] plotted against universe scale size. The red curves correspond with the CPL best-fit parameters of $w_0 = -0.90$ and $w_a = -1.49$ for IDE(a) α SMD(a) and $w_0 = -0.94$ and $w_a = -0.76$ for IDE(a) α SMD(a)$^{0.5}$.

The SMD and SMD$^{0.5}$ data illustrated in Figure 2 were tested against all CPL w_0 and w_a combinations; w_0 values in the range of +0.9 to −3.0 in steps of 0.01 were tested for each w_a value in the range of +0.9 to −3.5, also in steps of 0.01. As this was a log–log plot, any curve corresponding with a given w_0 and w_a combination was fixed in the log(a) abscissa direction, but could be moved in the ordinate direction to find the best fit. The best fits for each w_0 and w_a combination were determined by the position in the ordinate direction that gave the minimum value of the residual sum of squares (RSS). Then, that w_0 and w_a combination was assigned an R^2 coefficient of determination, given by $R^2 = 1 - (RSS/TSS)$, where TSS is the total sum of squares.

The w_0 and w_a combinations that provided the highest R^2 (or minimum RSS), both with maximum R^2 values of 0.93, are shown in Figure 2 for the two cases of SMD and SMD$^{0.5}$.

In Figure 3, each of the 121 SMD(a) measurements are plotted against the SMD(a) values predicted by the best-fit CPL curve at the measured a value. In both cases, the measured and predicted sets of values were related, with a Pearson correlation coefficient value of $r = 0.92$.

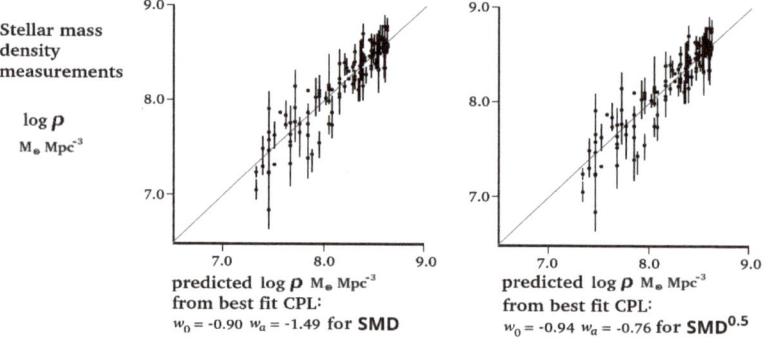

Figure 3. Identical plots of SMD measurements predicted by the best-fit CPL parameters against measured stellar mass densities at the same scale size for SMD and SMD$^{0.5}$. Both plots show a Pearson correlation of $r = 0.92$.

The maximum R^2 coefficients are plotted in Figure 4 on a colour scale for all of the above $w_0 - w_a$ tested combinations to show the extent of fit for different w_0 and w_a values for both cases.

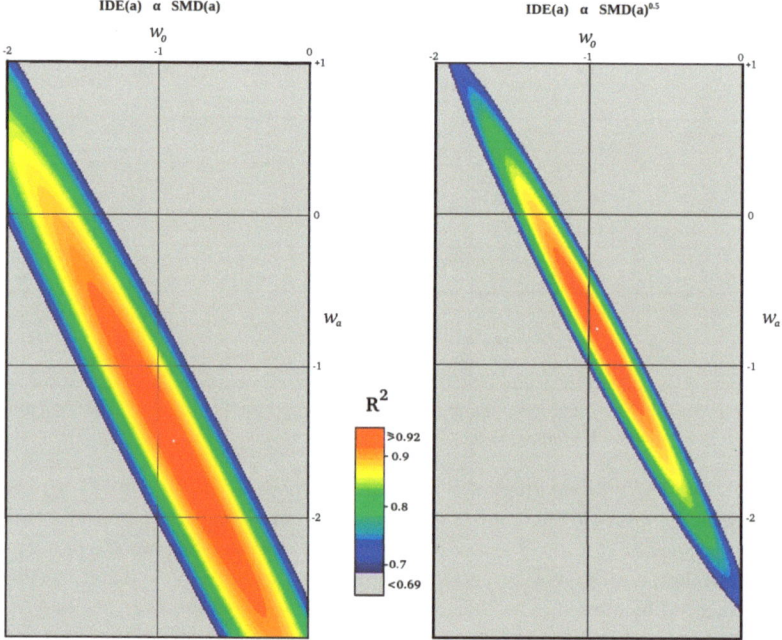

Figure 4. Plot of maximum R^2 coefficient of determination values in $w_0 - w_a$ parameter space in parameter steps of 0.01 for SMD(a) and SMD(a)$^{0.5}$. The best-fit $w_0 - w_a$ locations are identified by white dots.

3. Comparison of IDE Prediction with Experimental Measurements

In this section, we compare the IDE(a) contribution with several experimental measurements of dark energy. In Figures 5 and 6 we illustrate the expected information dark energy contribution in $w_0 - w_a$ space for the two cases of IDE(a) $\propto$ SMD(a) and IDE(a) $\propto$ SMD(a)$^{0.5}$ by re-plotting the $R^2 > 0.86$ and $R^2 > 0.92$ contours from Figure 4 in two shades of red, adjusted to the scales of the various published $w_0 - w_a$ experimental plots. Both IDE(a) predictions are compared in these figures directly with the results of *Planck* 2018 [54], Pantheon+ 2022 [22], the Dark Energy Survey 2024 [23], and the Dark Energy Spectroscopic Instrument (DESI) 2024 [24].

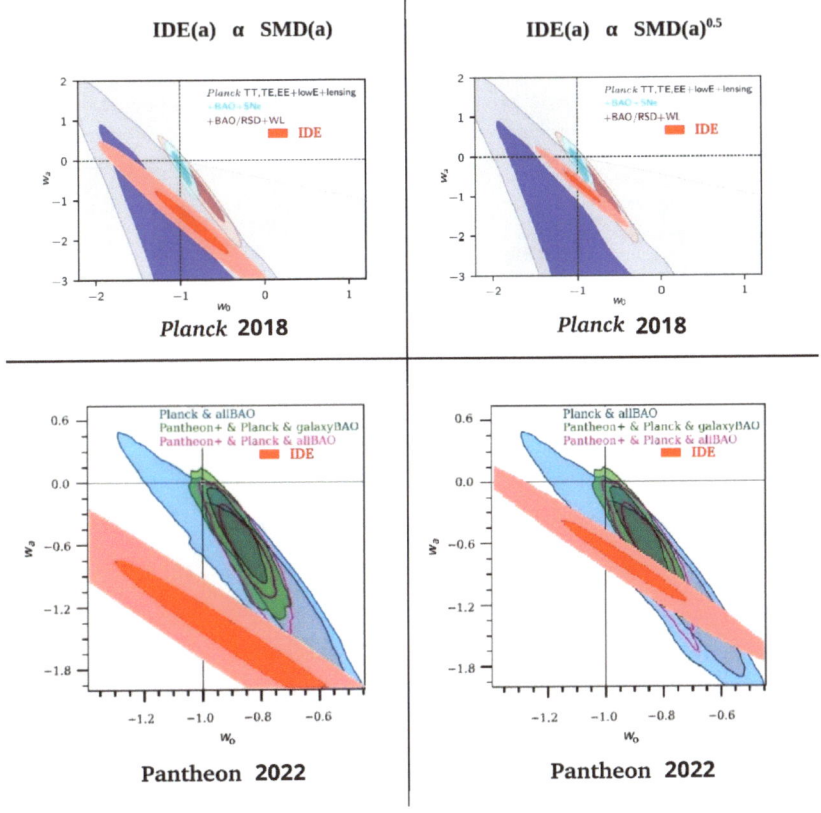

Figure 5. Information dark energy predicted contribution for the cases of IDE(a) $\propto$ SMD(a) and IDE(a) $\propto$ SMD(a)$^{0.5}$ compared in $w_0 - w_a$ space with *Planck* 2018 and Pantheon+ 2022 results. Adapted from *Planck*, Figure 30 of [54], and Pantheon+, Figure 12 of [22], under the Creative Commons BY 4.0 License.

These combined plots allowed the region of predicted IDE(a) in $w_0 - w_a$ space to be directly compared with the $w_0 - w_a$ space required to explain the experimental measurements of dark energy. In each measurement plot, there were several combinations of experimental techniques and different colours were used to differentiate between the different combinations, each with two shades per combination, corresponding with the 68% (stronger colour) and 95% (lighter colour) likelihood contours. The combinations included several different techniques, such as the cosmic microwave background, baryon acoustic oscillations, weak lensing, etc. The reader is referred to the cited publications for more information on these techniques and how data from the techniques were combined.

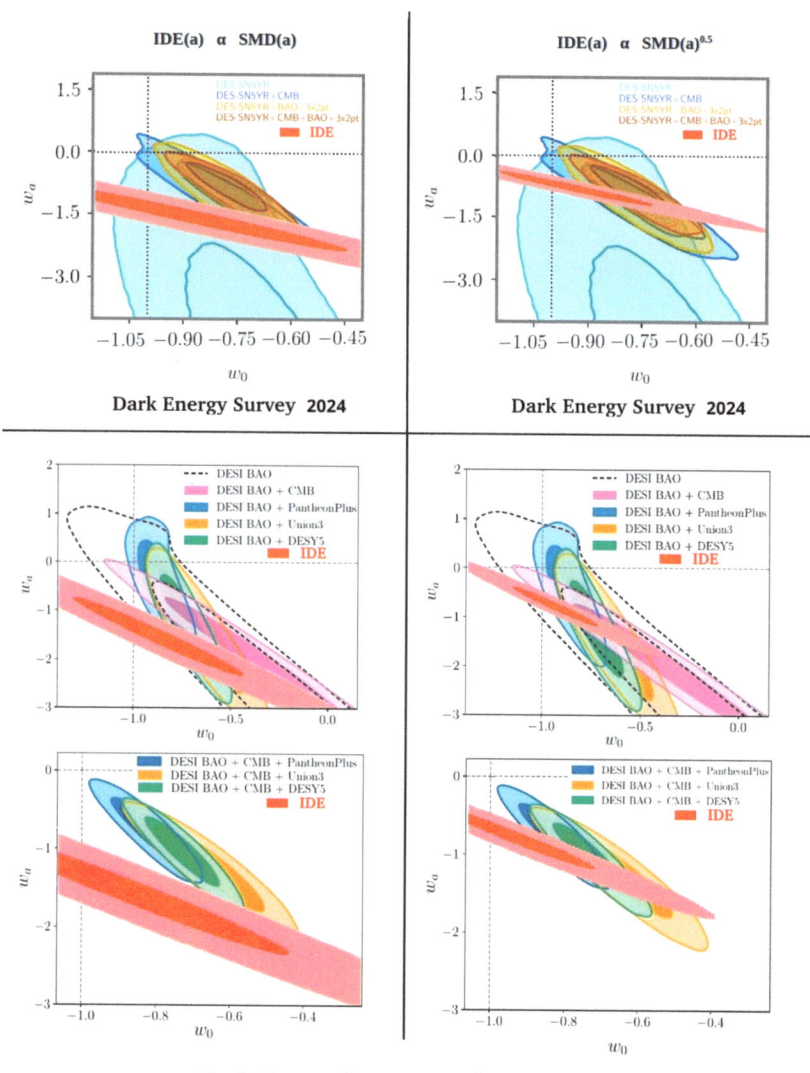

Figure 6. Information dark energy predicted contribution for the cases of IDE(a) ∝ SMD(a) and IDE(a) ∝ SMD(a)$^{0.5}$ compared in $w_0 - w_a$ space with Dark Energy Survey 2024 and Dark Energy Spectrographic Instrument 2024 results. Adapted from Dark Energy Survey, Figure 8 of [23], and Dark Energy Spectroscopic Instrument, Figure 6 of [24], under the Creative Commons BY 4.0 License.

The IDE predicted $w_0 - w_a$ spaces for IDE(a) ∝ SMD(a) in Figures 5 and 6 clearly show a strong overlap with the *Planck* plots of likelihood space, and lie close to, but with less direct overlap with, the more recent measurements of Pantheon+, the Dark Energy Survey, and the Dark Energy Spectrographic Instrument. However, the predicted IDE $w_0 - w_a$ spaces for IDE(a) ∝ SMD(a)$^{0.5}$ show an even stronger overlap in all plots. The best-fit IDE, $R^2 > 0.92$, overlaps the deeper-colour 68% likelihood area of all experimental data combinations in all plots.

4. Discussion

4.1. IDE Can Account for the Observed Dark Energy

While we might well expect a direct proportionality between IDE(a) and SMD(a), to exhibit the observed reasonable agreement in $w_0 - w_a$ space, we find that SMD(a)$^{0.5}$ provides an even better, fuller, agreement. In this case, two decades of SMD(a) mass density provide only one decade of IDE(a). Information energy, $N k_B T \ln(2)$, is proportional to temperature and we note that there are many cases in the universe where the temperature of objects scale approximately with the (object mass)$^{0.5}$ relation.

This approximate proportionality is observed over a wide range of scales, from the largest universe scales of galaxy clusters, to galaxy scales, and down to the much smaller scales of individual stars. In galaxy clusters, most of the baryons (60–90%) are found in the X-ray-emitting intracluster medium (ICM) at temperatures of 1–15 keV (approximately $10^7 - 1.5 \times 10^8$ K), with all the remaining baryons located in galaxies. Galaxy cluster masses over the two-decade range of 10^{13}–10^{15} solar masses, $M_\odot$, correspond closely with only a single decade of an ICM X-ray luminous temperature range of 1–10 keV, corresponding with $SDM^{0.5}$ (see Figure 15 of [55]). ICM accounts for most of the baryon entropy in the universe [56], and may make a significant contribution to IDE. The halo mass–temperature relation shows a similar temperature for α SDM$^{0.6}$ over a range of over three decades of mass for galaxy clusters, groups of galaxies, and individual galaxies (see Figure 4 of [57]; in that publication, it is deduced as mass proportional to $T^{1.65}$). At the other extreme of universe scale (in the main sequence stars), the temperature is again α SDM$^{0.5}$ because, over the two decades of star size from 0.5 $M_\odot$ to 60 $M_\odot$, the stellar photosphere temperature ranges over just one decade from 3800 to 44,500 K.

The two CPL $w_0 - w_a$ parameter combinations that best describe SMD(a)$^{+1.0}$ and SMD(a)$^{+0.5}$ show, respectively, a reasonable and a very good overlap with the $w_0 - w_a$ limits placed by dark energy measurements. This strongly supports the suggestion that there is a dynamic, phantom dark energy that is directly related to star/structure formation and primarily determined by temperature. Clearly, IDE can explain such a relation.

So far, we have shown that IDE(a) varies over time, with a relative variation that is consistent with the dark energy experimental results in Figures 5 and 6. We now need to show that the absolute energy density expected from IDE is sufficient to explain the observed dark energy effects. In Figure 7, we provide a survey of possible sources of information energy [16,17,56], with total information energies of these phenomena determined by their NT product. Their information energy relevance is illustrated by a comparison with the ~10^{70} joules mc^2 energy equivalence of the 10^{53} kg universe baryons. While there is much uncertainty in these NT values, it appears that the strongest sources of IDE—provided by stellar heated gas and by the intracluster medium—are approaching the baryon mc^2 energy. Therefore, this work establishes that IDE can account for the dark energy of the universe, very approximately accounting for the present energy density, but, more clearly and importantly, providing a clear agreement with the latest experimentally observed dark energy history in $w_0 - w_a$ space [22–24].

4.2. Cause and Effect

We have established a clear similarity between the history of dark energy and the history of star formation via the $w_0 - w_a$ parameter plots. This has led us to consider IDE as the source of dark energy. However, this similarity could also be explained by the reverse possibility, that dark energy might be responsible for some of the SMD(a) history. Indeed, the very recent reduction in star formation, reduction in galaxy merging, and reduction in general structure growth rate have been attributed to the accelerating expansion caused by dark energy [58,59]. This reduction in SMD(a) is evident in Figure 2 by the decrease down to $z = 0$ shown by the fitted CPL red curves, corresponding with a present equation of state parameter of $w_0 > -1$. However, we should expect that this would also happen if IDE is the source of dark energy. Increasing the star formation provided an increase in IDE energy density that eventually overtook the falling matter energy density to initiate the accelerating expansion. In turn, acceleration fed back to limit the star formation rate and IDE.

Over the late-universe history considered here, $a > 0.2$, there are two factors that support the main causal direction of SMD → IDE→ accelerating expansion. The first is the fact that SMD$(a)^{+0.5}$ provided the best fit in all the $w_0 - w_a$ parameter plots, corresponding with the temperature dependence expected for IDE rather than a mass dependence. The second is the close similarity in earlier growth rates, or similar w_a values, before dark energy was strong enough (relative to falling mass density) to affect the general structure growth rate.

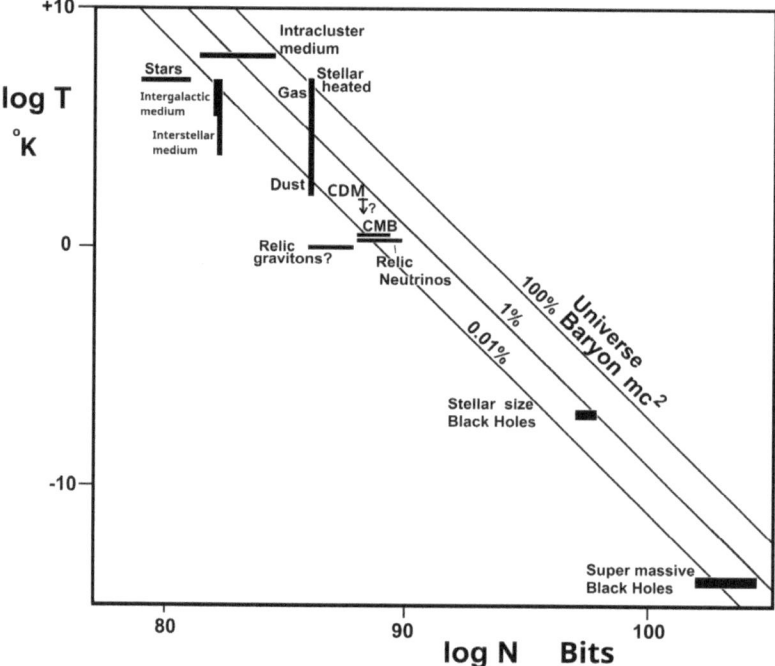

Figure 7. Sources of information energy with NT products compared with values that provide an information energy equivalent to the universe total baryon mc^2.

4.3. IDE Should Resolve Some Problems and Tensions of ΛCDM

Late-universe dark energy in the form of information dark energy was previously shown [15] to be able to address many problems and tensions of ΛCDM. Some of the most relevant are briefly restated here. A dark energy theory that can account for the observed effects of dark energy as an alternative to the cosmological constant would allow Λ to take the more likely zero value [60] and effectively solve the cosmological constant problem by Λ→0. Also, we see in Figure 6 that the cosmological constant ($w_0 = -1$ and $w_a = 0$) generally lies outside, or in some cases, only on the margins of, the $w_0 - w_a$ likelihood space of the recent experiments [22–24].

Late-universe dynamic dark energy that increases from $z \sim 2$ to the present energy density has been previously shown [61] to provide a possible explanation for both the Hubble and σ_8 tensions, similar to a transitional dark energy [62] or to a dynamic cosmological constant/running vacuum model [63]. The relatively fast increase in star formation between z = 2 and today combined with the a^{-3} fall in matter energy density effectively provides suddenly significant dark energy as it was previously insignificant at z > 2 relative to the matter energy density. The time history of IDE described here would have a very similar characteristic time history to a sudden turn-on of dark energy [64] and thus may also account for both tensions.

Dark energy that increased with star formation to become the dominant energy today naturally solves the cosmological coincidence problem. Increasing star formation also increased the probability of intelligent beings evolving to live in the dark-energy-dominated epoch, and to subsequently discover dark energy. Note that the observed value of Λ has been shown [65] to be too small to be compatible with a comparable anthropic reasoning when assuming ΛCDM.

4.4. IDE Can Also Account for Dark-Matter Attributed Effects

At the time of writing, the latest results from the most sensitive WIMP dark matter detector to date [66] managed to further limit the possible WIMP dark matter energy range, and still without any confirmed dark matter particle detection. Now, IDE has similar universe-wide total energy as matter and is primarily concentrated around stars and structures where it should have a local energy density at least as high as that from baryons. The General Theory of Relativity shows that space–time will be distorted by accumulations of energy in any form, not just by the mc^2 of matter, as illustrated in Figure 8.

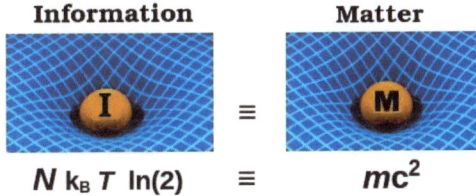

Figure 8. Space–time is equally distorted by an accumulation of energy in any form, comparing here the $N\, k_B\, T\, \ln(2)$ energy of information with an equivalent effect of mc^2 energy of matter.

Therefore, IDE in galaxies will have the same effect as an extra unseen dark matter component and will thus be difficult to distinguish from dark matter. The dark matter attributed effects in many galaxies have been shown to have their location fully specified by the location of baryons [67,68]. This observation is difficult to reconcile with ΛCDM, but it is clearly compatible with the effects expected from IDE and is also compatible with modified Newtonian dynamics (MOND). In a cluster of galaxies, the brightest and highest temperature galaxy is often found to have the strongest dark matter attributed effects [69], again consistent with an IDE source of the effects. When galaxies collide, the dark matter attributed effects generally pass straight through, remaining co-located with the stars and structures, while the gas clouds slow down with collisions [70–72]. This is also consistent with an IDE source of the effects.

New observations of early emerging massive galaxies and early clusters of galaxies require an accelerating structure formation at those times. This has been shown [73] to be difficult for the linear hierarchical galaxy formation of ΛCDM and more in keeping with the non-linear effects predicted by MOND. Equally, we should also expect similar non-linear effects with an increase in local attraction provided by IDE increasing with star formation.

The ΛCDM model assumes the acceleration continues to increase in our dark energy dominated epoch towards an eventual universe heat death, but IDE will lead to a different future. The stellar mass density is clearly starting to stop increasing (Figures 1 and 2). The future maximum star formation density may be only 5% above today's density [74]. This is also compatible with an analysis [75] of DESI data [24], which showed that dark energy density "reaches its maximum value it will ever achieve within the observed window". We can expect the IDE energy density to fall and, some time in the future, revert to a matter dominated epoch with deceleration. Perhaps this will eventually lead to a 'big crunch' or even an 'oscillating' or 'bouncing' universe.

IDE is the equivalent energy of the information carried by, or represented by, the matter in the structures of the universe. This close association of IDE with structures is not compatible with the normally assumed strong damping of dark energy perturbations. However, the IDE model leads us to expect the measured H_0 to vary depending on the distribution of mass and temperature along the line of measurement, and there is some evidence for possible directional anisotropies in H_0 [76] that would be expected with IDE. Also, distant quasars gravitationally lensed by closer galaxies yield H_0 values dependent on the lens redshift. This and other observations indicate a need to consider the possibility of both new late-time and new local physics [77].

Overall, we expect IDE to also account for at least some of the effects previously attributed to dark matter. Then, locally, IDE is attractive like invisible dark matter, but, universe-wide, IDE is repulsive as dark energy. These results are summarised in a simplified form in Table 1, where IDE is compared with other sources of dark energy and dark matter.

Table 1. Simple comparison of IDE with ΛCDM, scalar fields/quintessence, and MOND.

Required Dark Side Property	IDE	ΛCDM	Scalar Fields/ Quintessence	MOND
Account for present dark energy density	YES, order of magnitude 10^{70} J	NO, not by very many orders of magnitude	Only by much fine tuning	-----
Consistent with $w_0 - w_a$ experiment data	YES, very good agreement	NO, on margins of likelihood region	Not specific $-1 < w < +1$	----
Resolve Cosmological Constant problem	YES, $\Lambda \to 0$	NO	Only by much fine tuning	----
Resolve Cosmological Coincidence problem	YES, naturally	NO	Only by much fine tuning	----
Resolve H_0 and σ_8 Tensions	YES, possibly	NO	NO	----
Account for size of dark matter attributed effects	YES, same order of magnitude	NO, dark matter not even detected yet	----	YES, sometimes
Account for location of dark matter attributed effects	YES coincident with baryons	NO, not coincident with baryons	----	YES, Coincident with baryons
Account for early massive galaxies non-linear growth	YES, expect non-linear growth	NO, only linear, hierarchical growth	----	YES, expect non-linear growth

5. Summary

When compared in $w_0 - w_a$ space, the measured stellar mass density history, SMD(a), makes a very good fit with all measurements of dark energy history. This suggests that dark energy is directly driven by star and structure formations. The preference of fit for SMD(a)$^{+0.5}$ over SMD(a)$^{+1.0}$ further suggests that dark energy density is primarily determined by the temperature of structures at many levels of scale, whether galaxy clusters, galaxies, or stars. The dark energy dependence on structure formation, in particular with the dependence on temperature, is compatible with an information dark energy (IDE) explanation.

Funding: This research received no external funding.

Institutional Review Board Statement: Not applicable.

Data Availability Statement: Data available in a publicly accessible repository.

Acknowledgments: This work was enabled by the award of Emeritus Professor of Space Science from the University of Sussex. The author thanks the reviewers for their constructive comments.

Conflicts of Interest: The author declares no conflicts of interest.

References

1. Landauer, R. Irreversibility and Heat Generation in the Computing Process. *IBM J. Res. Dev.* **1961**, *5*, 183–191. [CrossRef]
2. Landauer, R. Information is Physical. *Phys. Today* **1991**, *44*, 23–29. [CrossRef]
3. Toyabe, S.; Sagawa, T.; Ueda, M.; Muneyuki, E.; Sano, M. Experimental demonstration of information-to-energy conversion and validation of the generalized Jarzynski equality. *Nat. Phys.* **2010**, *6*, 988–992. [CrossRef]
4. Berut, A.; Arakelyan, A.; Petrosyan, A.; Ciliberto, A.; Dillenschneider, R.; Lutz, E. Experimental verification of Landauer's principle linking information and thermodynamics. *Nature* **2012**, *483*, 187–189. [CrossRef]
5. Jun, Y.; Gavrilov, M.; Bechhoefer, J. High-Precision Test of Landauer's Principle in a Feedback Trap. *Phys. Rev. Lett.* **2014**, *113*, 190601. [CrossRef]
6. Yan, L.L.; Xiong, T.P.; Rehan, K.; Zhou, F.; Liang, D.F.; Chen, L.; Zhang, J.Q.; Yang, W.L.; Ma, Z.H.; Feng, M. Single Atom Demonstration of the Quantum Landauer Principle. *Phys. Rev. Lett.* **2018**, *120*, 210601. [CrossRef]
7. Wheeler, J.A.; Ford, K. *Geons, Black Holes and Quantum Foam: A life in Physics*; Norton: New York, NY, USA, 1998; ISBN 978-0393046427.
8. Zeilinger, A. A Foundational Principle of Quantum Mechanics. *Found. Phys.* **1999**, *29*, 631–643. [CrossRef]
9. Gough, M.P.; Carozzi, T.; Buckley, A.M. On the similarity of Information Energy to Dark Energy. *Phys. Essays* **2006**, *19*, 446–450. [CrossRef]
10. Peebles, P.J.E. *Principles of Physical Cosmology*; Princeton University Press: Princeton NJ, USA, 1993; ISBN 978-0691209814.
11. Gough, M.P. Information Equation of State. *Entropy* **2008**, *10*, 150–159. [CrossRef]
12. Gough, M.P. Holographic Dark Information Energy. *Entropy* **2011**, *13*, 924–935. [CrossRef]
13. Gough, M.P. Holographic Dark Information Energy: Predicted Dark Energy Measurement. *Entropy* **2013**, *15*, 1133–1149. [CrossRef]
14. Gough, M.P. A Dynamic Dark Information Energy Consistent with Planck Data. *Entropy* **2014**, *16*, 1902–1916. [CrossRef]
15. Gough, M.P. Information Dark Energy can Resolve the Hubble Tension and is Falsifiable by Experiment. *Entropy* **2022**, *24*, 385–399. [CrossRef] [PubMed]
16. Frampton, P.H.; Hsu, S.D.H.; Kephart, T.W.; Reeb, D. What is the entropy of the universe? *Class. Quantum Gravity* **2009**, *26*, 145005. [CrossRef]
17. Egan, C.A.; Lineweaver, C.H. A larger estimate of the entropy of the universe. *Astrophys. J.* **2010**, *710*, 1825–1834. [CrossRef]
18. T'Hooft, G. Obstacles on the way towards the quantization of space, time and matter- and possible solutions. *Stud. Hist. Philos. Sci. Part B Stud. Hist. Philos. Mod. Phys.* **2001**, *32*, 157–180. [CrossRef]
19. Susskind, L. The world as a hologram. *J. Math. Phys.* **1995**, *36*, 6377–6396. [CrossRef]
20. Buosso, R. The holographic principle. *Rev. Mod. Phys.* **2002**, *74*, 825–874. [CrossRef]
21. Chevallier, M.; Polarski, D. Accelerating universes with scaling dark matter. *Int. J. Mod. Phys. D* **2001**, *10*, 213–224. [CrossRef]
22. Brout, D.; Scolnic, D.; Popovic, B.; Riess, A.G.; Carr, A.; Zuntz, J.; Kessler, R.; Davis, T.M.; Hinton, S.; Jones, D.; et al. The Pantheon+ Analysis: Cosmological Constraints. *Astrophys. J.* **2022**, *938*, 110. [CrossRef]
23. DES Collaboration. The Dark Energy Survey: Cosmology Results with ~1500 new High-redshift Type 1a Supernovae using the full 5-year Dataset. *Astrophys. J. Lett.* **2024**, *973*, L14. [CrossRef]
24. DESI Collaboration. DESI 2024 VI: Cosmological Constraints from the Measurements of Baryon Acoustic Oscillations. *arXiv* **2024**. [CrossRef]
25. Li, C.; White, S.D.M. The distribution of stellar mass in the low-redshift universe. *Mon. Not. R. Astron. Soc.* **2009**, *398*, 2177–2187. [CrossRef]

26. Gallazzi, A.; Brinchmann, J.; Charlot, S.; White, S.D.M. A census of metals and baryons in stars in the local universe. *Mon. Not. R. Astron. Soc.* **2008**, *383*, 1439–1458. [CrossRef]
27. Moustakas, J.; Coil, A.L.; Aird, J.; Blanton, M.R.; Cool, R.J.; Eisenstein, D.J.; Mendez, A.J.; Wong, K.C.; Zhu, G.; Arnouts, S. PRIMUS: Constraints on star formation quenching and Galaxy merging and the evolution of the stellar mass function from $z = 0$–1. *Astrophys. J.* **2013**, *767*, 50. [CrossRef]
28. Bielby, R.; Hudelot, P.; McCracken, H.J.; Ilbert, O.; Daddi, E.; Le Fèvre, O.; Gonzalez-Perez, V.; Kneib, J.-P.; Marmo, C.; Mellier, Y.; et al. The WIRCam Deep Survey. I. Counts, colours, and mass functions derived from near-infrared imaging in the CFHTLS deep fields. *Astron. Astrophys.* **2012**, *545*, A23. [CrossRef]
29. Pérez-González, P.G.; Rieke, G.H.; Villar, V.; Barro, G.; Blaylock, M.; Egami, E.; Gallego, J.; Gil de Paz, A.; Pascual, S.; Zamorano, J.; et al. The stellar mass assembly of galaxies from $z = 0$–4: Analysis of a sample selected in the rest-frame near infrared with Spitzer. *Astrophys. J.* **2008**, *675*, 234–261. [CrossRef]
30. Ilbert, O.; McCracken, H.J.; Le Fèvre, O.; Capak, P.; Dunlop, J.; Karim, A.; Renzini, M.A.; Caputi, K.; Boissier, S.; Arnouts, S.; et al. Mass assembly in quiescent and star-forming Galaxies since $z > 4$ from UltraVISTA. *Astron. Astrophys.* **2013**, *556*, A55. [CrossRef]
31. Muzzin, A.; Marchesini, D.; Stefanon, M.; Franx, M.; McCracken, H.J.; Milvang-Jensen, B.; Dunlop, J.S.; Fynbo, J.P.U.; Brammer, G.; Labbé, I.; et al. The evolution of the stellar mass functions of star-forming and quiescent galaxies to $z = 4$ from the COSMOS/UltraVISTA survey. *Astrophys. J.* **2013**, *777*, 18. [CrossRef]
32. Arnouts, S.; Walcher, C.J.; Le Fèvre, O.; Zamorani, G.; Ilbert, O.; Le Brun, V.; Pozzetti, L.; Bardelli, S.; Tresse, L.; Zucca, E.; et al. The SWIRE-VVDS-CFHTLS surveys: Stellar Assembly over the last 10 Gyr. *Astron. Astrophys.* **2007**, *476*, 137–150. [CrossRef]
33. Pozzetti, L.; Bolzonella, M.; Zucca, E.; Zamorani, G.; Lilly, S.; Renzini, A.; Moresco, M.; Mignoli, M.; Cassata, P.; Tasca, L.; et al. zCOSMOS—10k bright spectroscopic sample. The bimodality in the galaxy stellar mass function. *Astron. Astrophys.* **2010**, *523*, A13. [CrossRef]
34. Kajisawa, M.; Ichikawa, T.; Tanaka, I.; Konishi, M.; Yamada, T.; Akiyama, M.; Suzuki, R.; Tokoku, C.; Uchimoto, Y.K.; Yoshikawa, T.; et al. MOIRCS deep survey IV evolution of galaxy stellar mass function back to $z \sim 3$. *Astrophys. J.* **2009**, *702*, 1393–1412. [CrossRef]
35. Marchesini, D.; van Dokkum, P.G.; Forster Schreiber, N.M.; Franx, M.; Labbe, I.; Wuyts, S. The evolution of the stellar mass function of galaxies from $z = 4$ and the first comprehensive analysis of its uncertainties. *Astrophys. J.* **2009**, *701*, 1765–1769. [CrossRef]
36. Reddy, N.; Dickinson, M.; Elbaz, D.; Morrison, G.; Giavalisco, M.; Ivison, R.; Papovich, C.; Scott, D.; Buat, V.; Burgarella, D.; et al. GOODS-HERSCHEL measurements of the dust attenuation of typical star forming galaxies at high redshift. *Astrophys. J.* **2012**, *744*, 154. [CrossRef]
37. Caputi, K.J.; Cirasuolo, M.; Jdunlop, J.S.; McLure, R.J.; Farrah, D.; Almaini, O. The stellar mass function of the most massive Galaxies at $3 < z < 5$ in the UKIDSS Ultra Deep Survey. *Mon. Not. R. Astron. Soc.* **2011**, *413*, 162–176. [CrossRef]
38. Gonzalez, V.; Labbe, I.; Bouwens, R.J.; Illingworth, G.; Frank, M.; Kriek, M. Evolution of galaxy stellar mass functions, mass densities, and mass-to light ratios from $z \sim 7$ to $z \sim 4$. *Astrophys. J.* **2011**, *735*, L34. [CrossRef]
39. Lee, K.-S.; Ferguson, H.C.; Wiklind, T.; Dahlen, T.; Dickinson, M.E.; Giavalisco, M.; Grogin, N.; Papovich, C.; Messias, H.; Guo, Y.; et al. How do star-forming galaxies at $z > 3$ assemble their masses? *Astrophys. J.* **2012**, *752*, 66. [CrossRef]
40. Cole, S.; Norberg, P.; Baugh, C.M.; Frenk, C.S.; Bland-Hawthorn, J.; Bridges, T.; Cannon, R.; Colless, M.; Collins, C.; Couch, W.; et al. The 2dF galaxy redshift survey. *Mon. Not. R. Astron. Soc.* **2001**, *326*, 255–273. [CrossRef]
41. Dickinson, M.; Papovich, C.; Ferguson, H.C.; Budavari, T. The evolution of the global stellar mass density a $0 < z < 3$. *Astrophys. J.* **2003**, *587*, 25–40. [CrossRef]
42. Rudnick, G.; Rix, H.; Franx, M.; Labbe, I.; Blanton, M.; Daddi, E.; Schreiber, N.M.F.; Moorwood, A.; Rottgering, H.; Trujillo, I.; et al. The rest-frame optical luminosity density, colour, and stellar mass density of the universe from $z = 0$ to $z = 3$. *Astrophys. J.* **2003**, *599*, 847–864. [CrossRef]
43. Brinchmann, J.; Ellis, R.S. The ma.ss assembly and star formation characteristics of field galaxies of known morphology. *Astrophys. J.* **2000**, *536*, L77–L80. [CrossRef] [PubMed]
44. Elsner, F.; Feulner, G.; Hopp, U. The impact of Spitzer infrared data on stellar mass estimates. *Astron. Astrophys.* **2008**, *477*, 503–512. [CrossRef]
45. Drory, N.; Salvato, M.; Gabasch, A.; Bender, R.; Hopp, U.; Feuler, G.; Pannella, M. The stellar mass function of galxies to $z \sim 5$ in the FORS Deep and GOODS-South Fields. *Astrophys. J.* **2005**, *619*, L131–L134. [CrossRef]
46. Drory, N.; Alvarez, M. The contribution of star formation and merging to stellar mass buildup in galaxies. *Astrophys. J.* **2008**, *680*, 41–53. [CrossRef]
47. Fontana, A.; Donnarumma, I.; Vanzella, E.; Giallongo, E.; Menci, N.; Nonino, M.; Saracco, P.; Cristiani, S.; D'Odorico, S.; Poli, F. The assembly of massive galaxies from near Infrared observations of Hubble deep-field south. *Astrophys. J.* **2003**, *594*, L9–L12. [CrossRef]

48. Fontana, A.; Salimbeni, S.; Grazian, A.; Giallongo, E.; Pentericci, L.; Nonino, M.; Fontanot, F.; Menci, N.; Monaco, P.; Cristiani, S.; et al. The galaxy mass function up to z = 4 in the GOODS-MUSIC sample. *Astron. Astrophys.* **2006**, *459*, 745–757. [CrossRef]
49. Cohen, J.G. CALTECH faint galaxy redshift survey. *Astrophys. J.* **2002**, *567*, 672–701. [CrossRef]
50. Conselice, C.J.; Blackburne, J.A.; Papovich, C. The luminosity, stellar mass, and number density evolution of field galaxies. *Astrophys. J.* **2005**, *620*, 564–583. [CrossRef]
51. Borch, A.; Meisenheimer, K.; Bell, E.F.; Rix, H.-W.; Wolf, C.; Dye, S.; Kleinheinrich, M.; Kovacs, Z.; Wisotzki, L. The stellar masses of 25000 galaxies at 0.2 <z <1.0 estimated by COMBO-17 survey. *Astron. Astrophys.* **2006**, *453*, 869–881. [CrossRef]
52. Madau, P.; Dickinson, M. Cosmic Star Formation History. *Ann. Rev. Astron. Astrophys.* **2014**, *52*, 415–486. [CrossRef]
53. Friedmann, A. On the Curvature of Space. *Gen. Relativ. Gravit.* **1999**, *31*, 1991–2000. [CrossRef]
54. Aghanim, N.; Akrami, Y.; Ashdown, M.; Aumont, J.; Baccigalupi, C.; Ballardini, M.; Banday, A.J.; Barreiro, R.B.; Bartolo, N.; Basak, S.; et al. Planck 2018 results. VI, Cosmological Parameters. *Astron. Astrophys.* **2020**, *641*, A6. [CrossRef]
55. Voit, G.M. Tracing cosmic evolution with clusters of galaxies. *Rev. Mod. Phys.* **2005**, *77*, 207–258. [CrossRef]
56. Basu, B.; Lynden-Bell, D. A survey of entropy in the universe. *Q. Jl. R. Astr. Soc.* **1990**, *31*, 359–369.
57. Babyk, I.V.; McNamara, B.R. The Halo Mass-Temperature Relation for Clusters, Groups, and Galaxies. *Astrophys. J.* **2023**, *946*, 54. [CrossRef]
58. Guzzo, L.; Pierleoni, M.; Meneux, B.; Branchini, E.; LeFevre, O.; Marinoni, C.; Garilli, B.; Blaizot, J.; DeLucia, G.; Pollo, A.; et al. A test of the nature of cosmic acceleration using galaxy redshift distortions. *Nature* **2008**, *451*, 541. [CrossRef]
59. Frieman, J.A.; Turner, M.S.; Huterer, D. Dark energy and the accelerating universe. *Ann. Rev. Astron. Astrophys.* **2008**, *46*, 385. [CrossRef]
60. Weinberg, S. The cosmological constant problem. *Rev. Mod. Phys.* **1989**, *61*, 1–23. [CrossRef]
61. Benevento, G.; Hu, W.; Raven, M. Can late dark energy raise the Hubble constant? *Phys. Rev. D* **2020**, *101*, 103517. [CrossRef]
62. Keeley, R.; Joudaki, S.; Kaplinghat, M.; Kirkby, D. Implications of a transition in the dark energy equation of state for the H_0 and σ_8 tensions. *J. Cosmol. Astropart. Phys.* **2019**, *12*, 035. [CrossRef]
63. Peracaula, J.S.; Gomez-Valent, A.; De Cruz Perez, J.; Moreno-Pulido, C. Running vacuum against the H_0 and σ_8 tensions. *Explor. Front. Phys.* **2021**, *134*, 19001. [CrossRef]
64. Akarsu, O.; De Felice, A.; Di Valentino, E.; Kumar, S.; Nunes, R.C.; Özülker, E.; Vazquez, J.A.; Yadav, A. Cosmological constraints on Λ_8CDM scenario in a typeII minimally modified gravity. *Phys. Rev. D* **2024**, *110*, 103527. [CrossRef]
65. Sorini, D.; Peacock, J.A.; Lombriser, L. The impact of the cosmological constant on past and future star formation. *Mon. Not. R. Astron. Soc.* **2024**, *535*, 1449–1474. [CrossRef]
66. Aalbers, J.; Akerib, D.S.; Al Musalhi, A.K.; Alder, F.; Amarasinghe, C.S.; Ames, A.; Anderson, T.J.; Angelides, N.; Araújo, H.M.; Armstrong, J.E.; et al. First constraints on WIMP-nucleon effective field theory couplings in an extended energy region from LUX-ZEPLIN. *Phys. Rev. D* **2024**, *109*, 092003. [CrossRef]
67. McGaugh, S.S.; Lelli, F.; Schombert, J.M. The Radial Acceleration Relation in Rotationally Supported Galaxies. *Phys. Rev. Lett.* **2016**, *117*, 201101. [CrossRef]
68. Lelli, F.; McGaugh, S.S.; Schombert, J.M.; Pawlowski, M.S. One Law to Rule them all: The Radial Acceleration relation of Galaxies. *Astrophys. J.* **2017**, *836*, 152. [CrossRef]
69. Viola, M.; Cacciato, M.; Brouwer, M.; Kuijken, K.; Hoekstra, H.; Norberg, P.; Robotham, A.S.G.; van Uitert, E.; Alpaslan, M.; Baldry, I.K.; et al. Dark matter halo properties of GAMA galaxy groups from 100 square degrees of KiDS weak lensing data. *Mon. Not. R. Astron. Soc.* **2015**, *452*, 3529–3550. [CrossRef]
70. Markevich, M.; Gonzalez, A.H.; Clowe, D.; Vikhlinin, A.; Forman, W.; Jones, C.; Murray, S.; Tucker, W. Direct constraints on the dark matter self-interaction cross-section from the merging galaxy cluster. *Astrophys. J.* **2004**, *606*, 819–824. [CrossRef]
71. Harvey, D.; Massey, R.; Kitching, T.; Taylor, A.; Tittley, E. The non gravitational interactions of dark matter in colliding galaxy clusters. *Science* **2015**, *347*, 1462–1465. [CrossRef]
72. Massey, R.; Williams, L.; Smit, R.; Swinbank, M.; Kitching, T.D.; Harvey, D.; Jauzac, M.; Israel, H.; Clowe, D.; Edge, A.; et al. The behaviour of dark matter associated with four bright Cluster galaxies in the 10 kpc core of Abell 3827. *Mon. Not. R. Astron. Soc.* **2015**, *449*, 3393–3406. [CrossRef]
73. McGaugh, S.S.; Schombert, J.M.; Lelli, F.; Franck, J. Accelerated Structure Formation: The Early Emergence of Massive Galaxies and Clusters of Galaxies. *Astrophys. J.* **2024**, *976*, 13. [CrossRef]
74. Sobral, D.; Small, I.; Best, P.N.; Geach, J.E.; Yuichi, M.; Stott, J.P.; Cirasuolo, M.; Jaron, K. A large Hα survey at z = 2.23, 1.47, 0.84 and 0.40: The 11 Gyr evolution of star-forming galaxies from HiZELS. *Mon. Not. R. Astron. Soc.* **2013**, *428*, 1128. Available online: https://academic.oup.com/mnras/article/428/2/1128/1000290 (accessed on 15 November 2024). [CrossRef]
75. Cortes, M.; Liddle, A.R. Interpreting DESI's evidence for evolving dark energy. *J. Cosmol. Astropart. Phys.* **2024**, *12*, 007. [CrossRef]

76. Migkas, K. Probing cosmic isotropy with a new X-ray galaxy cluster sample through the Lx-T scaling relation. *Astron. Astrophys.* **2020**, *636*, A15. [CrossRef]
77. Vagnozzi, S. Seven Hints that Early-Time new physics alone is not sufficient to solve the Hubble tension. *Universe* **2023**, *9*, 393. [CrossRef]

Disclaimer/Publisher's Note: The statements, opinions and data contained in all publications are solely those of the individual author(s) and contributor(s) and not of MDPI and/or the editor(s). MDPI and/or the editor(s) disclaim responsibility for any injury to people or property resulting from any ideas, methods, instructions or products referred to in the content.

MDPI AG
Grosspeteranlage 5
4052 Basel
Switzerland
Tel.: +41 61 683 77 34

Entropy Editorial Office
E-mail: entropy@mdpi.com
www.mdpi.com/journal/entropy

Disclaimer/Publisher's Note: The title and front matter of this reprint are at the discretion of the Guest Editor. The publisher is not responsible for their content or any associated concerns. The statements, opinions and data contained in all individual articles are solely those of the individual Editor and contributors and not of MDPI. MDPI disclaims responsibility for any injury to people or property resulting from any ideas, methods, instructions or products referred to in the content.

www.ingramcontent.com/pod-product-compliance
Lightning Source LLC
LaVergne TN
LVHW070000100526
838202LV00019B/2595